Echoes of Violence

HUMAN RIGHTS AND CRIMES AGAINST HUMANITY

Edited by Eric D. Weitz

Carolin Emcke

Echoes of Violence
Letters from a War Reporter

PRINCETON UNIVERSITY PRESS
PRINCETON AND OXFORD

Copyright © 2007 by Princeton University Press
German edition © S. Fischer Verlag GmbH, Frankfurt am Main 2004
Requests for permission to reproduce material from this work should be
sent to Permissions, Princeton University Press

Published by Princeton University Press, 41 William Street, Princeton,
New Jersey 08540

In the United Kingdom: Princeton University Press, 3 Market Place,
Woodstock, Oxfordshire OX20 1SY

Library of Congress Cataloging-in-Publication Data
Emcke, Carolin, 1967–
    [Von den Kriegen. English]
    Echoes of Violence : Letters from a War Reporter / Carolin Emcke.
        p.   cm.—(Human rights and crimes against humanity)
    ISBN-13: 978-0-691-12903-7 (alk. paper)
    ISBN-10: 0-691-12903-7 (alk. paper)
    1. World politics—1989– 2. Low-intensity conflicts (Military science)
3. Emcke, Carolin, 1967—Correspondence. 4. Journalists—Germany—
Correspondence. I. Title.
    D860.E5313 2007
    909.83—dc22

                                                            2006019003

British Library Cataloging-in-Publication Data is available

This book has been composed in Janson text with Helvetica Condensed
Family Display

Printed on acid-free paper. ∞

pup.princeton.edu

Printed in the United States of America

10 9 8 7 6 5 4 3 2 1

For Sebastian Bolesch

Only sheer violence is mute.

—*Hannah Arendt*

Contents

Preface

At first there was only speechlessness.

After spending a month and a half in Albania and Kosovo during the war, I returned to Berlin in the summer of 1999 and did not know what to tell my friends. How to convey my experiences in words that would not disturb them? How to describe this encounter with death and destruction? How to explain that war and violence inscribe themselves on your soul and continue to live with you?

My friends did not know how to ask, and I did not know how to respond.

In an effort to overcome my speechlessness, I wrote a letter that was sent to a circle of about twenty friends via e-mail.

I did not know then that the longing to tell my friends about war and its victims would become a ritual: after each haunting journey I would write a letter. Nor did I know then that this writing would eventually become a cathartic task, not merely an intellectual one. More and more, these letters became a means to reflect on my experiences and help me return to my life in Berlin.

Not all of the letters describe war itself—some portray the destroyed interior and exterior landscapes that war leaves behind. Two letters—on Nicaragua and on Romania—do not deal with wars in the narrow sense.

They discuss structural violence rather than immediate physical or military violence.

In the letters I tried to express something that is not found in traditional news coverage. The genre of the letter allowed me to combine different forms of narration: personal passages are followed by essayistic reflections; political commentary is interspersed with travelogues. I could not have written for publication in this way.

I wrote for my friends: artists and intellectuals around the globe with different religious and cultural backgrounds, whom I had met over the previous fifteen years.

At first there were no markers to guide me. I simply told my friends about my journeys, about what haunted me. I tried to answer their unspoken questions: What were my reasons for traveling to war zones? How neutral could I remain in such places?

Over the years certain themes and ideas became clearer: the war, its victims, and the witness. The letters give testimony about what I have seen, but also about me: the witness.

There were reasons not to censor my personal comments for publication. Over and over again, friends who read these letters responded with outrage and surprise: *this* they hadn't imagined, they told me. They had *no idea*, they said. All my friends were well informed—and yet through these letters they seemed to learn something different about the death and destruction at the fringes of the world.

Why?

In her book *Regarding the Pain of Others*, Susan Sontag writes about a phenomenon that I found among my friends:

Preface

viewers or readers who are confronted every day with images of horror from war regions *see* those pictures—but they cannot *situate* them in a meaningful context. They become numb after a while, and in the end they do not believe that these images really correspond to a violent reality.

Letters from a witness whom one can imagine, who becomes visible, who describes how one responds to violence, who wanders between different worlds and tries to translate between them—someone who also mentions what goes wrong, what embarrasses, what is unbearable—such letters can be credible testimony to the wars and their victims.

Echoes of Violence

Kosovo 1 (July 1999)

War kills. That is all it does.
—*Michael Walzer*

Dear friends,
I have been back for two weeks. I do not know how to answer the questions about my time in Albania and Kosovo—as if I hadn't been there or had not returned yet.

The experiences are present, the images, the smell, the sound—everything is clear and yet it is impossible to transform it into an adequate and intelligible narrative of horror.

We wish to believe that we are able to defuse threats by giving them a name. Rumpelstiltskin loses his power when we guess his name. But sometimes Rumpelstiltskin rages even when we know what he is called. Sometimes words cannot banish, and their failure only increases our sorrow.

Maybe I simply don't know where to start.

There: in the refugee camps where the deportees were stuck, the men silently sitting on the field, smoking, covered under colored woolen blankets, the women bent over plastic buckets, washing the only clothes they had; there: on the fields where the corpses were decaying in the sun, in the hospitals with this inimitable smell of disinfection and death; there: on the overflowing marketplaces, in the devastated mosques—there we all had the same horizon of experience. We were all stuck in this world of pain and destruction. Within this context, all these horrifying scenes made "sense." Of course, it all seemed unreal, and yet it was simultaneously too real for us to permanently call it into question. Our conversations and gestures were embedded in this context. It was a life within the same radius of violence.

Only now, back in Berlin, now when I am about to talk about this time, does its absurdity strike me.

In retrospect I can say: the experiences there are somehow separated from your reality here like the paste that I used to cut out with a biscuit-form on the cake tin at my grandmother's when I was a child.

Maybe that is why journalists are considered disturbed cynics: because the reality that they describe is so disturbed.

That is the burden of the witness: to remain with a feeling of failure, of emptiness because even the most accurate account does not grasp the bleakness of war.

The Task

We were in Tirana when the peace agreement was signed and the Serbian delegation agreed to pull out of Kosovo within forty-eight hours after the settlement and to withdraw to what was left of the Yugoslav republic. The air bombardment of the NATO alliance had lasted seventy-eight days, during which they flew attacks against government buildings in Belgrade, against positions of the

4

Serbian army in Kosovo—but also against civilian targets: bridges, factories, power stations, the television station of Belgrade, and various refugee treks, "collateral damage" as the propaganda unit in Brussels would call it.

At the end of the war, we could travel together with the ground troops that had been inactive so far and the thousands of Albanian Kosovar refugees returning to Kosovo—and write from there.

Our team in Kosovo included our Albanian driver Kuijtim Bilali; his nephew and our translator, Noni Hoxha; Joanne Mariner, of Human Rights Watch from New York, whom we had met in the refugee camps in Albania; the photographer Sebastian Bolesch; and me.

We remained two more weeks in war-torn Kosovo and traveled throughout the entire region. We saw young men—who had been hiding out of fear of the Serbian militia—returning from the mountains and dirty cellars. We saw famished Albanian Kosovar prisoners with sunken eyes tied together on a truck. They were supposed to be kidnapped to Serbia and had been forgotten. We saw how the Albanian Kosovars celebrated the end of the repression. We saw everywhere how the Serbian units had raged: the burned-down farmhouses, the demolished minarets of village mosques, the mutilated corpses where the Serbian myrmidons hadn't had time to erase the traces of their deeds and to bury their victims. We saw the Serbian troops during their withdrawal, drunk from stolen booze. But we also saw Serbian civilians fleeing out of fear of revenge. We also saw the neighborhoods of the Roma standing in flames.

Death and Destruction

Since my return, people ask me: "How do you cope with what you witnessed?" "How do you digest all the experiences?"

The answer is: you don't.

There are certain impressions you cannot "digest."

The sight of a seventeen-year-old girl in the hospital of Prizren in Kosovo. She had been shot by a sniper the day before the allied forces entered Kosovo. She had a brain injury and urgently needed to be transferred to the hospital in Prishtina. That night she had stayed in a room with five badly injured men: Serbs, Kosovo Liberation Army (KLA) fighters, and Albanians, the enemies of the war crammed together into one overheated room. You could hear her breathe. She would probably die within the next five hours because the hospital could not transfer her to Prishtina—the Serbian troops had stolen the only ambulance for their flight at the end of the war.

The sight of a charred back of a dead Catholic Albanian Kosovar between hundreds of books in his house in Koronica. The muscles in the shrunken body were still recognizable—it looked like one of those charts from biology class where all muscles of the human body are schematically displayed. Except the man in Koronica was brown-black; his burned flesh was porous and looked hairy like scratchy fur. Arms and legs were missing. Maybe they had been cut off, maybe they were burned completely, maybe it had been the dogs.

6

The Homeric heroes in the *Iliad* fear death less than the thought of being left unburied—outside the city walls— at the mercy of stray dogs. It always seemed rather strange to me that a living person would worry about his corpse being tattered by dogs. I could not imagine a world in which dogs would run around with human limbs in their mouths.

It was the brother of the dead man who brought us to this package of withered flesh. He walked from one room to the other, in a destroyed house, and talked as if it were still intact, as if that bundle on the floor still had anything in common with the human being he grew up with.

And one does not digest: the sight of corpses without heads, of cut-off body parts, contorted bodies that had been pulled behind a truck for miles (also reminiscent of Homer); the sight of bloated or burned corpses, some two months old, one week, one day.

There is this one image I cannot forget: the foot of a male body that we found in a ravine on a field near Meja. I still remember those two inches between the black leather shoe on his right foot and the blue cotton trouser, a peasant uniform such as I would see so often in the following weeks when looking at dead civilians. The corpse had been lying there, apparently, since April. In the meantime it had rained, and it had been as hot as it can be in a Yugoslav summer. One particular part of the image haunts me, a small detail: those two inches between the tied shoe and the hem of the trouser. Without the clothes that proved that this had once been a man, there were only two inches of dead, living flesh. Nothing else.

And there was this sound, very quiet, first unnoticed, and then so penetrating in its repulsiveness that no taboo, no shame, could repress my hearing it: parasites were eating the rest of a human being.

I cannot forget the ten-year-old girl in Gjakova who stood in front of the burned-out ruins of her former house and could not say two complete, intelligible sentences. She spoke without pause as if her speech were making sense, she did not stutter, did not hesitate; she formed one incoherent sentence after another. Finally, we understood that in this house her father, her brother, her aunt, and two cousins had been killed. Her uncle and her two other brothers had been arrested by Serbian units and deported the day before NATO troops—the Kosovo Force (KFOR)—arrived.

She told us that her father had fallen off the roof celebrating the long-awaited NATO intervention. He had broken his leg and could not move when the Serbian soldiers arrived at their house. They had told the girl and her mother to leave the house—and killed everyone else in it.

I cannot forget how she stood there in her pink shirt, in front of her former living room wall, slightly oblique because there was no flat floor anymore. And I cannot forget that she could not speak properly, and that she occasionally only stared at us and then continued to speak. And that she did not seem upset at all.

She was quiet and calm and only every now and then did she seem irritated—when she realized that she did not know the trick anymore, that trick that someone had taught her, years ago, in another time: how to form sentences

8

and make sense to others. Then she paused and suddenly felt like a stranger to herself, and then she seemed to tell herself that these words that came out of her mouth were unintelligible.

We were disadvantaged in comparison to other journalists who witnessed these images of death and destruction. Many reporters arrived in Albania or Macedonia only when the peace agreement was signed. But we had already been acquainted with the terrible events. We had been writing since April on the refugees and their fate, we had been listening to them: how their sons and husbands had been killed, what they had done before the crisis began, where they used to live, how they were expelled, how many hours they had walked till they had reached the border, when they had last seen their brother, where they were standing when a Serbian officer pulled a woman out of the throng of refugees, how they had been hiding in a barn.

At the end of the war, when we entered Kosovo, we knew exactly where to go and what to expect there. We had a map of killing in our minds—even before we arrived at the sites of the massacres.

But that meant that we could not relate to those tormented bodies as neutral bystanders toward anonymous corpses. After weeks of interviewing survivors in the camps in Albania, photographer Sebastian Bolesch and I knew the story of many of the dead; we knew whether their wives or children had survived on the other side of the border.

It also meant that we could imagine the corpses before us as fathers and brothers, as peasants or writers. We could imagine their previous lives, and sometimes we knew their relatives in Albania.

Impossible to gain distance.

But it was also conciliatory: to remember the real person, the living father or brother or cousin or neighbor; to ask for their story and narrate it; to recreate in writing a world that was supposed to be destroyed; to give each of these stinking, faceless bodies a name again and not to turn one's back.

Traces 1

The Serbian troops have pulled out the night before, and NATO units pass through the abandoned Serbian checkpoint at the border. The track vehicles raise dust and immerse the scene in a gray and yellow cloud.

The impatient Albanian victors cannot hold back their joy and longing to return faster than the convoy of army vehicles. Thousands are waiting with their cars and tractors on the side of the road, watching how the caravan of Western friends slowly winds up the pass to Molina, and then through the eye of the needle at the old checkpoint. Hundreds are queuing behind fences, behind the barbed wire, and the excitement pushes them farther and farther off the asphalt road. There are small welcome presents that the Serbian losers have left on each side of the border for the Albanian refugees. But the summer is a helpful friend, and so the hidden death is visible because the gray or green of the landmines is easy to distinguish from the dried-out grass.

10

Some Albanian Kosovars are dancing in the small offices of the checkpoint. What used to be the victims' repressed fear now bursts out: windows are soon destroyed. The men's silent impotence is now discharged in the joy of power, the joy of being able to destroy. Chairs are thrown, tables destroyed. A howling mob, celebrating the victory and mourning its price. Furious about the humiliation, now that it's over.

Anger is a luxury one can afford only in liberty.

Nobody in the joyful crowd pays attention to the pile of metal sheet in a corner next to the checkpoint: there are license plates, covered with dust, lying amidst broken glass. Hundreds of old car plates, ripped off the vehicles. It wasn't enough to pull Albanian women and their children from their farms and houses, it wasn't enough to steal all their belongings, rings, jewelry, and whatever cash they had left. No, at the last checkpoint, right before expelling them into a foreign country, the Serbian police officers completed their task and robbed them of the last proof that these people had ever lived in the province of Kosovo. They confiscated passports, driver's licenses, property documents—anything the Albanians had carried on their deportation.

This strategy was more than just symbolic violence. What happened in this repetitive scene at the border was not just a simple demonstration of power or humiliation of the defenseless victims. Whether the soldiers at the checkpoint acted on order of the chain of command, I cannot know. But the action was systematic enough to understand the intention behind it: never should the

11

refugees be allowed or enabled to claim a right to return. They were not supposed to keep any proof of their belonging to Kosovo.

There is reasonable doubt concerning the discourse of genocide in Kosovo, but the coordinated separation of an entire segment of the population, the apartheid measures that increasingly excluded ethnic Albanians from access to universities, schools, and work; the collective deportations that human rights groups had documented long before the NATO bombardment; and finally the mass exodus and the destructions and killings since March—all of these had a systematic character and aimed at the eradication of all traces of an ethnic identity.

Traces 2

"The blood will be a sign for you on the houses where you are. When I see the blood I shall pass over you, and you will escape the destructive plague" (Exodus 12:13–14).

The bloody sign at the doors of Christian Orthodox Serbs was mostly of black paint, painted or sprayed. Six times they had to start in order to finish the writing on the wall, two crossing lines and four half-circles (the letter *c*, in Cyrillic *s*) in the corners: the Serbian cross with its four Ss, *Samo Sloga Spasi Srbiju* ("Only unity saves Serbia"), was supposed to help them escape the plague.

That is the archetypical symbolism that indicates inclusion and exclusion, the protection of one's own people and the extradition of the others. Whether it is the blood on the doorframe, the writing on the wall, or the word *Shibboleth* that locals can pronounce but strangers cannot—numerous are the biblical stories and the historic accounts of the rescue of those who could declare themselves as members, and the banishment of those who could not read the signs. Religions and cultures do not differ in this respect.

But in the horror of this war, it was those small cowardly signs on the walls of Serbian houses that I found most disgusting.

While their ethnic Albanian neighbors were fleeing in thousands, while Serbian militia expelled mothers and children like cattle from their houses, while Albanian men were deported, kidnapped, or shot—there were some Serbian civilians who didn't have anything better to do than to mark their houses with the Serbian cross?

Nowadays the term *barbarity* is used to describe a particularly appalling archaic form of murder—a dubious usage, as if not all murders were "barbaric." As if the technical features of contemporary killing were a moral achievement, as if the weapons of mass destruction of the first world were somehow more civilized than the machetes of the Hutu in Rwanda.

But all those who deny the moral foundations of common belonging are barbaric. So it is not only the burning of entire streets, not only the shooting of the handcuffed Albanian, that indicates the barbaric, but all those tiny little actions and gestures that separate and exclude the neighbor.

13

Small and Big Gestures of Resistance

On my eighteenth birthday a friend and mentor of mine wrote a piece of advice on a tiny white business card, which she passed to me across the table of the restaurant where we were celebrating. She wrote: "What matters in life? To show dignified behavior under circumstances that suggest the opposite."

It is not always great deeds—as books and films want to make us believe—that make a difference in times of war. Sometimes it is small gestures.

W. E. Sebald writes in his controversial book on aerial bombardment and literature about a woman who stood amidst the ruins after an air raid, cleaning the windows of her intact house. Primo Levi talks about his Hungarian comrade in Auschwitz who urged Levi to wash himself against all odds. What seems like a lack of moral sensibility, what seems like a cynical dullness against all the pain and sorrow around, is sometimes merely a struggle for remnants of ethical or just aesthetic standards of a former life.

Sometimes human beings rescue themselves through their affection for another for whom they have to care, sometimes through their anger. Sometimes it is an ability, a habitus, that helps one to face the extreme; sometimes it is a metaphysical attitude, a belief in another world, that blunts some of the power of reality.

Here are some who showed dignified behavior under circumstances that suggest the opposite.

14

Kujtim

Kujtim was my driver and he is my friend. I met Kujtim on my first trip to Albania in April. My colleague Klaus and I had traveled from Skopje, Macedonia, to the Albanian border. We had crossed the border and hired a driver on the Albanian side and had asked him to drive us to the north, to Kukes. After hours and hours of driving through the mountains, on scary, winding, dusty roads, the driver suddenly stopped and got out of the car without explanation. We saw him standing in the road and waving to stop another car. When a gray Mercedes stopped, he spoke to the driver, returned to us and said that he couldn't continue driving, but this other car would take us to the north. Before we could say no, we found ourselves in a car that was already overloaded with people who didn't speak any language we could understand. We had no idea where we were, whether this driver was going to Kukes at all, and since it had turned dark by then, even the direction we were driving. Every half hour, the car stopped, and one of the girls who were now squeezed in between an old man and the driver jumped out of the car and vomited.

After about six hours of driving, we arrived in a town. The driver stopped in front of a bar, told us to go in and wait, and returned ten minutes later with a young boy, who spoke fluent English.

It was Noni, the driver's nephew. Kujtim asked his nephew to translate the following: "I don't know who you are, but you are foreigners. Your driver was a jerk, an unbelievable bastard who dropped you in the middle of the

15

night in a country you didn't know. But the two of you were in my car and you were talking and you were laughing all the time. Anybody else would have been scared to death. You have young and pure souls! I like you! I have arranged a place for you to stay, and I will invite you for dinner and then we can talk about what I can do for you." Kujtim became our driver for two weeks that first time. I wouldn't say that he saved my life—but he made me feel safe in each dangerous situation ever since . . . and there were some.

When I returned this time, I knew I didn't want to have anyone but him as my driver. It took me a half hour in Kukes to find someone who knew him, and ten minutes later he showed up. A half hour later, he had quit his job and asked me what we would do. I asked him if he wanted to travel with me into Kosovo, and he agreed right away. Noni would serve as our translator.

Kujtim was the best dancer in Albania and would loudly sing along with traditional Albanian and Kosovar sad resistance folk songs on his tape recorder. He had been hosting eleven refugees, complete strangers to his family, in his apartment since the beginning of the crisis, and had taken those three people in his car (the first time we met him) from Kukes to Tirana (a ten-hour drive) so that they could try to find relatives in the other camps (the vomiting of the girl that first night wasn't due to the winding roads, but to trauma).

When we arrived later in Kosovo, in Prizren, for the first two days the Serbs were still in town. On the second day, the Serbs left in a huge convoy. That night, Joanne

Mariner noticed that about one hundred families had missed the chance to leave in the convoy and were now hiding in the Orthodox church in the center of Prizren. Joanne came to me and said that they were civilians, families, who were scared to death that the Albanians were going to take revenge and kill them all. Kujtim was listening without understanding more than that Joanne was upset. I told Noni, who then translated to Kujtim.

We are talking about the second day of the liberation. We are talking about the end of the first day on which we had seen what the Serbs had done to the people and their homes. We are talking about the end of the first day that we smelled the stench of death.

Kujtim said: "O.K. What are we going to do about those Serbs? We have to help. They are the same as all the other refugees who are hiding in my home back in Kukes."

Emine

I met Emine in the heat of a summer afternoon in the women's tent in the camp Piscina in Tirana, Albania, eight days before the war was over. She was forty-six, a former lawyer who was denied the right to work by the Serbian government about seven years ago and has had no legal job since then. Emine fled her home town of Mitrovica two months ago. She had friends in Tirana who offered to let her to stay with them in their flat, but she refused. She didn't want to have the comfort all to herself and would

17

rather stay with all the others in the dirty, hot tents of the camp, facing the heat, the nightmares about the past, the fears for the future, and the snakes in the tents. She had volunteered to work for Medica Kosova, a project organized by the German nongovernmental organization Medica Mondiale, which takes care of raped women. Half of Emine's family was missing, disappeared for two months; she had lost her house, her belongings, her passport—but she smiled when she talked to me.

"We have won," she said at a time when the war was still going on. "We have won, already now, we have won because we survived."

When I asked her what she meant, she replied that it had been Milosevic's only goal to completely wipe out the whole Albanian population: the fact that there was one, one hundred, maybe thousands left was not enough, but it was enough to make her a proud victor over a racist ideology. "His ideology and his policies wanted me dead—but I'm alive. We have won!"

And then she went on to envision her life after the war, how she will return to her destroyed house, how they will start a new life: "We will start anew but we will never be the same again. We will never be the same, but we will start to talk with the Serbs again. We have to. We have to have survived for something better."

Sefer

In the corner of Sefer's tent in the camp in Kukes, in northern Albania, sits an old man. He can't talk; he is mentally ill. His grandniece is jumping on his legs, but the old man doesn't seem to care. He doesn't because he is paralyzed. He owes his life to his nephew, Sefer. Sefer and his family had left their home town, Gjakova, when the Serbs forced them out and destroyed their house. They flew to Koronica, a small town west of Gjakova. When a Serbian officer from Koronica was shot by the KLA, Sefer and his family left Koronica as well—he feared the revenge of the Serbs. Since the old man was paralyzed, Sefer carried his uncle on his back all the way to Orise. On their way, the Serbs stopped them and forced Sefer to "throw down his uncle," then they arrested Sefer and about two hundred other men and stuck them into a two-yard-deep ditch. "They wanted to bury us alive," says Sefer. When some old men were released and let out of the ditch, Sefer managed to escape. He returned to the place where he had left his uncle, and continued to walk, with the old man on his back, in the direction of Meja. When he finally arrived at Meja, he saw the dead: two lines of bodies lying on the main road, all with their hands behind their heads, face down, all shot.

Sefer was a witness to the massacre of Meja where, according to Human Rights Watch, about three hundred refugees had been killed on the 27th of April. During the morning hours of the 27th, the Serbs rounded up the people between Junik and Gjakova and killed them on the main road and in a field next to the Meja road.

"If I hadn't had to carry him," says Sefer, "I would have been in Meja a few hours earlier."

In fact, it was the paralyzed old man who had saved Sefer's life—not the other way round.

Witnesses and Testimonies

"Nobody testifies for the witness," Paul Celan writes.

Writing on the war in Kosovo, the reporting from the refugee camps from across the borders was problematic.

We were not eyewitnesses, but rather were dependent on the testimony of others. The stories could not be verified through images or documents—only through independent testimony from other witnesses.

It was morally and politically delicate reporting since our stories about the war crimes did not rest within a local context, but we transported them into the public sphere of the international community. We did not work in a vacuum, but rather in a political-military conflict, and we reported, of necessity, from only one side. Although there was a correspondent who wrote from Belgrade and whose articles could challenge and oppose ours, nevertheless we covered the situation in Kosovo solely through the testimony of one party: the Albanian Kosovars.

During the first European war that was justified through the discourse of "humanitarian intervention" alone, our dispatches on the human rights violations against the Albanian Kosovars were appreciated by the belligerent parties of the NATO alliance. Especially among the German public, which traditionally opposed international missions of the Bundeswehr, Germany's armed forces, such stories of the suffering of the ethnically persecuted Albanian Kosovars could be used as a moral trump card in the rhetorical battle for war.

The public relations machine in Brussels fabricated polarizing reports from early on: the murderous acts of the

Serbs on the one side; the virtual, clean military actions by an air force that intervened only for humanitarian reasons on the other side.

Nevertheless, with all due caution toward the conditions and effects of our writing, with all due criticism of the NATO propaganda—the events in Kosovo could not be perceived ahistorically. The ethnic campaigns of Slobodan Milosevic had already destroyed Bosnia, UN troops had already failed in Srebrenica and allowed the massacre of about six thousand men, Sarajevo had been besieged, and the systematic deportations and human rights violations against Albanian Kosovars had been documented long before March 1999.

Should we now refrain from writing about the wounded refugees, the abused men and women that crossed the border in thousands into Albania? Were the war crimes we could reconstruct via the testimony of the victims not trustworthy—just because they were useful to NATO commanders?

We reported on the human rights violations committed by Serbian soldiers or militia—even though it served NATO. Just as we reported on human rights violations committed by Albanian Kosovar civilians or militia—even though those reports did not serve NATO.

When we were finally able to enter Kosovo, we were nervous.

The first town we saw, Prizren, was hardly destroyed.

Had we written false accounts? Had we been fooled by horror stories? Had we contributed with our reports to a war that was fought because of the suffering of refugees—and did their stories now turn out to be wrong?

21

Well, Prizren was to be an exception.

Other villages were almost completely destroyed. The accounts of the refugees—no matter how traumatized or disturbed they may have sounded—turned out to be amazingly accurate. Not only the numbers they had suggested but also their descriptions had been so precise that we were able to reconstruct a number of the sites of war crimes: there was the railway track they had mentioned, there the river that the train crosses, a hundred yards farther on there is a cornfield, and then . . .

Absurd Normalcy

Nothing on these trips happens as planned. Research leads to nothing, scheduled interview partners never show up, you cannot find the place you are supposed to go to, the entrance to the refugee camp is closed, everything takes longer than expected. And it is never really one's own desert if something good or reasonable works out.

It is details and accidents that decide success or failure, sometimes whether you are harmed or unharmed. A car accident can save lives when you arrive late where it was dangerous before. It is strangers whose knowledge and generosity are indispensable. Whether they welcome us or whether we meet them in the first place is pure coincidence. Sometimes there is some resemblance between us and their lost children, sometimes there is simply the desire for a cigarette or a conversation, and suddenly it is there, this atmosphere, this opening. It is not in our hands.

You can plan what to read before departure, you can

pack carefully. I am ready to admit that I am a particularly paranoid organization freak and that I take everything with me: from old and new maps of the region, Japanese mint oil, an edition of the Qur'an, and a compass to a reserve pair of extralong shoelaces.

But once on the road?

It is pure luck whom you encounter, whether you advance faster or slower. It is unconscious actions, coincidences, that gain particular importance in areas of war. If our stupid taxi driver hadn't kicked us out, we would never have met Kujtim Bilali. And without Kujtim, we would never have understood the story of Kosovo, we would never have taken so many risks, and without our trust in him, we probably would not have escaped unharmed as we did.

We—Kujtim, his nephew Noni, the photographer Sebastian, Joanne Mariner, Markus Matzel, another photographer, and I—lived together in the Thelande, a rather dubious hotel. The six of us lived together in one room with four beds—and a bunch of cockroaches. Soon I had adopted Fred, my personal cockroach. We got along quite well, particularly after I had taught him a few rules of living together. So after two days, he was so polite that he would leave the bathroom early in the morning when I wanted to go in. Unfortunately, I have to report that Fred had a tragic accident at the end of my bed one morning.

We didn't have any food those first days and hardly anything to drink but coffee and schnapps. Fortunately we had brought some food from Albania. Since our group was growing daily and since all the other journalists in this hotel were hungry as well, our supplies didn't last very long. But we had some wonderful picnics on the terrace of the hotel—tanks passing by every two minutes, making conversation impossible; KLA fighters passing by, celebrating the victory and the end of the war by shooting in the air; returning refugees on tractors passing by in front of us, while we were having dry bread and sardines and beer for breakfast.

Certain goods and abilities became highly desired or envied: whoever had been given a combat pack by the allied soldiers (who felt pity for us) was considered lucky: a combat pack is a survival kit that contains absolutely disgusting stuff, only slightly varying according to the nationality of the army (certainly the French combat pack had the best food, and rumor had it that the Italian one included condoms). The Germans, of course, had the worst: it contained crackers and three different sorts of disgraceful sausages in tubes and tins.

After one week of one massacre site after another, after one week of anticipation that each burnt house and each newly discovered crime site with tortured and murdered Albanian dead would only increase the tension between the remaining Serbs and the returning KLA fighters and refugees—after that first week of hardly any food or sleep, after dreamless nights and nightmare days, we all needed a break.

The war was over, but peace had not arrived yet—and we were simply exhausted.

We decided to organize a party.

Joanne and I went from each crowded and dirty room of the hotel to the next and invited people and said that

24

we would provide music (which was a lie) and attractive women (which was at best an exaggeration) but they would have to bring the alcohol.

The key was James, a South African technician working for the European Broadcasting Union (EBU), who had a talent for making different technical parts and equipment look and sound like a CD player. We collected and brought all we had: *ABBA Greatest Hits, Dance of the 80s,* Talking Heads, Billy Joel, Louis Armstrong, the Cure . . . it was amazing what dreadful music journalists and barkeepers in Prizren and the cleaning women of our hotel were listening to. Kujtim somehow managed to organize bottles of whiskey, gin, and schnapps, and the BBC opened their secret emergency box and donated plenty of Guinness.

For once, we stopped talking about the dead and mines and started to talk about our lives "out there," in this other world, so far away from Kosovo.

In itself, the idea of a party in this landscape of death and destruction probably seems macabre.

Bad movies and allegedly progressive media critics enjoy designing the image of the cynical war reporter: a macho guy, divorced or impotent, with his shirt wide open so that you can see his hairy chest. During the day, he (it is always a "he") sits unshaven and bored in a café at exactly the moment a bomb explodes in the street in front of him. At night, he sits in the bar of his hotel drinking whisky (as if that were available in these regions), unmoved by the world around him, only keen on a "story."

The truth is that it is hardly possible to spend more then five or six hours in the hotel—the other eighteen hours a day you are on the road. And you—yourself already a victim of these haunting images—you long for any form of cynicism that could protect you.

Everything exists at the same time in areas of violence: everyday life with its routines, its small ridiculous features, overcomes all shame. When war has become a companion of life, then normal hierarchies of sorrow wear off, the lines between normal and abnormal vanish.

When death and destruction are daily experiences, it does not become more acceptable. It is normal in a quantitative, not a qualitative sense.

You count on it.

But this expectation does not go along with moral acceptance. It is a habitual expectation—just as you walk around in winter with shoulders pulled up to your ears, against the cold, but you don't shiver any less.

Whereas the extreme paralyzes you in the beginning, whereas at first it blocks you completely, this cramp slowly disappears and you begin to search for the point of fracture, for the disruption of war. That's where you discover spaces and playgrounds that (out of context) seem absurd.

In Kukes, Albania, the town gravedigger had led us to an untreated piece of land that served as a cemetery. It was pouring rain and we were stumbling behind the man with his purple umbrella from one hole in the ground to the next. While he mumbled and complained about the war, about the nameless dead who were brought to him every day from the nearby hospital or directly from the frontier, about dying in exile and the lack of assistants, he maneuvered elegantly with his white shoes through the soaked earth around gigantic puddles and pointed to the deep, fresh graves that awaited new nourishment with open jaws. While we were walking through the clay mud, more and more red earth clustered together underneath our boots. Our steps became heavier and heavier, and we tried without much success, slightly disgusted, to get rid of the sludge. We trampled around between the graves, and we were overwhelmed equally by shame and anguish. The earth underneath our soles seemed to pull us downwards, and we hectically rubbed our boots against grass or stones— and suddenly we had to laugh. It was half-frantic, half-desperate laughter. The gravedigger and Kujtim turned toward us. Of course, there was absolutely nothing funny in this situation, everything was tragic, but nevertheless or because of that we had to laugh about its absurdity.

Roma

Already on the first day in Prizren it was predictable that the Roma would become the first victims of the new conflict in the new Kosovo.

When the first convoy with Serbian families left the city, a crowd had gathered on the pavement and threw stones at the refugees. About one hundred Albanian Kosovars were standing on the steps in front of the hotel, yelling at the trucks and cars filled with terrified Serbs. After about ten minutes, I finally understood what they were screaming: "Ci-ga-ne, Ci-ga-ne!"

In this outburst of sheer hatred, they chose the word *Gypsy* to taunt the Serbs. It seemed to them, apparently, the most evil insult that they could think of in their rage.

From early on, everything indicated that the Roma would once again be the *homo sacer*, as Giorgio Agamben calls it, the figure that can be killed without punishment being meted out later.

In the eyes of the Albanian Kosovars, the role of the Roma destined them for acts of revenge.

Certainly, the Roma never were, either individually or collectively, in a politically dominant or even influential position. Certainly, they were socially much too marginalized themselves to participate in the discrimination of Albanian Kosovars. They had not given any pretext, any motive for this violence disguised as revenge.

But they had not been deported by the Serbs. They had been spared. That alone was considered "collaboration" by the Albanian refugees.

The eternal stigmatization and persecution of Sinti and Roma has always been a scandal of history. Kosovo, unfortunately, was not different from other regions of the world. But in addition to all the old harassment against the Roma, there was something else in Kosovo.

The Roma here had been forced by the Serbs to work as carriers of the dead. They were called when someone had died; they had to collect the corpses and bring them to the morgue. In times of war, the Roma were ordered from the graveyards to the massacre sites and asked to cover all traces, to bring the bodies to some clandestine place and bury them. The Roma lived in old-fashioned settlements, mostly on the fringes of cities or directly on the graveyards where they worked.

In the unconscious of the Albanian Kosovars, the Roma were associated with death—and were feared.

. . .

We traveled to Kosovopolje in the north of Kosovo. Hundreds of Serbian families had withdrawn to this region. The atmosphere was extremely explosive, as is always the case immediately after the end of a war, a military coup, in this phase of transition, in which one side has lost privileges, influence, territory, and the sense of security and the other takes it all over.

There is never any "vacuum," as this transition is often thoughtlessly called. Power does not simply pass into a vacuum, just as energy in the physical realm doesn't get lost—it gets transferred.

The Serbian civilians were terrified, furious, helpless. They felt unjustly persecuted by the entire Western world, abandoned by their troops, which had withdrawn to the Republic of Yugoslavia, and they all were in that state of aggressiveness that is rooted in fear and impotence.

For security reasons, we left Kujtim and Noni in the car, because we did not want to provoke the Serbs with Albanian companions—and walked to a former schoolyard.

We discovered about two thousand Roma crowded together in old classrooms and in the yard. They had been expelled from their homes in the neighboring towns of Mitrovica, Podujewo, and Prishtina. They had been beaten out of their houses by returning Albanians, who had stolen their last few belongings. Now they were hiding in this school building without water or electricity. They didn't know where to go because they knew that nobody wanted them.

One of them, Naim, an eighteen-year-old boy, told me in fluent German: "We understand that the Albanians are

29

angry after all that was done to them. It was horrible. But why are they mad at us?"

Naim invited me to come inside the building with him. Sebastian with his camera should stay outside. Photographers were not wanted. Before I could coordinate with Sebastian, they pulled me inside.

The rooms were almost bursting—people were lying, sitting, standing on the floor, in the hall, in the former classrooms; there were sick and old, children and babies all lying on the cold floor. I was surrounded by a huge group that guided me, squeezed in the middle, always one hand holding mine. Old women came up to me and touched my forehead and nose as if to bless me, mothers came up and asked me for aspirin and told me of their hunger and their fear. They all talked at the same time, pushing and pulling at me, till one of them called for order again. I almost fainted because it was so hot in there and because there were so many pressing me, but there was always someone holding me from behind and Naim tried to shovel space for me to breathe.

They looked at me as if I were an alien and constantly thanked me for talking to them. I think they were touching me to find out if I was real, or maybe they were testing whether I would be scared.

It was as if they had been taught to think of themselves as leprous, and as if they were surprised that someone came who did not fear contamination, threat, or theft.

More disturbing than their living conditions was the judgment of themselves that I, in a double reflection of external perception and self-image, could read into their surprise. In mimetic assimilation, they had almost become what others had seen in them. They already anticipated our rejection of them and were amazed when someone did not see them in the distorted mirror of centuries-old prejudices. What shocked me wasn't, of course, their touch, but rather their learned fear that I would be scared of them.

Ethnic Conflict or Circle of Violence

Shortly afterward, we drove into the west of Kosovo, to Peja, the birthplace of the Serbian Orthodox Church. In its religious-political importance, Peja can probably be best compared with Rome's importance to Catholicism. If separation of Kosovo was to be the political solution for the conflict, then Peja *had* to be Serbian. For religious or political reasons, the fleeing Serbs could leave every city, every village in Kosovo—but not Peja. It was logical that Serbs seeking protection would assemble at this symbolically meaningful town. When we arrived there, hundreds had gathered inside the cathedral.

We walked inside and talked with them. The desperate Serbian Kosovars were sitting and standing in the yard, behind safe walls, and Orthodox sisters in black offered us mocha in tiny cups. We learned that a KLA commando had killed three Serbian civilians the previous day. The feared circle of violence.

We drove immediately to the neighborhood they had described to us, and found the small farm. The three dead men were still lying there. Each of them had been killed with a single shot right between the eyes. A precise execution.

Of all the dead that I saw, these were the most "intact" bodies, and yet the sight of one corpse in the first floor of the building was more disturbing than anything I had seen before. This man had still been alive twenty-four hours earlier, and now he was lying in his bedroom, on the floor, hands folded on his belly as if a priest had done his duty. There were photos on the wall next to his bed, and a framed diploma at the end of the bed. It was absolutely quiet in this room.

Suddenly, I was overcome by the shame of an intruder, as if that cold body on the floor were still alive: quite different than in the case of all those mutilated corpses, I suddenly felt confronted with a human, the house had not been burned down, everything seemed alive and inhabited. I had entered the private rooms of a stranger uninvited. Too late I realized that I had nothing to do at this scene—and ran out of the house.

When we were just walking out of the garden, back onto the road, five military vehicles arrived and the Metropolitan of Montenegro (who was substituting for the Patriarch of Peja) arrived together with two other priests. The Italian soldiers were securing the road and the little farmhouse, and within five minutes, three wooden tables had been placed in the center of the garden in front of the house, and the three dead men were brought outside and thrown onto the tables. Some Serbian neighbors dared to come out of their hiding places and the Metropolitan mixed the oil and the wine in a beer bottle and began his improvised ceremony. We were watching this scene from the edge of the garden when suddenly one of the priests came up to me and gave me one of those small honey-colored candles all the mourning neighbors were holding in their hands.

I hesitated.

For whom should I mourn? Who were these three men with the clotted blood on their foreheads? What crimes were they guilty of? Who had executed them? Why? Were these paramilitary fighters who had participated in massacres of Albanians? Or were they innocent civilians who had become victims of arbitrary Albanian violence?

Should I reject the candle?

The Italian soldiers stared at me just as the stricken Serbian faithful did.

Would I tolerate their earlier crimes if I accepted the candle, or would I tolerate their execution if I rejected it?

It was a religious funeral for three men who had been murdered and I was asked to hold a candle for the dead . . . and I took it.

Later we questioned witnesses, and what the differing accounts had in common were trivial facts: it had been at 5 PM the previous day when ten KLA fighters in uniforms had entered the farm and had killed the three immediately.

Everything else: the background, the meaning, the assessment of the deed—everything disappeared in the biased perspectives based on the ethnic identity of the witnesses. Guilt or innocence—everything dissolved in contradictory testimonies.

The Albanian neighbors declared that the three dead had been paramilitaries who had participated in burning houses of Albanians. The KLA in their headquarters in Peja said that this neighborhood had been famous for paramilitaries and had participated in a massacre in which thirty people were killed. When I asked them about these three men in particular, they just replied that it had been the whole town that was notorious for those crimes.

The old Serbian neighbor said that she was sure that these were completely normal, innocent civilians who had never committed any crimes.

Maybe it was naive to think that after this ethnic rampage there could still be a multicultural life, that the former victims could distinguish between the ethnic policy from Belgrade, the systematic killing of the Serbian militia, and uninvolved Serbian civilians, that the crimes of the past had to be remembered but not revenged.

I don't know.

What's certain is that we experienced both during these weeks: the consequences of a politically constructed ethnic hatred and the birth of a new myth of allegedly justified killings, disguised as spontaneous rage and revenge.

It is always the same pattern that turns victims into murderers: with reference to real or imagined persecutions, justifications are created for the eternal circle of violence. The inability to live a different future is rooted in what the American political theorist Wendy Brown calls a "wounded attachment," in an attachment to the wounds of the past; tied to their own humiliation, to former disgrace and persecution, they justify deeds that make them more and more similar to their former tormentors.

We left Kosovo without hope. Without relief about the end of the war—even though we had longed for it in the name of all those nameless Albanian refugees. The streams of fearful wanderers were now moving to the north, not the south anymore.

What happened to Emine, I don't know. But I hope for her and for Kosovo that she keeps her promise and begins the dialogue, because only sheer violence, Hannah Arendt once said, only sheer violence is mute.

Lebanon (October 2000)

Desperation is the mainspring
of war.

—*Simone Weil*

Golan Heights
Territory controlled by
UN troops
Sheeba farm

Telkalakh
Halba
Tripoli
Hermil
Batrum
Bsharri
Labwa
Qartaba
Mediterranean
Juniye
Ba'albek
Beirut
Zahle
Ed Darnur
Zebdani
LEBANON
Sidon
Jezzin
Rasheiya
□
Damascus
Merj Uyun
Tyros
SYRIA
Bint Jubeil
El Quneitra
ISRAEL
Akko
Safad
Haifa
0   25   50 km
Lake of Gennesareth

Dear friends,

Sometimes we are magically drawn to the things we do not understand.

Lebanon, that legendary cedar state with its hybrid, defiantly flourishing capital, Beirut, has always been a place of irresistible attraction. Ever since childhood I have been fascinated by the disturbing images of ghostly house-to-house combat in the embattled city. Aside from the pictures of the Schleyer kidnapping and of the leaden autumn of the Red Army Faction, it was images of the Lebanese civil war that captivated our entire family night after night. It was my first genuine political television experience.

Unless I'm mistaken, it was the first war that I experienced on TV, as it was taking place, and it was the first war that I understood *as such*.

So this was war?

In my parents' living room, the various waves of killing in that faraway country soon became blurred and indistinguishable: the fighting between Maronite Christian Phalangists and Muslims after 1975, the Syrian invasion in 1976, the Israeli invasion in 1978, the air attacks on Beirut, and finally the massacres of Chatila and Sabra in 1982. Everything began to merge into sequences of images without contours, into the recurring greenish yellow glow of bombardment until, suddenly, there were no more images of entire cities—they had been replaced by tiny segments, fractions of scenes filmed through a gap or a break in a wall that could barely have provided adequate cover.

It had long since become impossible to tell things apart in this seemingly endless conflict, to figure out where the fighting was taking place, who was being killed and which militias were being celebrated or feared at any given moment, and why.

Once Upon a Distant War is the title of a book by William Prochnau about young war correspondents in the early days of the Vietnam War. That was what Lebanon once represented for me—an absurd war in a faraway place.

Although the strange images I saw on TV seemed unreal and almost harmless, I could never forget the horrible sounds of death and destruction: artillery fire, at times sharp and immediate and at times muffled and distant, and the lighter crackling of machine guns.

Even as a child, I was more impressed by sounds than images. Oddly, visual and acoustic perceptions seem to operate separately in my mind. I was able to store the images of gun battles in Beirut *without* attaching any meaning to them.

My colleagues and friends would add that this is the reason I write such miserable news stories, stories that lack the visual element that has become so all-important today. But I became aware of the acoustic imprint of war, in all of its gruesome polyphony, the first time I heard the sound of Katyusha rockets.

It wasn't until years later that I finally traveled to this country, still mysterious to this day.

40

The war had ended and the senseless violence had subsided. The Boujri, the central square in downtown Beirut, had become a peaceful place again. Elegantly dressed people sit once again in the cafés on the Corniche, Beirut's famous promenade bordering the magnificent bay, and at night everything sways to the beat of Arab pop music or French techno booming from the city's bars and nightclubs. In the old city, rebuilt houses now cover the traces of civil war, but the war lives on in the gestures and habits of Beirut's inhabitants. Just as West Berliners, a full ten years after the fall of the Berlin Wall, still take absurd detours along a now-imaginary wall, some Beirutis still avoid some of the most embattled streets of the civil war, streets long since peaceful, while others walk more quickly than necessary, their painful memories still acting as a cautious guide in the new Lebanon.

I went to Lebanon a few months after the Israeli army had withdrawn, in May, from the "occupied zone"/"security zone" (this is where disputes over terminology begin: *security zone* is what the Israeli government called the territory in southern Lebanon controlled by its troops, while the Lebanese civilian population called the region the *occupied territories*).

We were interested in the still-unstable new order in southern Lebanon. What had changed since then? What kind of situation would we encounter in this area—without the Lebanese army and mainly controlled by Hezbollah? What is Hezbollah? Is it merely an organization of fanatical terrorists who kidnap and murder Israeli soldiers, or is a political party to be taken seriously? How are the 260,000 to 350,000 Palestinian refugees faring in the camps? How does someone feel who has been confined to a refugee camp for fifty-two years? How secure is the border? Will there finally be peace? And when it comes to peace, whose decision is it—Hezbollah's? The Syrians'? Iran's?

The media pay little attention to this area, even though evidence of virtually every remaining disputed issue in the Middle East comes to light on Lebanese soil: Hezbollah, financed and supported by Iran, admired by Christian and Muslim Lebanese alike for its successful "resistance"/ "struggle" against Israeli forces; the violent struggle against Israel; the Palestinian refugees who are being held in camps but long to return to Palestine and Israel.

The multiethnic state of Lebanon is a society without a clear majority (all ethnic groups are equally represented in the population).

Syria is also worth mentioning in this context: the protective power, the great "friend," originally brought in at the request of the Lebanese president Suleiman Franjieh to prevent Lebanese citizens from killing one another. In fact, Syria appears to be both a "protective power" that acted against common enemy, Israel, and an "occupation power" that today holds Lebanon in its octopuslike tentacles.

How We Traveled

Our team on this journey through Lebanon consisted of three people: our driver, Mohammed, a melancholy Muslim Lebanese who spoke only Arabic and whose preferred topic of conversation was his tragic love life; our photographer, B., a warm-hearted Maronite Lebanese, fluent in Arabic and French; and Marwan, a charming, half-Muslim and half-Christian, twenty-two-year-old Palestinian who had studied political science at the American University in Beirut and spoke Arabic, French, and English.

All we needed was a Syrian and we would have had all of Lebanon in our gigantic, gold-colored Mercedes.

But even without a Syrian in our little group, we were constantly embroiled in minor civil wars in the car. Each of us held a different view of the Syrians' role, each had a different way of looking at the causes and events of the civil war, and each entertained different hopes for the future.

Luckily, there were some things we did have in common. One was our passion for good food at almost any time, day or night. Each of us loved to make the occasional stop at one of countless roadside stands to eat flatbread with cheese, *kibbé*, olive paste, bread with warm cheese and honey, *foul* made of dried beans with olive oil and lemon, *shavarma* and salted yoghurt.

One could write an entire book about the hospitality of the Lebanese, about the obvious pleasure they take in giving and about their delectable dishes, about their sensuous love of color and about the fragrances of their breads, about their sweets and baked goods.

We drove south along the coast almost every day, returning to Beirut in the evening.

My conversations with politicians, intellectuals, and religious leaders in the capital during my first few days in Lebanon prepared me for spending time in the south, and it was only through these conversations that I was able to prepare myself for this beautiful and angry, sad and exhausted, lively and violent country.

Blinders

It's impossible to report on Lebanon without writing about Israel, the dispute over the Holy Land, the refugee question, and protection for persecuted Jews and displaced Palestinians.

In many of us, these issues conjure up deeply entrenched convictions and open wounds. One cannot write about this region of the Middle East without causing offense, displeasure, or unease; one cannot express words of understanding without being accused of downplaying the issues; one cannot express criticism without being accused of aggression.

But at least some degree of damage control can be achieved by first disclosing a few limitations:

We find it all too easy to imagine that we can consider various cultures, historical facts, and convictions with the same respect, open-mindedness, and circumspection.

It would be dishonest of me to write this report about Lebanon without first confessing to my own unacknowledged biases about the Middle East, biases that I have tried to revise again and again as a result of the impressions I have gained on many trips to Muslim countries.

This is not as obvious a conclusion as one might perhaps assume.

Of course, it seems appropriate that a German of my

generation, whose entire political socialization was shaped by discussion of the Third Reich and the Holocaust, would feel a special obligation to the Jews who were driven to settle in Israel.

Contrary to what the neoconservative discourse surrounding the relevant pronouncements by Peter Sloterdijk or Martin Walser would have us believe, I find this shaping of public thought by the Holocaust to be neither bothersome nor restrictive, but instead necessary and instructive.

Among my generation, opinions about our relationship with Israel remained split between those who, seeing the Holocaust as grounds for collective responsibility, developed a special concern for protecting the Jews (worldwide, not just in Israel), and those who, acting on the same motives, felt especially guilty about the situation of the Palestinians, whom they see as the last victims of Jewish displacement from Europe and the founding of the state of Israel. Few are able to reconcile the two views.

But my personal understanding of the Middle East was also influenced by my affection for a Lebanese friend of many years, Nayla Wiegand. She was the one who impressed on me the fate of the Lebanese, caught between civil war and emigration. Constantin, her second son, is my godson. A few years ago, acts of terrorism claimed someone who was close to each of us in the very same month. Monstrous violence had broken into our lives and that of our friends, a violence both cowardly and mute, destructive and pointless. And although the circumstances of our respective losses were completely different, we have remained bound together in our sorrow ever since.

I believed that I was morally prepared for the challenges I would face in Lebanon. Armed with this close personal relationship with my friend in Lebanon and a deep sense of connectedness to Israel's fate, I believed I could be impartial. By my trip was to expose my sheer ignorance.

When you drive south from Beirut, you see the Mediterranean on your right, while orange, lemon, and banana plantations extend along both sides of the road. You drive through the old cities of Sidon and Tyre, and at some point you arrive in the former "security zone," the "occupied territory."

The towns here seem desolate, because very few of their former inhabitants have dared to return to their old farms.

The landscape gradually changes, becoming increasingly barren. The ground is dry and hard, a few shepherds watch their flocks as they graze on rocky hills, and the only plants that continue to thrive here are olive trees and tobacco plants.

After a two-hour drive, we arrived at a higher elevation that affords a view of this dusty, mountainous region, the Golan Heights off to the east and Israel directly in front of us. Although the north, with its fertile, irrigated farms, is far more beautiful, I was filled with joy as I gazed at this landscape.

As I looked at the olive trees lining the hills farther south, the word *Canaan* rose from some deep, hidden corner of my being, and I felt something akin to a homecoming.

I am neither Jewish nor deeply religious, but as I stood there on the border, I suddenly discovered just how deeply my thoughts and emotions have been influenced by the archetypical images and stories of the Old Testament.

I had never realized what a profound effect these images and stories—which I had always perceived as tales of childhood or sediments of education—had shaped my associations.

Perhaps this is how religion, the constant repetition of religious acts and motives, works—irrespective of our faith: we become familiar with the stories, and as we read them we imagine the main characters, their lives, their pain, their conflicts, and everything we read and hear finally becomes a constitutive part of our emotional being. I will never be able to eat a cucumber sandwich without thinking of the hypocrisy of the characters in Oscar Wilde's *The Importance of Being Earnest*, will never look at someone with a birthmark without recalling Saul Zurata's empathy in Vargas Llosa's *The Storyteller*, and will never smell lilacs again without thinking of Thomas Mann's unrequited love in *"Fallen."*

I needed the trip to Lebanon, and it was important that I stand on the other side of the fence. It was the only way I could comprehend just how strongly Israel, this promised, shattered land, and its myths have informed my being in the world.

The Palestinian Camp

In the tiny shop in Ain el Hilweh, Lebanon's largest Palestinian refugee camp, not far from the city of Sidon, a black-and-white television set sits wedged between bags of sugar and flour, emitting a bluish glow. Hattin Tawfic's entire family crowds together in front of a table, watching stone-throwing children turn into dead martyrs who are wrapped in flags and heaped with praise.

In the evening, when the day's heat slowly subsides in the camp, the neighbors converge on the shop to talk about the tiny incidents in their eventless lives.

The TV set, with its images from Palestine, provides neither comfort nor diversion, only deepening a sense of sadness and longing among its viewers.

Knowledge doesn't feel at all like power here, no matter how often Hattin Tawfic watches the images broadcast by CNN. All he feels is his own powerlessness.

He is tired. His eyes have been ruined by the contaminated water in the camp, gout has stiffened his joints, and when he watches the evening news he becomes angrier than a man his age should be.

He has been a refugee for fifty-two years, and although he has lived in the same place the entire time, although he has never moved on in fifty-two years, he always feels as if he were still traveling and had never arrived.

In 1948, he left Palestine and walked all the way to Lebanon. He spent his first four years on Lebanese soil living in a tent with the fifteen members of his family. Now he is eighty-one, too old to derive strength from the hope of ever laying eyes on his native town of Tabara again.

The refugee camp has since grown into a small city, complete with houses and streets, shops and mosques. The streets are narrow, apparently built just wide enough to allow for the passage of two Mercedeses at the same time.

Hattin's family no longer lives in a tent. Instead, he and eleven other family members live in a two-room apartment.

The camp lies in a clearly demarcated valley. The Palestinians are not permitted to settle anywhere outside its walls or venture for long past a checkpoint where guards watch everything that comes or goes. Although they are allowed to leave the camp for visits, they are not permitted to live anywhere else.

"Our land is in flames," says Hattin's wife, and the people standing around in the shop nod silently. "We want to fly there and help."

A group of children causes a scene in front of the shop. Spotting a journalist taking notes, they've quickly come together to stage a protest. They pretend to be angry, to show that they are prepared to go to war. We pay as little attention to them as possible, because we don't want to contribute to the irresponsible circular dynamic in which media interest encourages aggressiveness because aggressiveness attracts media interest. The children are between seven and thirteen, and they wave the Palestinian flag. One boy ties a Palestinian headscarf around his head, mimicking his brothers on CNN, and the children begin shouting so loudly, yelling anti-Israeli slogans, that it becomes difficult to hear what Hattin has to say.

Because television fatally thrives on moveable images, thoughtless cameramen prefer filming the staged spectacle of a group of bored children instead of portraying the motionless sorrow of the camp's elderly refugees. Their images convey the impression of Palestinian refugees as a thoroughly brutalized society of murderous children, and not as a vegetating, imprisoned people.

Just around the corner, a few hundred yards away, Aayed Attwat waits for his flatbread to finish baking. He stands in front of a pizza oven and refuses to speak with me, thinking that I'm Jewish. I refuse to deny it. Why would I? Is the fact that I am not Jewish a criterion for conversation?

The interpreter wants to tell him that I'm German, but I decline this ticket into the Arab world—not just because there are no mutually exclusive identifying characteristics between being German and Jewish, but also because it is a truly abysmal twist of history that Germans should be welcomed because of their presumed anti-Semitism.

Then it occurs to the old man that I could be English (apparently the second-worst option for Palestinians)— and he still refuses to speak with me.

Meanwhile, the screeching children with their simulated hostility have arrived at the pizza parlor, screaming even louder than before. Fortunately, Marwan has a low tolerance for both noise and impolite behavior, and he quickly dispatches the gang around the next corner.

Aayed takes the opportunity to scream at me in Arabic. From the few bits of his tirade I can make out, I understand that he is holding me responsible for the crimes of the British. Finally, I become irritated and ask him, "Do I look British?" (a coup, I find, given my rather un-British appearance). Marwan translates, and the old man responds: "How do I know you're not from Israel? You look like you could be."

Which takes us back to square one.

The pizza baker, who has been watching the entire exchange in silence, sympathetically gives me a piece of bread, and when I say one of the ten Arab words in my vocabulary—*shukran*, thank you—Aayed suddenly wants to talk after all.

Long ago, earlier in his life, he was a lemon farmer. But now he is seventy-five, his country is lost, and all that remains for Aayed is bitterness.

"Hezbollah is the most honest party," he says. "Our own officials are the traitors." Like many other Palestinians in the camp, he despises Yasser Arafat, because, as they believe, he "sold" the Palestinian refugees by signing treaties with Israel.

The eternal refugees of Ain El Hilweh feel isolated in a foreign land. Most Lebanese, Muslims and Christians alike, still associate the Palestinians with instability and civil war, and many have trouble forgetting the actions of the universally hated Arafat, who arrived in their country and behaved as if he were its ruler, not its guest.

Although many Arabs are quick to invoke Arab brotherhood when issuing vehement declarations and engaging in joint attacks against Israel, by no means does it lead to solidarity with the Palestinians, offers of assistance, or even the integration of Palestinian refugees. The Palestinians have been living under the most wretched conditions possible for more than forty years. They are constantly being used as political tools, their displacement described as deeply lamentable and unfortunate—and yet they are not welcome in any neighboring country in the Middle East.

Their situation has only deteriorated further as a result of Israel's withdrawal from southern Lebanon and the ongoing intifada in Israel. The enemy, whose presence established a bond between the Palestinians and their Lebanese surroundings, no longer exists on this side of the border.

But, more important, the Lebanese, weary of perpetual war and domination by another state, long for a return to normalcy. But it is precisely this longing for normalcy that runs counter to the interests of the Palestinian refugees. They are the leftovers of a long war, and in the misery of exile they endure, surviving in the knowledge that as long as the intifada continues, they will not forget, and as long as the occupied territories remain an open wound, they will continue to hope for a better life. This is why the Palestinians worship Hezbollah, which, in its acts of violence, continues to destroy any sense of normalcy and upholds the Palestinians' belief in a return to the Promised Land.

In Er Rashidieh, another camp along the coast farther south of Tyre, Sultan Abu al Aymaiin, Al Fatah's representative in Lebanon, agrees to meet with us. At the entrance to the camp we are greeted by three Al Fatah soldiers wielding Kalashnikovs. But first we must pass through the Lebanese checkpoint. When we reach the second, Palestinian checkpoint, the three guards keep us waiting under an enormous poster of Arafat.

The security measures are not surprising. Sultan al Aymaiin has been sentenced to life imprisonment in absentia by a Lebanese court, on charges of having founded a terrorist organization.

Despite the court's ruling, the Lebanese authorities have never even attempted to arrest Al Aymaiin. The camps remain essentially off-limits to local authorities. Despite the fact that he is a terrorist who has been officially sentenced to life in prison, we had no trouble calling Al Aymaiin on his mobile phone from Beirut to schedule an interview. In addition to tolerating the presence of people such as Al Aymaiin, the Lebanese authorities turn a blind eye to weapons in the Palestinian camps.

Al Aymaiin has his own interpreter, who monitors Marwan's translation. Al Fatah is in a difficult position. Despite having fought for so many years, Al Fatah's soldiers are losing more and more respect with each passing day. Many Palestinians believe that Hezbollah is the only force capable of defeating the technologically superior Israeli army, while Al Fatah's aging fighters sit around "uselessly" on the Lebanese side of the border.

And so Abu al Aymaiin can do little more than repeat stories from the past. He sits in this camp, watches the violent clashes of the new intifada on CNN every night, and touts Al Fatah as a symbol of resistance—a symbol, nothing more and nothing less, because all that remains for Al Fatah's leader is to feed the fantasy that Hezbollah is merely a copy of the original.

As we converse, the small gold model of the Al-Aksah Mosque on Al Aymaiin's desk suddenly lights up, and a mechanical muezzin begins to pray. The only thing that prevents me from laughing out loud is the bodyguard's Kalashnikov.

But there really isn't anything to laugh about, because the tiny mosque, a constant reminder of a faraway home, represents precisely the core of the issue in this conflict.

Five times a day, this ugly, ridiculous plastic mosque reminds Al Aymaiin that the Palestinians are not where they belong, that their exile can never be home. Five times a day, the automated voice whines "Allahu Akbar," the squawking muezzin a reminder of what Jerusalem means to the Palestinians.

One of the key questions of the future will revolve around the potential danger emanating from these despondent Palestinian refugees in their camps.

Timor Güksel, the commander of UNIFIL (the United Nations Interim Force in Lebanon), sees more misery than despondency in the camps. Nevertheless, a single frustrated individual attacking the border could trigger the uncontrollable dynamics of violence and retribution at any time. And no one could prevent it.

Hezbollah 1

The reality of Hezbollah is confusingly complex.

Anyone who attempts to describe this organization as a homogeneous social entity underestimates its power of attraction and the fact that it is deeply rooted in the society of the south, as well as the dangers it poses.

There is nothing complex about Hezbollah's violent, cold-blooded, and repugnant attacks.

As I describe life in southern Lebanon, Hezbollah's social network and its charitable activities, I do so with absolutely no intention of playing down the fundamentally appalling nature of its violent crimes. But without acknowledging the many layers of this ambivalent entity, it would be impossible to understand why its members are so obviously revered, why its members of parliament are praised, even by politicians from other parties, and why it is so difficult to fight Hezbollah.

Before departing for the south, we contacted Hezbollah to notify the organization that we would be traveling in "its" territory.

How does one go about notifying Hezbollah?

Beyond its terrorist network, Hezbollah is a surprisingly well organized party in Beirut. To set up the meeting, Marwan simply called Hezbollah's press agent, Sheikh Ata, explained that we planned to travel to the south, and asked whether we could pay him a courtesy visit first, partly to enhance our own security in the Hezbollah-controlled zone. We drove to a suburb of Beirut, where we saw veiled women walking through the heavily populated, winding streets. Sheikh Ata met with us in a run-down, inconspicuous building.

He stands under a portrait of Khomeini and apologizes for not shaking my hand, nodding his head instead (which doesn't lessen the insult of his religiously motivated refusal to shake the hand of a presumably unclean woman, but at least he appears to be aware of the offense).

Sheikh Ata proves to be a friendly, helpful intermediary. He offers to contact a few important Hezbollah officials in the south, gives us some telephone numbers, and promises to arrange a meeting I have requested with Mohammed Raad, the chairman of the Hezbollah faction in the Lebanese parliament.

He offers to provide us with a "helper" in the south, but we thank him and decline the offer. Traveling in the company of a member of Hezbollah would be impossible. It would destroy any sense of neutrality and make it impossible for us to hear voices critical of Hezbollah. Besides, no former member of the SLA (South Lebanon Army, the Lebanese militia that joined forces with Israel and fought against Hezbollah) would want to talk to us.

Although Sheikh Ata is shrewd enough to understand why we prefer to travel alone, he nevertheless proves to be both cooperative and efficient.

Few in Lebanon see Hezbollah as a terrorist organization, because they don't see Israel as a peaceful neighbor. It is not just the destruction the Israeli army left behind in southern Lebanon that redeems Hezbollah's fighters in the minds of the Lebanese. UN Resolution 425, which calls for the withdrawal of the Israeli Defense Forces (IDF), also elevates the members of Hezbollah to the status of resistance fighters rather than terrorists.

Even large portions of the Maronite Christian upper class in Beirut are convinced that Hezbollah plays an important role for the poor, unemployed Muslims in the smaller cities of the south. Not only is Hezbollah treated as the liberator of the south, but also as a party that takes care of its supporters. In southern Lebanon, Hezbollah has helped build the local infrastructure, administers a vital healthcare system that operates the region's hospitals, and runs a construction company that helps rebuild destroyed houses and roads.

Absurdly enough, I was treated in a hospital run by Hezbollah. From daily exposure to anti-Semitic remarks in countless conversations, I had developed a psychosomatic blister on my tongue that was making it increasingly difficult for me to speak. Finally, our photographer assured me that the doctors would treat anyone, regardless of their religion or nationality. Under a giant portrait of Khomeini, a veiled nurse patiently dabbed Piralvex onto my swollen tongue and didn't even bat an eye when I provocatively paid my bill in U.S. dollars.

Search for Traces

Moujib Termos is twenty-eight but looks forty-five. His forehead is studded with deep scars. He has been a member of the Hezbollah since the age of seventeen. He was arrested by the SLA shortly after he joined Hezbollah, and was detained in Khiam. He spent the last eleven years in the notorious prison at Khiam, which has been condemned repeatedly by the International Red Cross and by Human Rights Watch for its cruel conditions and physical abuse. He was released a few months ago when the Israeli army withdrew and the SLA militia just left the prison unguarded.

Maybe he remains here at the prison in the service of Hezbollah propaganda, so that foreign visitors learn of the crimes of the Israeli army and its ally, the SLA. Maybe he simply does not know what to do with his new freedom and the joblessness in the south. Maybe his traumatic experiences behind these walls continue to haunt him. Maybe all motives are intertwined.

Moujib guides us through the empty hallways and cells of his former prison and describes how he was brought to the interrogation room every day during the first six months, with a hood over his head, where he was beaten before he was even asked a question. The barren room radiates nothing: no horror, no darkness, a disinterested witness of daily abuse. Nothing else.

He had to kneel on the floor, Moujib says, like this . . . and each question about Hezbollah was accompanied by a blow to his head, he says. Three times a day he was brought to this room, he says, three times a day the same questions, the same beatings. After two months, electric cables were attached to his ears, fingertips, and genitals, he says, and then electroshocks were sent through his body.

Twenty times a day, he recounts, he fainted, long after he had lost all ability to speak. Whoever thinks torture is about statements and confessions is naive. Beyond vicious physical torture there is nothing but stammer, whimper, and unconsciousness.

Moujib shows us his cell where, he says, he was locked up for six months: a small dungeon of 4.6 feet × 2.6 feet, stone floor, metal door, only one small hole on top of the cell so that fresh air—and rain—could enter.

There was no toilet, no running water, no window. When the door is closed fresh air enters only through the hole. A small bucket for excrement was emptied every ten days; the guard could open a small bolt in the door to control the detainee.

The guards used to pass by the cell any hour of the day, he says, and kick against the metal door from the outside— so that if the isolation and darkness and limited space hadn't been enough, the noise of the banging against the door would definitely drive you mad.

Shall I repeat this?

He spent six months in this cell, 4.6 feet × 2.6 feet, unable to stretch, stone floor, no window, no toilet, just a hole on top. Six months.

Secretly, I was searching for reasons to doubt his story. Worse, I searched for reasons to justify his treatment. Hadn't he been, according to his own account, a member of Hezbollah? What kind of crimes had he committed? How much more sadistic had his actions against Israeli soldiers been in comparison to his detention? Wasn't it necessary for the troops in Lebanon to defend themselves against ruthless terrorists like Moujib? Maybe he had never lived in this dungeon. Maybe the Hezbollah had dictated every single word he told us.

We stared into this dark cell and did not want to, did not want to believe it—simply because none of us wanted to imagine it. Self-protection needs doubt of the painful truth as an escape agent. That is how we respond as TV viewers, when we cannot bear the suffering of others, when the images are too overwhelming, and so too we journalists react when confronted with injustice and violence.

I tried to distract myself from the inner horror through the alleged precision of research. That's a trained technique of contemporary journalists: in particularly disturbing contexts, we suddenly focus on details to increase our investigative credibility, the so-called authenticity of our subjective narratives. Then you suddenly find license plates, car types, colors, and brand names in the stories and reports—which are only in rare exceptions of any relevance.

So I tried to whitewash my own shame about the endured pain of the other by pretending professional activity. I went inside the cell in order to measure the size with my feet—when Moujib asked me whether he should shut the door for a moment, just so that I could see how dark it was.

He closed the door, and after three seconds I wanted to scream.

I knew they were standing outside, knew that they didn't have keys to lock the door, knew that they were my friends, knew that I would be quickly out of there again, and yet I lost my nerve after just a few seconds.

More?

There was a steel power pole in the prison. It stood next to the barracks where the prisoners were detained if they had survived the first six months of interrogation (by the way, apparently there was no interest in killing the prisoners; they were tortured just long enough to destroy them, but not long enough to kill them).

Anyway, there was this steel power poll next to the barracks, and it had a little mistake. Some inattentive steelworker years ago had unintentionally cut the crossbeams a little too long so that they were hanging over just by a few inches. An irrelevant tiny mistake for the power pole, but a crucial few inches for the prisoners who were handcuffed and tied to this pole. When they were beaten, these few inches cut into their heads and backs. That's where Moujib's scars came from.

Over the years approximately 3,500 prisoners have been mistreated in Khiam prison, and considering what was done here, it seems surprising that "only" twenty-four detainees died.

60

Under pressure from two human rights groups in Israel, the Association for Civil Rights and the Center for the Defense of the Individual, the Israeli Ministry of Defense has admitted its involvement in the torture and interrogation practices at Khiam prison. It was also confirmed in an affidavit by Brigadier General Dan Halutz, who was in charge of the IDF's operations in south Lebanon.

My sense of solidarity with Israel as a German does not make me blind or deaf to Israeli offenses. What the sometimes shrill debate on anti-Semitism and anti-Zionism neglects is the critique that is rooted in emotional proximity to and worry about Israel, rather than in anti-Semitic hatred or denial of Israel's right to exist.

A Discussion of the Lebanese Nation

The Maronite patriarch, Cardinal Nasrallah Sfeir, resides in a huge castle on a mountain in the east, overlooking Beirut and the bay.

He speaks out for those who demand the withdrawal of the Syrian army from Lebanon. He is eighty years old, but his sparkling brown eyes give him the look of a man thirty years younger. Nevertheless, it seems as if his perceived closeness to God and death has eliminated any fear he would otherwise have of the Syrians. He is also convinced that there has been a fundamental shift in the attitudes of Lebanese society ever since the Israeli withdrawal. By now, both Muslims and Christians share the sentiments many Christians had previously expressed privately. On the Lebanese day of independence, students held vocal demonstrations, demanding that the Syrians return to their own country.

It's a new and controversial discussion.

Many traumatized families still fear that if the Syrian army were to withdraw, extremists from all possible religious communities could plunge the country into another civil war.

On the other hand, Syrian control over the country has become so pervasive that even the Lebanese who once felt the greatest sense of gratitude to the Syrians are outraged. Syria interferes in the country's internal political affairs as it sees fit, imposes constraints on the fragile Lebanese economy with its export restrictions, and uses Lebanese territory for its war against Israel, instead of waging its costly battles on its own soil.

Moderate voices like those of Nassib Lahoud, Lebanon's former ambassador to the United States, and Nayla Moawad, the widow of the murdered former president René Moawad and a member of parliament herself, have at least spoken out in favor of a public and open discussion of relations between Syria and Lebanon. And yet even their relatively tame dissent is considered scandalous in this Syrian satellite state.

They know that a certain strategic dependency on Syria is for the time being necessary, in light of the Arab-Israeli conflict, but they also see the need to renegotiate the terms of Syria's presence in Lebanon.

Everyone looks with anticipation to Damascus, where the relatively inexperienced Bashar Assad holds the key to Lebanon's future. Whether Lebanon will be able to govern itself at some point in the future depends in large part on Assad.

Hezbollah 2

Mohammed Raad likes to be called "Hajj" Raad, because this honorary title indicates that he has made the pilgrimage to Mecca, an accomplishment of which he is proud. Indeed, he has made the pilgrimage twice.

When I ask Raad what the trip meant to him, he responds: "I would like you to be able to experience it. It cleanses the soul." It's a somewhat ambivalent remark, since it remains open as to whether he intends to convey regret for the fact that I, as a woman and an infidel, will never have this experience, or whether he feels that my soul could use cleansing.

Raad, the chairman of the twelve-member Hezbollah faction in the Lebanese parliament in Beirut, is an intelligent, crafty politician. He knows that his organization has gained respect in recent years, especially in the last few months, when the acts of revenge and retribution Western experts expected in the wake of the Israeli army's withdrawal failed to materialize. Although he feels confident of the recognition his party and movement have attained, he is also clever enough to recognize the dangers. After all, Hezbollah can only lose in comparison with its current position.

Hezbollah gets its funding from Iran and a few wealthy Lebanese Shiite businessmen in West Africa. But it also depends on Syria's presence in Lebanon, because it was the Syrians who prevented the Lebanese army from being stationed in southern Lebanon.

UN Resolution 425 calls for the stationing of official national forces, not the Hezbollah militia. During a meeting of the UN Security Council in October 2000, an angry Kofi Annan criticized the Lebanese government for abandoning the entire south to Hezbollah's control. The Lebanese, who couldn't publicly admit to Syria's influence, reacted by simply reinterpreting Resolution 425, arguing that Israel had not yet withdrawn completely, because it still occupied the Shebaa Farms area, which supposedly belonged to Lebanon. A second line of argumentation ends in the question: Why should the Lebanese army protect Israel and its borders?

For Nayla Moawad, these arguments are ridiculous. She says: "It's quite simple. We have an army, and I believe it is the normal duty of military forces to be stationed on the borders of my country. Period."

In reality, it appears that Syria has no interest in Lebanon having peaceful borders. Syria still wants to recapture the Golan Heights, but without having to fight for the region on its own territory. This is why the open wound of the Lebanese border is needed, why Hezbollah is needed to handle the fighting (although Hezbollah cannot be too successful, because this would make Syria dispensable for Lebanon), and why the "Lebanese" Shebaa Farms are needed, to give Lebanon an excuse to prolong its conflict with Israel.

Shebaa Farms is a dusty area that is currently part of the Israeli-occupied Syrian territory southeast of Lebanon. According to the United Nations, there is not a single map of Lebanon or Syria from the 1950s or later that could be used to document that this is Lebanese territory. In other words, Lebanon has no legitimate claim to the region.

As Timor Güksel of UNIFIL explains, no one laid claim to the area when the resolution was signed, nor had any serious claims been filed by the time Israel withdrew from southern Lebanon. Richard Norton of Boston University, one of the leading Western experts on Hezbollah, describes Shebaa Farms essentially as a blatant diversionary tactic. But apparently it's one that works.

Hezbollah refuses to respond to questions about the condition of the Israeli soldiers it has kidnapped, instead pursuing a strategy of "information in return for information."

"We are prepared to negotiate over the prisoners, independently of the Shebaa Farms issue," says Raad.

But until then, one will simply have to wait. No one seems to care about what this means for the kidnapped Israelis. When asked about the issue, Hezbollah officials are quick to cite the statistics of how many prisoners on the one side are offset by kidnapped Israelis on the other. Statistics to legitimize injustice.

Human rights are not applied generally here, only relatively.

Hitler

Never before have I been confronted with so many people who admire Hitler. Unfortunately, one of them was our photographer.

I spent a day and a half listening, quietly, to his occasional anti-Semitic rants, his occasional praise for the Nazis, and his pronouncements of sympathy for Hitler.

When I was a child, it was a normal phenomenon that when we were on class trips to the Netherlands or Denmark, other children would throw stones at us, cursing us as Nazi kids. We couldn't hold it against them. For us, it was perfectly normal that we didn't speak German in certain situations in other countries, for fear that it would remind people of their experiences during the Holocaust.

But the fact that Germany's shameful past was suddenly being talked about as something laudable, that we were suddenly being praised for disgraceful crimes—that was outrageous.

It seemed difficult to explain my rejection of Nazism and my relationship with Jews or with Israel to our photographer, B., and others without losing their confidence in me as a fair-minded journalist, as someone who could report just as critically about Israel and its human rights violations as about the terrorist activities of Hezbollah and authoritarian Syria.

After two days, during which I suffered in silence, just as we returned from Khiam and were all still shocked by the stories of abuse that had been committed there, B. suddenly blurted out: "I would have preferred it if Hitler had killed them all, the Jews."

Where could I begin?

I asked Mohammed to stop the car.

How was I to set the historic facts straight and explain the special significance these crimes have for me? And not just to anyone, but to people who were directly affected by the displacement and exodus of European Jews?

How could a dialogue about such irreconcilable experiences succeed? In a car? On a highway? In such a short period of time? Hopeless.

Jews have always been Israelis, and Israelis have always been perpetrators, not victims—this was the distorted formula of many in the Middle East. Those who subscribed to it ignored Jewish or German history, the immeasurable suffering the Jews experienced.

They had to be coaxed into a story that requires them to *imagine* Jews as defenseless, marginalized, displaced, and finally murdered victims. Accustomed as they were to fear and rejection of Jews, it took a slow, careful telling of the story of the Holocaust to open their minds to understanding and perhaps even compassion.

I talked for a long time.

Finally, I told B. that he could curse me as a German, he could blame us for our crimes, for the wars we have forced on the world, for the destruction of Jewish life in Eastern Europe, for the disgusting, unbelievable industrial extermination of millions of people, and for the Holocaust— and rightfully so. But he should never again dare to praise Hitler and his unprecedented crimes in my presence.

I thought that was it. But the conversation couldn't possibly end there.

And then all of us, one after another, began talking about our pasts, about the real and imagined experiences of each our societies.

We talked about how difficult it is to free oneself from the special treatment of these roles as victims—and not to become indifferent to others.

The experience of injustice all too often immunizes against the suffering of others.

The painter Francis Bacon completed a series of paintings in the 1940s that illustrates how violence and suffering register in our bodies and consume us. In Bacon's disturbing oil paintings, titled *Heads*, disembodied figures and distorted faces hover in an almost depthless space, imbued with agony and suffering, while torn-open mouths seem to scream in pain. What is missing in Bacon's images—and I am reminded of this on our journey through Lebanon—are the eyes. These mistreated figures are no longer capable of gazing outward. Their agony absorbs everything, displacing their perceptions into their inner selves—and the outside world becomes invisible.

On the plane ride home, as I was looking out the window, I asked myself how I would feel if I were to stand on the other side of the border, in Israel, on my next trip to the region. How would I react to the view of the fertile hills of southern Lebanon? Would I be filled with the joy of familiarity? With the fond memories of the hospitality I had experienced, of that war-torn society whose members are nevertheless able to pull off this astonishing generosity day after day?

Nothing will change my deep sense of closeness to Israel, but new impressions have been added. The stories, images, and friendships that form our identities have been expanded.

Russel Hardin speaks of the epistemological comfort of home. But what he does not explicitly mention is that home is not necessarily a single, stable place.

It is the encounters with people who tell us about themselves, their stories of myths and legends, the suspicions that build over generations, but also the hope that refuses to dry up, the songs and spices that we come to know, the way the twilight suddenly sharpens the contours of objects and figures, the sound of language, books—all of this together forms the experience of home. It is many-layered, interrupted, dynamic.

Lebanon has become a part of it.

Nicaragua (April 2001)

Violence is to be found in any action
in which one acts as if one were alone
to act.

—*Emmanuel Lévinas*

Dear friends,

Nicaragua?

That means first of all wind!

There is always, perpetually, everywhere wind. It accompanies you, your thoughts, it ensnares you when it plays and flirts with your body, it cools the pearls of sweat on your skin, and yet it presses, it torments; it harasses your breath, your hair, and your eyes. The wind brings the dust, and it brings trouble.

You also hear the wind at night when the branches of the bushes and trees knock and stroke the window of your hotel room; it's not loud enough, this knocking, to keep you awake, but it's not quiet enough to let you feel alone in an unknown silence in a strange country. It seems to demand attention, and it seems to protect you.

Desperation 1

The time frame of hope for a daily meal on the streets of Managua lasts for exactly the duration of one red light. It is the slice of time between the amber and the red when the beggar on the little island of pavement can approach the drivers in the waiting cars for some córdobas. He has lost his legs and is tied to a wheelchair, and when he sees me opening the window, his motionless face is suddenly filled with life and he bends forward with the upper part of his body: at the same time a gesture of respectful greeting toward me in the car and the anticipation of the movement of a body that cannot move, an indirect movement that begins with his head, which physically seems to pull the rest of his body behind it—first the chest, and then the arms move the wheelchair toward me. After a few feet he stops, pushing forward with his head, somewhat ridiculously moving without having any effect on the body/wheelchair anymore. The streets in Managua are not made for wheelchairs; there are huge holes in the asphalt surrounding him, and whichever way he tries to turn his vehicle, he remains stuck. His arms cannot bridge the gap between the position where the wheelchair got stuck and my hand with the bills. The light has already turned green by the time he has given up hope and rowed backward to his pariah island on the pavement, far away from the pickup trucks, far away from the córdobas behind closed windows, and far away from a meal.

Desperation 2

For the first time in my life I was bitten by a dog.

The dog belonged to Alberto.

The place where Alberto lives has no name. Alberto's neighborhood is beyond the last town that is still worth a name, it is beyond the last bus stop, it is even beyond the last stop of one of the old East German trucks that carries workers, *campesinos*, on the loading platform. He lives in a geographical void, a no-go neighborhood. And so Alberto has to walk the last miles to his corrugated iron hut. The hut is empty, just nine children (one is away, four are his, and five belong to his sister-in-law, who still has a job in the free zone Las Mercedes near Managua) fill it with life. There are two reddish iron chairs, a rolled-up hammock somewhere in the dark, and one lonely electric bulb that does not work hanging from the "ceiling." Alberto takes a wooden stick and walks out of the house to hit at the electric cable on the street. The light in the hut turns on, for about two minutes, and then fades out. There is nothing to eat; we talk standing outside the hut. The sticky heat of the day has been pent up inside.

In the middle of the night, Alberto's dog shows up, a strong-muscled gray-brown bastard with black ears, which jumps up and down with joy at seeing his master.

Suddenly, he smells something unknown; he raises his snout, turns around, and then discovers what's strange: me, standing among the family members as if one of them—and suddenly, without any growling or teeth-baring warning, he bites the back of my right hand.

Shocked, Alberto pulls him aside: "I am sorry. But he does not know guests. Nobody who does not have to live in these conditions dares to come to this area."

Nobody in Nicaragua would come out of curiosity or friendship to a neighborhood without a name, without streets. No stranger would voluntarily come to the favelas, the towns that are not found on any map, invisible to anyone who is not forced to live here. Separated from everything and yet without borders. Frontiers of shame prevent any contact.

Friendships and visits remain within the same radius of

misery; nobody travels beyond the dusty fringes of the collection of huts—except for work. In the early, cool morning hours, a human herd leaves along the small paths between the huts, into the traceless vastness of the dried-out area surrounding their neighborhood, past miles of garbage dump, to the unmarked post next to an old tree that gives shade, till the truck stops here and picks up the workers to take them to the first street where an official bus stops.

How could Alberto's dog possibly know what a guest is?

The Task

We flew to Managua, the photographer Thomas Müller and I, in order to do a story on the exploitation of workers in the free zones.

In times of globalized capitalism, management strategists of multinational corporations invest more and more money in marketing campaigns and corporate identity. In such a management culture that is more interested in corporations' image than in the quality of their products, the budgets for materials and personnel are reduced to a minimum. Since legally protected employees in our countries are considered expensive and inflexible, the production process is transferred abroad to cheaper, less regulated areas.

During the 1990s, free zones (in the Philippines, China, Mexico, Vietnam, Sri Lanka, El Salvador, and Nicaragua) were established as quasi extraterritorial zones where subcontractors from the United States or Taiwan produce goods in sweatshops for Wal-Mart, the Gap, Nike, J. C. Penney, or Tom Tailor—without any local authority inferring, without any limitation by national labor or tax laws.

Worldwide, there are more than two thousand such zones, controlled by private security companies behind barbwire fences and walls. Almost twenty-seven million people globally work in such zones under condition that invoke images of Manchester capitalism.

According to a 1998 study by Charles Kernaghan on sweatshops in China, You Li Fashion Factory in China, for example, paid thirteen cents per hour to workers who had to sew products for the label Esprit seven days a week, from half past seven in the morning till midnight.

In the microcosm of the maquiladora (a sweatshop in a free zone in Nicaragua), you discover the reality of globalization of capital without the universalization of law: thousands of Nicaraguan workers produce T-shirts out of Taiwanese cloth on Japanese sewing machines under Chinese supervision, for an Asian-owned company.

After the bitter experience of imperialist repression, notorious underdevelopment, a decades-long dictatorship under General Somoza and his dynasty, military and economic intervention from the United States during the civil war in the 1980s, and widespread corruption under Daniel Ortega—the temporary hopes of the Sandinista revolution of 1979 have at last been destroyed.

The World Bank considers Nicaragua to be the second poorest country of the Western hemisphere (after Haiti). To cover its enormous foreign debts, neoliberal governments have begun—under the pressure of the fiscal demands of the International Monetary Fund (IMF)—to sell out the country.

Nicaragua, once admired for its rich biodiversity, cannot afford to carefully steward its treasures of tropical wood, cotton, and minerals. Of the estimated eight million hectares of rainforest in 1950, only four million have escaped cultivation. Experts suggest that the Nicaraguan rainforest will be completely destroyed within the next ten to fifteen years.

Demands for strict fiscal policies by international credit grantors have led not only to massive cuts in the budget for social programs and massive layoffs resulting from the privatization of various state-owned companies, but also to the selling-out of fishing and mining licenses to foreign investors. Ecological standards have been ignored, as have the land rights of the indigenous Mitskito, Mayanga, and Rama, who traditionally inhabit the rainforest and mining regions. Even though the territorial rights of the indigenous are constitutionally guaranteed, the government has sold concessions and land in areas that did not belong to the state.

In the post-Sandinista Nicaragua of Violeta Chamorro and Arnoldo Alemán, more and more free zones—the so-called *zonas francas*—have been created year after year.

Whereas in 1992 Nicaragua exported goods worth about 12.8 million dollars, in 2000 the foreign producers in Nicaragua exported goods worth 250 million dollars.

But the free zones that allegedly were intended by the IMF as a rescue operation for the impoverished country and that brought forty thousand jobs do not benefit the local economy. The garments, textiles, and machines that are needed for production are all imported from abroad; local subcontractors or natural resources are not used—Nicaragua contributes only cheap human labor. Nothing else.

The Maquiladoras

The red light is blinking. Fraught with danger. An error in the machine is an accident, a defect, sand in the system's teeth. Row C falters. The trousers are already piling up at the table in front of the Musashi 21, the modern Japanese sewing machine. Usually, the Musashi can turn three green-and-white pieces of cotton within seconds into the bottom pocket. But the red light alarms the Chinese technician, who hurries to keep the production on pace.

Seven hundred pairs of trousers per day, that is the new norm. A couple of weeks ago, it was still five hundred. But then row C had reached the goal on the one-hundred-yard track they call their own—from the first table, where the jeans fabric is cut on templates, to the last table, thirty-seven operations and tables further along, where the label is sewed into the finished trouser. Five hundred per day. This wasn't possible during normal working hours from 7 AM till 5 PM, and so they had to work overtime till 9 PM. It took them weeks before they had the rhythm, the cut, the norm.

When they reached that goal, the norm was changed. Now it is seven hundred trousers per day, and they won't be able to achieve that today. Each minute that the red light is blinking costs them. Though a technical problem may be an accident, the workers won't be paid for the lost production. Whoever falls behind gets paid less. It is a simple calculation, and the eighty women of row C have to pay for it today. "This is theft," says Nedia, 25, who irons the jeans at the beginning of the row, "We're not workers, we are just slaves."

The traders at the entrance of Las Mercedes, the biggest free zone in Nicaragua with more than twenty-eight thousand workers and ten factories, are sleeping in their hammocks, surrounded by an assortment of matchbox cars, fried bananas, and Lux soap. They are ready for the end of the shift. Business is confined to those twenty yards between the end of the working day beyond the barbwire fence and the yellow former school bus that is waiting with its motor running on this side of the zone to pick up the women and take them home.

The jobless rate is around 60 percent in Nicaragua; the only people who have money to spend are those with jobs (and even they don't have any money to spend), and the free zones provide jobs. But the zones swallow more and more minutes and hours of the time and lives of their workers—by the time the shift is over, there is neither energy nor time left for the women to "go shopping." The free zones not only cut out more and more of Nicaragua's territory (forty-eight factories in ten free zones by now) and turn it into quasi extraterritorial states, they also attract traders to their borders, where they settle for hours of the beginning and end of each shift—and as a result, they drain the towns of their lifeblood.

It is already dark when the shift ends and the twenty-eight thousand workers of the free zone Las Mercedes slowly fill the streets inside the zone, and are swallowed and carried away, like jetsam. Private security companies control the border of the zone. The security officer places his foot next to the inside of the worker's foot to stay balanced and in control, and then he searches the tired men and women one by one. After exploiting them for fourteen hours a day, the companies cannot refrain from checking whether any worker has stolen a needle, a piece of fabric, or a pair of jeans.

The workers are being paid 2.574 córdobas, or twenty cents, for one pair of jeans that sells in the United States for $21.99. Business using cheap labor in Nicaragua is booming: in 1993, companies from the free zones exported clothing worth 10.3 million dollars to the American market; in 1996, the exports of clothing were worth 67 million.

Guillermina, Alberto's sister-in-law, is slowly moving toward the exit; she cannot afford any of the goods the traders offer to her. She is making two hundred córdobas per week at Fortex, her Taiwanese employer. And she already spends ninety-one córdobas per week for the hour-and-a-half bus ride each way between her home and the factory. Today her eldest son, Wilfred, is waiting for her. Wilfred's father abandoned the family, and since there hadn't been enough money to marry years ago, Guillermina is now left without any support. During the day, Wilfred takes care of his four siblings, but there isn't much to do. "There isn't money for more than one meal per day," says Wilfred. He bites off the corner of the plastic bag that one of the traders has sold him for a córdoba and sucks out the cool water.

He tried to get a job in the free zones but was rejected. When I ask him what he really wants to do, he says "computers," but the courses for computing are private, and they cost money the family does not have. Wilfred never complains about his life. He hardly talks at all. What about? It is this speechlessness, this desert of words, this dried-out and lost hope that I find the least bearable, this "impeccable credential of old pain" (as Audre Lorde phrased it) in someone so young—Wilfred is only eighteen.

The bus is traveling west, down Route 266, the workers are squeezed into their seats, and nobody talks. "The body isn't prepared for such working hours," says Alberto, and despair weighs down his voice. "When you finally arrive at home, you are actually too tired to fall asleep."

When you ask the women in the bus what they do, they never say simply: I work for Chentex, or Roo Hsing as a sewer or washer; instead they say: "Mine is the back pocket," "Mine the seam on the right leg," "Mine is the main vertical seam"—the production sews the labels of their identities, the work divides them into zones: the seams, the pockets, the front or the back part of the pants.

Time Layers 1

Nicaragua does not know addresses.

There are hardly any street names in Managua, so what you get is a reference system with prominent points of orientation, like: from the Church Santa Maria, one block up and then twenty to the south. Or: at the Palacio Nacional, two blocks up and five to the north. This is a pretty good system in a country with a high rate of illiteracy. Unfortunately though, this is also a country that was twice devastated by earthquakes in the twentieth century and also by Hurricane Mitch a couple of years ago. Mitch destroyed some of the buildings that were reference points. So now there is an imaginary map of the past that still guides people: where the Church San Marco used to be, two blocks down and three to the south. And definitely never, ever try to meet someone after nightfall—there is no way to tell where south or north is.

"History is an object of construction," writes Walter Benjamin, "whose location is not formed by homogenous or empty time but by the present."

The view of Nicaragua's past is distorted by the view of its present.

Nicaragua used to be for many an almost mythical place of utopia with an earthly address, it was Ernst Bloch's "not-yet." It seemed particularly unreal to go there to report on Manchester capitalism in the twenty-first century and the exploitation of workers.

Because of the Sandinista past, I projected a particular potential for resistance against neoliberal policies. An illusion.

Rather, the despair among the people in Nicaragua seemed to weigh so much more, since they had already learned a language of rights. It wasn't an unshaped, imprecise longing for something better. They knew they were being denied something that they deserved. They experienced the present not just as bitter, but as a loss.

Too Old for Prostitution

There is a tired silence in the bus.

"Every single move in the factories is regimented," explains Alberto, and the others in the bus join in our conversation and confirm his statement. Even going to the restroom is arbitrarily permitted or forbidden by the Chinese supervisors who patrol between the lines. As Wolfgang Sofsky writes in *The Order of Terror*, "By social definition, the slave is not a member of human society." The slave not only loses control over his or her work but over him- or herself. "I was pregnant," recounts Jeannette, 21, "and I fell badly. They would not let me go to the hospital. They simply would not allow it." She continued to work for four days. Then she started bleeding. She lost her child at the Roberto-Huembes Hospital in Ciudad Sandino.

Time is eating up the paint on the wall of the emergency unit. A nurse is bored and sings along with the song by José Luis Perales playing on the old Grundig radio. Estella, 28, sits in front of the radio and Dr. Juarez and talks to her about her pain. A bladder infection. The usual diagnosis for factory workers in the free zones. Many women simply don't drink enough anymore because they are afraid that they will be forbidden to go to the toilet. They suffer dehydration as a result, and often bladder infections.

Estella will be able to take care of herself now. She has been sacked by Chao Hsing, together with nineteen of her coworkers. First they had met secretly, after work, to debate their situation at Chao Hsing. Finally Alberto and

Estella went to the Ministry of Work and applied officially to form a union at Chao. Union work is a constitutional right in Nicaragua. Two weeks later, the Ministry sent an inspector to the factory. The official explanation was that the "workers' papers had to be checked." But only Estella and the other cofounders of the union (whose names were on the letter they had given to the Ministry of Work) were checked. One week later, Alberto was sacked. A couple of days later, Estella lost her job. They were given no explanation by the Taiwanese boss.

Maribel Gutierrez, 35, who is also in the bus, has four children. She says, "We had everything in Nicaragua: we had war, storm, corruption, our own people stealing from us, now foreigners stealing from us." She says, "We work because we are hungry. Only the younger ones are able to reject the job at the free zones—they can still work as prostitutes on the streets. . . . We're too old for that." Nobody in the bus seems to even consider the possibility that the government might defend its citizens' rights against global capital's power.

"The Taiwanese think they can do what they want," says Carlos Borje, the general secretary of the union. "They think this is their country."

Chinese Nicaragua

The Chinese state inside Nicaragua wants to be protected. Only the purple bougainvillea fight their way over the wall of the Asian enclave, near Managua's airport. A steel door prevents entry and insight. Chu-Ching Feng,

38, has lived in this luxury ghetto for three years. An agency in mainland China offered her the job as a supervisor at Chentex; work permit and visa were already included. She has no children, and her husband is still in China. For three years, she has patrolled the aisles at Chentex, watching over the speed of the Nicaraguan workers. She has not seen much of her new homeland: neither the poverty in the corrugated iron hut settlements nor the beauty of the volcano landscape around Lake Managua. Chu-Chin's Nicaragua reaches from the enclave with her Chinese colleagues, the Asian restaurants, and the wall surrounding it to the free zone and the factory a few hundred yards farther on. Her Spanish is as good as it was on her first day; she is still talking of "zonas flancas," but she does not need many words to pressure the women in the factory.

It is unclear whether Chu-Ching Feng ever considers what she actually does here. It is unclear whether she simply believes that this is the best job she could get. Who knows what her living conditions were like in China. Maybe she would be more concerned or critical if her Spanish were better.

This is a multizone: there are territorial zones, social zones, cultural zones, language zones—and there is no trespassing across the demarcations. The pain in the back of my hand reminds me of the closeness of the borders every day and night.

It is a class struggle wrapped in the vocabulary of ethnic prejudice.

"The Chinese have a different mentality," says Steven K. Chang, 54, the manager of the Roo Hsing factory. "If two people who know each other bump into each other in a park in China, they don't greet each other. The people here in Nicaragua cannot understand that." Indeed, the Nicaraguans cannot understand that. They think all Taiwanese and Chinese are alike—they are all *Chinos*—and "the only contact we have is aggressive," says Nedia, 25.

In the beginning, all our attempts to enter the free zones failed. One impenetrable security ring after another prevented any entry. Calls at the Ministry of Labor were as useless as written requests to the secretaries of Asian managers. Out of sheer desperation and with the help of Thomas's contacts with staff at the airport, we hired an old helicopter to fly over the monstrous free zone Las Mercedes in the early morning hours, a semilegal and semismart action. The zone touched the airport directly, and chartered helicopters have no right to fly over the runway. While flying over the sealed-off zone, the pilot crossed the airport's only runway. Via headphones we could hear screaming air-traffic controllers from the tower telling us to move our rotor out of the approach lane.

In order to give Thomas a better view, the pilot had taken out the helicopter's side door. Immediately before departure, he handed us a roll of sticking plaster with the advice: the tape should be of use, since the safety belts were a little fragile.

After a couple of days, it finally worked out that we got into the most notorious of all factories. The Taiwanese manager of Chentex, the most aggressive garment producer in Nicaragua, granted us an interview and asked us to visit him in the factory.

It was like accompanying Dante to the deepest circles of hell—we had to travel from one security zone to the next, one ring to the next. We had to pass the main entrance, we had to pass the barbwire fence, we had to pass the security officers' questioning and control of our passports, we had to pass the entrance of Chentex, a main entrance with a locked steel-plated door and an armed security officer, and at the entrance of the factory itself we had to pass another security check and receive special passes in order to be able to enter the factory.

Chentex has received a new order of jeans today. Chentex can produce twenty to twenty-five thousand pairs of jeans per day, six million per year, for big American retailers such as Kohl's, J. C. Penney, and Wal-Mart.

Kou-Chuen Yin, 40, the vice-manager of Chentex, is running up and down the gallery on the first floor of the Chentex factory. He has a Ph.D. in veterinary medicine. His expertise was the breeding and treatment of pigs, and it seems, quite frankly, that he applies that expertise to the human species. "We can work all night long in China," he complains. "Unfortunately, we cannot do it the Asian way here. At least workers are better here than in Mexico—there, they are only lazy."

Yin talks to me despite the fact that Chentex has already been featured prominently in the *New York Times* as the worst example of slavery in the free zones; he talks to me despite the fact that he is currently involved in one lawsuit filed by him and one against him. He has sued former workers at his factory, who were legal members of a union and tried to organize a legal strike—he not only sacked them but also filed a suit against them for "sabotage and terrorism."

Still, the manager makes no attempt to hide any of the

exploitation, the denial of basic rights, and the struggle with the unions. He does not even need questions as excuses to launch tirades against lazy workers, dreadful communists, and the Sandinistas, who were nothing but a degenerate horde of revolutionaries ("As a German, you know how difficult it is to deal with those communists—they think people are equal. But that is impossible").

It is amazing. The entire conversation rests on his implicit racist assumption that "we," from the "industrialized world," know what "we" are talking about. He assumes a consensus between "us"—"we" capitalists know how to rule the world, and "we" know that one just has to show the dirty communist unionists where they belong.

"They should be grateful here in Nicaragua that we came," he says. "We came because the government asked us for help. We don't even know yet if we can make money here."

He lies.

The fact is that Taiwan has given 180 million dollars to Nicaragua as development aid since 1992—a fraction of the profits from its sweatshops over the years.

Against all threats and risks, union workers such as Carlos Borje and Pedro Ortega still battle for the rights of every single worker.

There are black lists with the names of "troublemakers" circulating among the managers of foreign companies—those workers will not be employed at any of the factories. The practice resembles a professional ban because neither the national laws nor the international treaties such as the North American Free Trade Agreement (NAFTA), in which freedom of association, the right to form unions, and the right to strike are guaranteed, protect the workers in the free zones.

"This is where you see the inhuman face of globalization," says Charles Kernaghan, the director of the American Committee for Labor. "If the union fails here, it sends a bad message for other places."

Kernaghan got a sense of what to expect during his last trip to Nicaragua: he was already sitting in a plane in San Salvador that was about to depart for Managua when the Nicaraguan government denied him entry. After a half hour of negotiation, six security officers boarded the plane and "accompanied" him off. Activists for workers are not welcome in Nicaragua.

Time Layers 2

The black silhouette of Augusto Cesar Sandino rises above the Loma de Tiscapa, the national park that has become a memorial, a volcanic mountain in the center of Managua.

The statue of Nicaragua's freedom fighter overlooks and outlasts the fate of his successors in the eternal circle of reforming and destroying violence.

Carlos Borje wanders with us along the serpentine path up the hill, and narrates the story of Sandino, a story that is continually reinvented in the collective memory composed of individual voices.

The myth of Sandino is nurtured equally by followers and by enemies. They all refer to the legendary figure: some in order to continue the struggle against American influence, against corrupt tyrants, and against exploitation of the poor rural population; others in order to prevent this inheritance of Sandino.

Borje searches for the beginning of this circle, he wonders whether it might be Nicaragua's geographical situation that has made it so interesting for foreigners since the sixteenth century, or whether it might be its natural resources. Whether it might be the personality and biography of Sandino, who agitated against the conservative government and the American marines in the 1920s.

"But here on this hill," says Borje, stroking his black moustache, "it was only dictators who reigned here." He greets the uniformed guard, who seems to be bored in the company of the mute, iron statue of Sandino. Borje begins his account: how in 1934, Anastasio Somoza García ordered the assassination of the rebellious Liberal Sandino with the help of the National Guard (which had been trained by American military personnel), how the authoritarian Somoza clan dominated and terrorized the country for decades afterward.

When Borje begins to describe the seizure of power by Anastasio Somoza Debayle, he pulls up his shoulders as if he was still expecting the blows of the despot's henchmen. "The Tiscapa symbolizes the terror regime of the dictator, who installed his military headquarters with its notorious torture chambers here," says Borje, and then he recounts the names of the members of the opposition who were killed in the cellars on this hill.

Originally we had intended to climb the Tiscapa only to admire the view and to take some pictures of Borje—but now the walk turns into a history lesson in the shadow of Sandino.

For Borje, the narrative is indispensable; without the stories and myths of the history of Nicaragua, the union leader could not return to his small, dark office every day and listen to dismissed workers. He cannot offer them anything but his words of the revolution, the past one and the one that is still to come, like an old unredeemed promise. That's why Borje talks about the old Sandinista vision, here, on top of the hill above Managua, less to us, strangers, than to himself.

How finally in 1979 the guerrillas (who fought in the name of the murdered hero of the 1930s) kicked out the last of the Somoza dynasty. How not even the American supply of weapons and money for so many years was ultimately able to prevent the victory of the Marxist Sandinista Front. Borje speaks proudly of the alphabetization campaigns, and he talks a little bit louder so that the clandestinely listening guard under the statue can understand everything.

While Western governments and even the American administration under Jimmy Carter at first welcomed the Sandinistas (and all, other than the Soviet Union, immediately donated eight million dollars of emergency aid), U.S. policy turned after the Republicans captured the White House in the 1980 election: propaganda of the alleged emergence of a second Cuba in Nicaragua followed economic sanctions. Cold War fantasies of a Soviet bastion in close proximity to the United States rhetorically prepared the way for military support for the Contras in Nicaragua and for the brutal civil war that ensued.

We can complete the sad story ourselves. On the Tiscapa you can read Nicaragua's latest past: the detested symbol of Nicaragua's dictatorships was declared a national park by Violeta Chamorro. In 1956, Chamorro's husband had been detained and tortured in the cellars on the Tiscapa—and now the Tiscapa was supposed to become a monument of liberation and the silhouette of the father figure Sandino should rise above it.

Today, Taiwanese investors practice an unexpected form of "demilitarization" at the bottom of the hill: a gigantic shopping mall and the renovated Hotel Intercontinental are indications of the neoliberal conquest of Nicaragua.

When Borje finally arrives at the present, his narration slows down.

He not only weighs each word, but he also considers how it fits in with earlier sentences; he uses not just terms to describe social or political phenomena, but also quotations that echo a tradition and evoke memories.

The rash analysis of his European guest cannot pressure the unionist. He situates each contemporary event in the genealogy of repression that has to be told slowly and precisely. With each sentence of this history, he seems to lose his pace, as if mourning the impotence of the people burdens his tongue.

He sounds a little dusty when he talks about the lawless conquest of Nicaragua by foreign investors; the vocabulary of political economy that runs through his language seems old-fashioned, wooden, a discourse from the 1970s with worn-out stereotypes.

You have to listen to him for a while with the patience of an ignorant stranger, you have to travel through Nicaragua, and you have to have witnessed the boundless injustice in order to understand his timeless rhythm.

The almost embarrassing antiqueness of the language with which he expresses his lament is rooted in the worries he faces. The conflicts with which Borjes struggles are old conflicts, unworthy of this century. It is not his language that is stuck in the past, but the social reality surrounding him.

Only a European traveler can be so disturbed by the dissonance of the simultaneous.

The fall of the Soviet Union has distracted us from the analysis of economic relations; the critique of capitalism has gone out of fashion, buried under debates on the recognition of cultural identities or questions of internal or external violence. Even the critics of globalization often shy away from using the classic concepts of political economy. Notions such as "exploitation," "slavery," and "strike" seem to entertain the bored reader like old hairstyles or costumes.

And then there is this slowness.

Even when Borje talks about the injustice in the maquiladoras, you wish to hear more vibrant anger from him. He has lost hurried bustle in the years of resistance. He seems, like Job, to take every shattering bit of news imperturbably; nothing surprises him anymore and the indignation of a foreign guest amuses him. "It is good if you can still express rage," says the union leader on the way down the hill toward the city. "But what is needed even more is stamina." His sedate friendliness does not reduce his commitment; his critical attitude is not dulled by the perpetual experience of suffering.

Each cruelty still counts for Carlos Borje, he still wants

to register each detail, each action, no matter how many there are.

In his presence I recall a line from Felix Mendelssohn's Second Symphony, the *Song of Praise*: "Who counts our tears in times of misery."

Borje still counts—like a bookkeeper of injustice.

Alberto, meanwhile, walks the last miles to his hut through the dust. He has already lost all hope for a victory of the workers. "We in Nicaragua," he says, "we had everything already. We had to learn Russian in the times of the Sandinistas, English for the Americans and their Contras. It seems it is time now to learn Taiwanese."

Kosovo 2 (October 2000)

One source of violence is the power of imagination.

—*Wolfgang Sofsky*

Dear friends,
I am back from Kosovo, and still slightly disoriented.

Everything seems to be calibrated for the world of experience over there: skin and nerves are porous, over-
attentive, irritable in the expectation of a threat at any
moment. Body and perception are still conditioned by
perpetual danger. Every movement, every sound is registered and quickly examined.

It is strange to be back in an environment of silence.
Even the hectic consumerism in Berlin suddenly seems dis-
concertingly slow and smooth; I perceive, see, and feel as
if through a thick heavy curtain. Everything appears dead-
ened. Without the border controls, checkpoints, barbed
wire, yelling, loud folk music, and army vehicles that surrounded me till yesterday, I feel as if I were deaf.

Still tuned to the enmity of postwar Kosovo, the simple
possibility of crossing the street without thinking is an in-
credible luxury.

A Return to What?

Only one year had passed since my journey through the
war-torn province with its refugee treks, mass graves, and
burned houses, first of the Albanians, then of the Serbs.
Only one year had passed since the victors joyfully danced

in the marketplace of Prizren, celebrating the end of the ethnic slaughter.

And now we returned to Kosovo to witness the first local elections in the peaceful part of the republic.

Suddenly, the old Kosovo seemed as unreal as the new.

The stories were more complex, the images less shining, and the frontiers less clear-cut. The pain was real and imagined, the emotional landscape was multilayered, and the apparent normalcy was illusory. Suddenly, there were "official" people—politicians, police officers, United Nations Interim Administration Mission in Kosovo (UNMIK) staff, party members—who dominated the discourse. There was an official language now, a virtual script that organized collective thinking and speaking—you had to find the periphery, the splinters, the fragments of individual lives and language, to understand what was really happening.

Last year, I could listen to individuals telling me their story, their experience, the chronology of the last days, weeks, months—depending on when they had been driven out of their homes (the further north they had lived, the longer their stories, the longer their flight). Detailed, epic descriptions of what had happened to them.

One year later, the recent experiences of the Albanian Kosovars were of apparent normalcy, not worth mentioning. They do not talk about their individual experiences anymore, but about their collective claims, about the interpretation of past suffering and their longing for the future. It is old pain and their past status as victims, however, that guide their understanding of themselves and their vision for the future.

The present remains locked up in a blind area of their perception.

The former victims do not want to acknowledge that the persecuted of yesterday, the Albanian Kosovars, have become the dominant, protected group, whereas the former oppressors, the Serbs, live isolated in ghettos.

The past stays alive, is repeated, a counterpoise for the future—but the present is faded out.

Election Day

Certainly, there were also moments of joy; there was also a sense of reconciliation during this disappointing journey of return.

How the Albanians queued for hours on election day in front of the polling stations, for example. They arrived at seven in the morning, couples holding hands as if to tame their civic enthusiasm, others slightly afraid, in disbelief as to whether this gift of free elections were really true.

I remembered what they had looked like in northern Albania, the thousands in the mud, later in tents, with no belongings and no hope, in dirty sweaters, one on top of the other, because all they could take with them on their flight was what they could carry on their bodies. I remembered how they all looked alike in their sorrow, searching for a loaf of bread, a piece of soap, or an injured relative.

What a change to see them now in their happy excitement on election day, proud, individuated according to wealth and status, and not just according to their losses;

how they stood in front of schools, courthouses, and administration buildings, quietly whispering as if one of the international election supervisors could still drive them away, as if their newly gained right could be taken away from them at the last minute.

Many did not know what options they had, did not know that they could have refrained from voting. The logistics arranged by the Organization for Security and Cooperation in Europe (OSCE), the body with responsibility for nation building in postwar Kosovo, were a disaster: There were not enough polling stations, the identification procedures were ridiculously complicated (one of the consequences of the Serbian policy from 1999 to take all identification papers, vehicle license plates, and other legal papers from the fleeing Albanian Kosovars), and nobody was prepared for the people's anticipation and excitement.

The patience of these first-time voters was amazing: how they stood in front of closed doors, eager and happy about a privilege that to most of us in our saturated Western democracies seems like a useless duty. And their elegance: they all arrived in their Sunday clothes, a gesture of respect for themselves and for the long and painful path to these elections.

At the same time, their patience was also very much tactical and not just emotional: they wanted to be good pupils, to behave well, to be the way the West wanted them to be, so that they would receive the reward for their good behavior: independence from the detested Yugoslav Republic.

They all knew: any violent act would have harmed their image, destroyed their democratic credibility—and damaged the prospect of international recognition.

After the War/After the Elections

Prishtina has changed in the last year: from an ugly, gray, half-destroyed, half-empty city to an ugly, gray, half-destroyed, overflowing, and lively city. The cafés are full of speechifying men. There are Internet cafés and bars with names such as St. Pauli, Blair, or Toni; illegal copies of Sting and U2 CDs; this fall even Foreigner sells, as do fake Marlboro cigarettes with the *Kosovo* signature.

The Grand Hotel definitely has no *grandezza*, but it is currently the only place with real bathrooms and, occasionally, a working telephone line. It is run by KLA veterans and some obscure figures. The foreigners staying here avoid the hotel bar, where Albanian businessmen loaf about and settle dubious transactions. Water is available only at certain times, but at least this year the elevator does not get stuck all the time. There is a monstrous TV set in each room, and the porn magazine in the desk drawer offers "phone sex with mature women" in a country with no functioning telephone lines.

On the streets of Prishtina, in particular on Mother Teresa Street, booksellers display their war memorabilia. Their small folding tables are full of diaries of KLA fighters and history books on Albanian martyrs and heroes. When I ask them what sells, they laugh: not the old stuff—the English-Albanian dictionary is the best seller, and not only among young Kosovars.

The myths of the past are useful only for conversations over a glass of strong Raki in dark pubs—but English is the official language in a Kosovo run by the United Nations, and every reasonably well-paid job in the province requires language skills before any other qualification.

The province is run and overrun by hordes of international aid staff. Institutions and organizations have spread across the country and any functioning local structures are suffocated by conferences, rules, and meetings with the megalomaniac bureaucracy.

"What's the difference between the Albanian Mafia and the UN administration of Kosovo?" goes an often quoted joke: "The Albanian Mafia is well organized."

After the elections there were no celebrations, no election parties, no parades of honking cars, no shootings in the air, no singing. Everything was eerily quiet. The post-election mood was like a cigarette after bad sex: the bored, businesslike satisfaction of being done with it.

The elections had already taken place, they had been peaceful, and now the great event had lost its importance. Suddenly, the elections appeared as what they really were: a ritual of delusion, a gesture of the international community, which waveringly wanted to redeem the province from its violent past of apartheid (and to get rid of its own shameful role of passive observer of Milosevic's war spectacle), but was not willing to allow for real democratic processes.

The self-determination of the predominantly Albanian population in Kosovo would lead to independence from the Republic of Yugoslavia (or, in the paranoia of some American strategists, to a Great Albania), and that is why there were only irrelevant communal elections.

The specter of secessionist wars has long haunted the power headquarters of many multiethnic, multireligious states, frightening their leaders. Out of fear of the fragmentation of cumbersomely put together nation-states, every single case of potential independence movement in the world is being repressed. Even if they are peaceful, democratic movements, they are hindered despite international agreements. Even if the grounds for secession are not ethnic or racist, but pragmatic. Even if other ethnic identities are granted minority rights and a multiethnic state could result from the sought-after independence. The fear of secession is always out there.

Different historical and cultural movements are lumped together, so that the terrorist actions of one separatist group neutralize the peaceful demands of another.

And so a hermaphrodite Kosovo is kept alive, and Albanian Kosovars must stay together with the imploding carcass of Yugoslavia.

Serbian Enclaves in the New Kosovo

As we arrive at Gracanica, the Swedish KFOR soldiers at the checkpoint are in a bad mood. They do not like it when journalists take notes. Their post is shielded by sandbags and barbed wire; they are having a bad day, for whatever reason. They ask me for my passport, my press card, my KFOR accreditation. It is never enough.

They don't like my attitude—and if I were they, I probably wouldn't either. I tend to lose my temper when having to deal with bullying by border guards, flight attendants, soldiers and policemen.

Perhaps as a punishment for my cross-grained attitude,

the control procedure drags on. Now a soldier is checking the car in a deliberately slow and painstaking manner: the trunk, the interior trim, the doors, and even the filthy floor mats are inspected before they finally let us pass.

Gracanica is a spectacular monastery from the fourteenth century, Serbian architecture in the most beautiful Byzantine style. Three round arches with high narrow windows draw visitors in. Inside, in a devout dimness, wonderful sixteenth- and seventeenth-century frescos and icons illustrate believers' prayers.

Destroyed and reconstructed from ruins again and again, Gracanica is for religious Serbs a symbol of both the vulnerability and the survival of their community. King Milutin's dedication is inscribed on the south wall of the sacristy: "I saw the devastation and fall of the church of the Holy Theotokos of Gracanica and I had it rebuilt from the foundation stone."

A poster at the main entrance displays a caricature of a hunter with a rifle: "Please no weapons in the church."

Alexandra's baptism is taking place today, but the six-year-old is afraid of the portentous ceremony. She is wearing jeans, sneakers, and a colorful jacket, and does not dare to come forward from the protected space between the legs of her parents, who are dressed in black. There is no community, no relatives, no friends celebrating this day with Alexandra.

Gracanica is an enclave, a ghetto with six thousands Serbs trapped inside. There is a market on the main street where four farmers sell tomatoes, cauliflower, and onions; the people living in the ghetto never leave the enclave.

They do not dare even to go to the supermarket in the

nearby town. Prishtina is only three miles away, but the risk of being recognized as Serbs seems too high. They live off their miserable crops and the aid they receive from UNMIK.

Inside the church, a young woman hesitantly approaches me, in the rather submissive way that seems to be expected from the terrorized Serbs—sadly, that is how you can recognize even utterly innocent individual Serbs in Kosovo, in their humble demeanor, an attempt to conceal all gestures of their previous supremacy. Her name is Tamara.

She asks if I want to know anything about the icons and is glad to find someone interested in Orthodox culture. Whispering so as not to disturb Alexandra's baptism, she tells me about the myths and stories behind the images and the artists who painted them, as we move from one saint to another.

The Serbian Orthodox saints on the paintings have no eyes. "When the Turks conquered this area, they scratched off the color of the eyes." We learn about the many times the monastery was attacked by the Turks between 1379 and 1382, which eventually also led to the destruction of the building's dome.

Tamara's English is a bit rusty, but fine. She speaks slowly, so slowly that you think she has not slept in years, and she seems older than she probably is. She is tired, awfully tired of the war and its consequences.

She wears spectacles with a black, misshapen frame and thick lenses. Her right eye is constantly moving; her left one can focus on you, but the right one is searching for another reality it cannot find, homesick without a home.

She is an Orthodox Christian and believes in God's will.

For her, the fate of Serbs in the current apartheid system of postwar Kosovo is divine punishment for the crimes committed by Serbs against Albanian Kosovars.

Tamara is thirty-two years old and teaches chemistry at a medical school in a town nearby. She is from Nis, in Serbia, and moved to Kosovo only two months ago, because she could not find a job in Yugoslavia. Although they share her ethnic origin, she feels like a stranger among many of the Serbs in Kosovo. Some of her Serbian neighbors in the enclave cling to a rigid nationalism that she has not heard for a long time at home in Nis. She comes from a family of doctors critical of the government; she tells us stumblingly that her parents opposed Milosevic not just after the revolution in Belgrade, but long before, when Serbian civilians still cheered nationalistic warmongers.

She acknowledges the crimes of the Serbian army and the paramilitaries in Kosovo without being asked about it. She gets upset about her compatriots' unwillingness to even consider the harm they inflicted on the Albanian population.

Her critical position toward Milosevic, ethnic cleansing, and the narrow-mindedness of her fellow countrymen, however, will not protect Tamara from the consequences of the collective punishment imposed on Serbs. She is a Serb, and like the others, she must stay trapped in the ghetto, soaked in fear of the Albanians, of attacks, of the night.

Tamara is the ideal translator for our planned trips into the Serbian territories in Kosovo, and the following day I persuade her to work for me. The 120 German marks I offer her for a day of translating equal her monthly salary as a chemistry teacher.

In Gracanica, Tamara takes us to Father Sava, the spokes-man for the Serbian community and the voice of the criti-cal Serbs in Kosovo, who has created an island of hetero-geneity. In the office of the monastery, which also serves as a living room, a priest is sitting at a computer. He is playing a videogame and Carlos Santana is blaring through his headphones. Behind him, an oil painting of an 1894 Serbian rebellion against the Turks hangs next to KFOR's Ethnic Distribution Map.

Father Sava studied English at Belgrade University, and his English is so excellent that, if it were not for his long reddish beard and his black cowl, you could mistake him for a member of the British royal family.

He pleads for a symbolic joint visit to the massacre sites by representatives of Albanians and Serbs. The Serbian representative would acknowledge the crimes committed by his people and officially apologize for them—provided that afterward they both would go to a destroyed Serbian Orthodox church, where the Albanian would condemn the devastation of Serbian cultural sites (as many as ninety churches were destroyed by mines and hand grenades be-tween the end of the war and October 2000 alone).

Everybody in this country talks about apologies. Con-stantly. Both sides are always demanding apologies from one another, as though words could undo the facts, as though the wounds could heal and the victims' complaints could cease.

I sometimes wonder whether they demand these sym-bolic gestures only because they expect the other side to reject them—so that they can stay in their outraged sense of injustice.

Only a few, like Father Sava, try to break through the circle of accusations; only a few understand that there can be no hierarchy of suffering if Kosovars are to have a common future.

But all creative ideas proposing some form of joint or combined action by Albanians and Serbs continue to get lost in the gaps between the zones and ghettos of a disabled province.

Traveling between the Zones

The first four Albanian drivers in Prishtina say "no" when you tell them that you will be traveling with a Serbian translator. But you cannot find a Serbian driver in Prishtina. The fifth one agrees for a higher price.

We drive north to pick up Tamara at the school in Kosovo Polje where she teaches.

Kosovo Polje is mainly Albanian, except for one Serbian neighborhood called Bresje. The borders are not clearly set, so Tamara can never feel totally safe. Neither does she know which language she should speak so as not to attract attention. A few KFOR soldiers guarantee some security during the day. At night, outside the ghetto, Tamara is easy prey.

She is so exhausted from teaching that she is almost unable to speak or walk. On the way to the car, she tells us that two boys had misbehaved during the chemistry class and she had to kick them out. "They have no interest in learning," she explains. "They do not know what they are learning for. What for, in this country?"

110

She has no answer to that question.

Once inside the car, the driver and Tamara do not speak a word to each other. Tamara cannot speak Albanian and the driver does not want to speak Serbian, the language of the former oppressors. To avoid any unwanted closeness, Tamara sits in the back with me and the photographer; Joanne Mariner, from Human Rights Watch (who, like last year, has joined us on this journey), sits in front, next to the driver.

It is quiet in the car until a huge monument appears on our right.

We ask Tamara whether this is a monument commemorating 1389, the crucial battle on the Field of Blackbirds, the myth feeding the wounded Serbian attachment to Kosovo.

Tamara does not know the monument; she does not know the symbol of the Serbian claim on Kosovo. She, a Serbian woman working in Kosovo, has never seen this monument; without any hesitation (and before we can stop her) she asks the Albanian driver in Serbo-Croatian what that monument is.

Everybody else in the car freezes.

A terrorized silence. The whole history of ethnic hatred, of the war, of the ignominy suffered in the Field of Blackbirds, of the cycle of death and expulsion, separates the front from the back seat.

The driver stares first into the rearview mirror and then over his shoulder, in disbelief, wondering who this woman with the misshapen glasses and the fleeing eye could be, this woman who has dared to ask him in Serbo-Croatian about the symbol of Serbian oppression.

And then he seems to lose control.

In Serbo-Croatian, the forbidden language.

Still frozen, we follow the incomprehensible dialogue between the two unequal figures. We are nervous: who knows if the torrent of words will enable any further joint undertaking, if the mutual contempt of their respective groups will make any kind of understanding possible, if the proletarian, business-minded Albanian driver and the intellectual, devout Serb, this improbable duo, will be able to communicate, of all things in front of us, in a rickety, rusty car.

They talk uninterruptedly for about a half hour, totally forgetting us, while we try to read, at the least in their facial expressions, the emotional color of their conversation.

Finally, Tamara saves us with a translation: she had apologized to the driver, explaining that she did not know the monument because she came from Serbia.

As soon as she is done with the translation, the driver wants to continue their conversation.

Two hours later, our driver confesses to Tamara that he has had an extramarital affair with a Serbian woman for more than four years. His Serbian lover had supported him throughout the war, and had brought food and clothes to his hideout in Prishtina. Now it was his turn to help her and support her in the Serbian ghetto.

We drive to Mitrovica, the divided city in the north of Kosovo.

Mitrovica is divided naturally by the river Iber: the north bank is Serbian, the south side Albanian. There is only one bridge joining the two sides, but only journalists, KFOR soldiers, and suicides cross the fence watched by Spanish soldiers.

112

Ninety thousand Albanians and eleven thousand Serbs live on either side of the river; the town and its population are divided by the river and by the experience of war. In the beginning, international soldiers tried to escort Albanian women so they could go shopping in the remaining stores on the Serbian side, but in the meantime they have given that up.

We leave our Albanian driver at the south end of the bridge and escort Tamara the twenty yards up to the no-man's-land. A sign reads, "Welcome to Hollywood— Restaurant 40 meters to your right." This area is the "zone of confidence," as it is officially called—a cynical joke.

We cross the bridge and Tamara is safe for the first time since she has joined us. Very few Albanians live here; the land north of Mitrovica is mainly Serbian.

If Kosovo actually were to be partitioned, this is where the line would be. The Iber is almost a natural border between Albanian and Serbian Kosovo—if it were not for the small Serbian enclaves and ghettos in Gracanica, Orahovac, Kosovo Polje, and other towns in the south.

Mitrovica North is an independent city; it is lively, almost self-sufficient, and full of shops with a wide offering of consumer goods. There is no visible lack, fear, or restriction as in the isolated enclaves in the south.

With their Serbian motherland at their back (i.e., north), the people feel safe. Conflicts with the Albanian Kosovo start and end on the bridge over the Iber.

Everybody we meet is friendly and ready to talk. Guests from the other river bank accompanied by Serbs are not common.

Only when I stroked one of the little pink pigs that were

113

squeezed on an open truck did the grim farmer give me a distrustful look. Maybe he could read my thoughts. I considered stealing one of the cute animals sleeping on straw. I could hide it under my arm and run with it over the bridge to the Muslims, who will not eat pork. But the wary Christian farmer does not take his eyes off me, so I just pat the hairy pig and obediently follow Tamara, who has already arranged for a new car for us.

We travel farther north.

The landscape is beautiful, yellow and red, foliage colors at their peak.

Our destination is Leposavic, a small town in the hills, twelve miles before the Serbian border and formerly a center of resistance to Milosevic. Nenad Radosavlevic, the governor of the town, was the only one who asked the Serbian citizens to vote. While all the other Serbian communities boycotted the elections, he asked them to register and vote.

Radosavlevic looks like Clint Eastwood; he has steel-blue, flat eyes, wears a denim shirt of the same color, and understands more English than he admits. He starts answering before the translator is done with the question.

"It wasn't about the elections. They are not important. It was for the historians and the statistics. In fifty years' time, when all Serbs have been driven out of this region, the historians should know that we were once here."

Of all Serbs we have met, he is the only one who recounts the story of Albanians and Serbs living together peacefully before the war, of the perversity of the alleged eternal hatred among the people of Kosovo. "We were neighbors and had no problems with one another," Ra-

114

dosavlevic says, "until some fool decided to burn the Albanians' villages."

But moderate voices cannot be heard amidst the chorus of radicals.

Few Serbs responded to Radosavlevic's appeal to vote. Many were intimidated by extremist Milosevic supporters.

Oliver Ivanonic, the notorious radical Serb leader from Mitrovica North (who now, of course, pretends to be a strong supporter of the new government in Belgrade), organized demonstrations against Radosavlevic in Leposavic, spreading such fear among the people that few dared to sabotage the sabotage.

Since the UN administration did not want to leave the Serbian minority without representatives, Bernard Kouchner, the head of UNMIK, simply appointed Serbian representatives for the Serbian municipalities, despite the fact that the communities had not voted.

This is how Radosavlevic became governor of Leposavic: he accepted the job. The first thing he wanted to do when he took office was to make contact with the Albanian municipalities. Father Sava and Radosavlevic are the hope of Kosovo. They are the subversives at the periphery of the country, their ethnic groups, and their enclaves, disrupting the official cartography of zones and borders.

Books 1

When we return to Mitrovica North, it is already dark. Tamara is scared.

We have to cross the bridge to the other side, to those

who are "the others" for Tamara. Once we have crossed the border, we arrange for an Albanian driver and Tamara becomes silent again.

We do not tell the driver where we have to drop Tamara off and simply ask him to drive us to Prishtina. Only shortly before Kosovo Polje do we ask him to make a turn and then give him further directions.

When we arrive at the Serbian neighborhood of Kosovo Polje, he gets angry and refuses to continue driving. With charm and money, we persuade him to drive on. When it becomes clear that we will not be able to drive Tamara home, and since it would be too dangerous for a young Serbian girl to walk home at night, she calls her boyfriend using a mobile phone and asks him, in English, to pick her up at the Orthodox church.

We stop at the fenced church, but no one is there.

While Joanne tries to distract the increasingly impatient driver with her talk, I walk with Tamara through the night.

We have finally realized that there must be two churches and we are at the wrong one. In spite of wild threats and insults, Joanne succeeds in convincing the driver to wait for us with the engine on, while Tamara and I look for the right place. When we arrive, her friend is so relieved, he almost starts crying when he sees us.

We say goodbye and part.

During dinner in Mitrovica, Tamara had asked for our addresses and telephone numbers, and a book recommendation. After thinking what could be good for her, I wrote down *Fugitive Pieces* by Anne Michael and *Disgrace* by J. M. Coetzee. On my way back to the car in the dark, I

116

realized that she will not be able to get them: there are no book stores in the ghetto, and she cannot cross the ethnic borders without a foreign escort.

Books 2

Linda was my Albanian translator in Prishtina. She spoke excellent English and was a quick, accurate translator.

I had spent the whole day with her, interviewing Albanian intellectuals, writers, journalists, politicians, people in the street, policemen, old and young men. I had asked them about the elections, the future, the war, their feelings toward the Serbs, toward Ibrahim Rugowa and independence.

We had spent hours together without exchanging any personal words. Finally I asked her what kept her busy in her "normal" life.

"Philosophy." We both laughed when I told her that I had a Ph.D. in philosophy.

Linda was a sociology and philosophy student at Prishtina University, currently struggling with Hegel's phenomenology. She explained that Prishtina University's professors were old communists from the time when they were still allowed to teach, in the 1980s. They did not teach any contemporary texts, because the library did not contain any new literature.

Then it suddenly burst out of her: "Can you believe it? It was only two months ago that I learned about Foucault! Can you believe it? His text changed my life—and two months ago I didn't even know he existed."

Linda had traveled to Turkey in order to buy *Archaeol-*

117

ogy of Knowledge, the only Foucault she had read so far. She knew about his other works, but could not get them.

While we made our way through the streets of Prishtina, she asked me about the life and the other books of the French philosopher. Walking slowly among loud street hawkers and the diesel stench of cars, we talked about Foucault's texts and influence. Linda kept asking questions and looked for connections between *Archaeology of Knowledge* and *The Order of Things*; she became so loudly angry that people stared at us: "This is a human rights violation, to have to live without his texts!"

Her professors had offered her a position at the university, but she would rather go to New York to continue her studies there—and to get other books by Foucault.

No Forgetting/No Forgiveness

The raped wives from Velika Krusa and Krusa e Male demonstrate for their disappeared husbands. The fleeing Serbs had taken them hostage at the end of the war and they have disappeared since then: nobody knows if they are still vegetating in Serbian prisons or if they were hastily buried in mass graves.

The widows until otherwise confirmed stand outside the government building of Prishtina and passersby simply cast down their eyes to avoid seeing them.

The women seem like people from the past, with their headscarves, their gray and brown coats—they do not fit anymore in this lively, glaring city with its dynamic, young people. They stand close to one another on the walkway, like a herd of scared sheep, seeking one another's protection, hugging one another's fears and sadness. Nobody pays attention to them, nobody sees them.

The same politicians who are unwilling to talk to these poor women, however, do not hesitate to mention their fate when they can exploit it in their speeches about independence and the impossibility of settling differences with Serbian civilians.

The history of these women is of general political importance—but the women themselves are not.

The crime committed against them is useful, but the victims of the crime are overlooked. Nobody wants to be reminded of their pain. Their sight irritates the general desire for normalcy.

Only a kind activist takes care of the old women, who are terribly disappointed that nobody wants to listen. They had traveled for hours by bus from the south of Kosovo, and now nobody cares. They are too tired and frustrated to even lift up the signs they had prepared with their husbands' names and yellowed photos.

The story of the hostages, of the Albanian prisoners in Serbia, is the thorn in the side of any reconciliation attempt.

When in the fall Vojislav Kostunica finally released Flora Brovina, the most prominent prisoner, the Albanians only shrugged their shoulders, rejected the importance of the gesture that they had been demanding, and asked for all the other prisoners.

Being back in Kosovo is depressing.

One year after the war, there are not only territorial ghettos, but mental ones as well. It is a country of bitterness. States of real and imagined injustice are kept alive.

On the Albanian side, I could not find anyone who would admit that the fate of the Serbs in the ghettos was cruel, unfair, and sad—the only answer I heard was their demand for independence and the request for more time.

"We know what you mean," said Ramiz Kelmendi, 70, an elegant, fine intellectual and a cofounder of Rugowa's LDK (Democratic League of Kosovo). "But it is still too early. Look at what the Serbs have done. The international community wants to recognize the so-called new Belgrade as soon as possible, and we still don't have our independence."

After ten years of apartheid, eleven months of persecution, and four months of killings, Albanians are still overwhelmed by fear. They are unwilling to talk about the rights of the Serbs or about a future multiethnic Kosovo as long as they do not have their independence from Serbia.

Interestingly enough, their rejection of the Serbs is mostly not of a racist nature. They are full of anger against the perpetrators and, because the nature of the perpetrators' code and of their crimes was ethnic, they reject them collectively. At the same time, Albanian Kosovars always stress that innocent Serbs could certainly stay in Kosovo.

But every attempt to get them to admit that the attacks on Serbian churches and people have to stop is in vain. They do not even answer and just repeat over and over their demand for independence.

Creating a truth commission (like the one in South Africa) to investigate the crimes committed under the Serbian regency, and also the killings committed after the war by former KLA fighters and by Albanians, would have been more useful than the provisional judicial system that was actually set up. The international administration decided to employ three hundred Albanian prosecutors and judges, right after the war, to build up a judicial system with local people. Nice thought.

These judges had been educated in the 1960s or 1970s, and have not practiced law since the 1980s. Rolf Welberts, the head of the OSCE's human rights division, says that the judges lack basic qualifications: "They are simply not familiar with the rights of the defendant. It is common practice that the defendants don't see their attorneys before the first hearing."

What is even worse and sadder is that the judges are not ethnically fair. Very few Albanians dare to seek criminal prosecutions of former KLA fighters—they are too scared and bitter to properly consider charges of crimes against Serbs. The few international judges (I believe there are nine total) that were flown in to help are not enough to correct or even avenge such injustice.

Power

Edita Tahiri is officially Ibrahim Rugowa's foreign policy advisor and the only high-ranking woman in the LDK.

We pick her up in a café where she is sitting among black-clad party officials, chain-smoking and talking. Now and then, passersby or unknown people in need approach her asking for advice or help. She wants to meet with us in a quiet place, so we go to her nearby office. At first, she sits behind a large wooden desk, but later she comes nearer, so as to have a better chance of passing on to us her love for Kosovo. She stirs her already empty coffee cup with a small spoon, as though that will help her bring ahead the history of her country.

Edita Tahiri talks about her life dream: independence. She does not trust Kostunica. The new government in Belgrade still has to prove how democratic it really is. She prefers Zoran Djindjic—she respects him for his courage in standing up to Milosevic on behalf of Kosovo.

She openly addresses the crimes by KLA veterans and the Mafia structures some of them have established in certain areas of Kosovo. She knows that there will be talks between Kostunica and Albanian representatives—but she does not want to be the first to shake his hand.

This is a war about symbols, about timing, and about not giving in first.

But Edita Tahiri is also developing ideas for a future constitution of a semi-independent Kosovo (she imagines a limited independence under a protectorate system, similar to the one in East Timor) that guarantees constitutional rights to Serbs.

As her talk becomes more and more passionate, there is suddenly a power shortage and we sit in complete darkness. Her voice keeps flowing, unaffected, in the dark: "Did you know I used to be an electrical engineer?" she asks, and I notice that she is fumbling for something under the table, next to my feet. "Power also depends on independence," she keeps on talking, and pulls out a small flashlight. She places it on the table, smiles, and explains that Kosovo's electric power station should also be run by Albanians.

Her political commitment, however, is of a deeper nature and not just enlightened self-interest. The rule of law

122

should protect not only Albanians, but everybody in Kosovo: "We need institutions that take care of the past and the future," she says, "so that people don't think they can punish crimes by themselves."

Her secretary knocks on the door and walks in carrying a small candle, but Tahiri proudly points to her flashlight.

She wants the Serb delegates appointed by Kouchner as the heads of the local Serb municipalities to cooperate and work constructively together. She is the first to say so.

Angelus Novus

"To articulate the past historically does not mean to recognize it 'the way it really was.' It means to seize hold of memory as it flashes up at a moment of danger," says Walter Benjamin. People continue to pile up the wreckage of the past and do not make any efforts to articulate "the way it really was." In Kosovo, people are so attached to their past that they fail to notice that the danger is long gone.

In my first days in Kosovo, I never understood why I never received a direct answer to my questions about the fate of the Serbs, why the discussions about the ghettos had nothing to do with the ghettos.

The reaction was always either silence or a lecture on the importance of independence.

The Albanian angel of history leaves the memory of the past behind while staring at it—it moves backward toward independence.

Albanian Kosovars see their memory in light of the real or imagined danger of Serb domination—and they never talk about what is happening right in front of their eyes. They never talk about the present, the current Albanian domination and the repression of the Serbs.

Staring at the past, they fear the danger of a return to the Serbian motherland, to Serbian oppression—and fail to see their own progress.

The farther away the danger is, the weaker their fears, the wider their visual field, the more focused their perception, and the greater the scope of their plans.

That is the future and I hope it begins sooner rather than later. In the meantime, Father Sava, Edita Tahiri, Tamara, Nenad Radosavlevic—they all have begun to clear away pieces of the wreckage. One by one.

Romania (August 2001)

In the beginning, there was similarity.

—*Edmond Jabès*

Dear friends,

Usually, I feel like a different human being when abroad.

I love the sensation of being a stranger, of my own metamorphosis, of sharing time, food, convictions, and listening for hours on end. I am simply happier the moment I arrive at any foreign airport in the world, I am thrilled to see the light and colors, I love to dive into the difference and make it my own, to travel around, meet people, and—sometimes—become befriended like a dog.

After twelve hours in Bucharest, all I wanted was to run home.

It was the first time when what I saw did not sow the seeds of a deep desire to see more.

All I wanted was to get out of there and to wipe out the memories, to erase all images from my inner screen.

The Task

I flew to Bucharest in order to write for a cover story on "trafficking in children." A team of reporters from our magazine had decided to write a report on the global trade in children: for sexual exploitation, illegal adoptions, trafficking of organs, labor exploitation. My colleagues from Africa, Latin America, and Asia contributed, and I—for the Eastern European section—chose Romania.

An estimated one to two million people are trafficked each year worldwide, according to a U.S. Congressional

Research Service report. Most of them are women and children. The trafficking in people for prostitution and forced labor is one of the fastest growing areas of international criminal activity. It is considered the third-largest source of profits for organized crime, after drugs and guns, generating billions of dollars annually.

Trafficked children are kidnapped by force or seduced by deception or fraud—they are told stories of lucrative jobs as babysitters or housekeepers, they disappear on the way home from school, they are taken from orphanages, from home, from the street. You would think that most of the time, these kids were violently separated from their parents or their home.

Sometimes, if they are street kids, the promise of a warm meal is enough, sometimes it's only the taste of sweets, sometimes the brothers and sisters of a girl envy her when her mother sells her to a stranger for fifty dollars.

The traffickers are hungry scavengers of the battlefield; they live off poverty, despair, war, and ignorance. Often they come with the bombs, as part of the "humanitarian intervention." Once the troops move into the newly built garrisons in Vietnam, Bosnia, Macedonia, or Kosovo, girls are brought in to feed them.

In the era of HIV, sex customers' erroneous belief that children are too young to be infected has forced traffickers to recruit younger and younger girls.

Bucharest

I had only false images of Romania in my mind. The only real pictures I knew were of December 21–22, 1989, with a delusional Nicolae Ceauşescu standing on the balcony of his palace, talking to demonstrators who were no longer afraid of him. On my inner screen, I always associated Bucharest with the dark colors, the washed-out gray and brown, of Krystof Kieslowski's Warsaw (*A Short Film about Killing*). It was cold in my Bucharest, and it was perpetually raining, I had to be wrapped up in plenty of layers of clothes. My Bucharest had no fragrance, no aura between ugly, six-story Stalinist buildings.

The real Bucharest is spectacular at first sight. It is full of parks and gardens, it has wide, grand avenues with big old trees, and stunning turn-of-the-century architecture with plenty of Art Deco windows and doors. There was gorgeous weather when I arrived and throughout the whole trip. Wonderful hot summer days, the people on the street were extremely friendly; it was lively, and charming.

We stayed in one of the typical luxury hotels with all the comforts and the same interior design as all over the world.

I had a driver who would not talk, a translator—Mihai—who would not do anything unless he had his baseball hat on, and a car whose engine would not start unless we were in no hurry. Excellent.

Liberté Toujours

Augustin is free. He is free of the beatings from his father, free of the cold he felt when his father made him stand in the snow to punish him, free of the longing for his dead mother, free of any linear memory. Augustin is seventeen, and he lives on a little island of green and bushes near the traffic lights, at the metro station Grozavesti, on the outskirts of Bucharest.

He does not recall when he left home, he does not recall how long he has been living on the streets, and he does not recall when he ran away from his first refuge on the street: the asphalt floor in the north train station, because of the raids, the murders, and the pedophiles. He does not know how long he has been living on this little dirty spot, far away from the city center, surrounded by a satellite colony, right next to the traffic lights and below the huge billboard above his head, where Gauloise cigarettes promise *"Liberté toujours."*

A small breeze of wind carries the haze of yeast from the bread factory across the river Dimbovica, some fifty-five yards away, but Augustin does not notice the wonderful, tantalizing scent. His freedom rests in the small plastic bag he presses to his mouth. The bag quickly changes its shape and size when he breathes—like an animal struggling with death. Augustin is struggling with life, and the Aurolac (paint thinner) helps: it helps him to forget his memories, his hunger, his needs.

When he talks, his eyes move quickly, he can hardly focus, he is mentally always on the run, he wants to tell me something, he wants it to be important, he wants to give it some weight, some meaning, but whenever he is about to finish a sentence his concentration is already gone, and he does not recall how he got to the middle of that sentence, what he wanted, and where he is in that sentence, and then he frantically presses the plastic bag back against his mouth and nose and inhales, it rustles like wrapping paper, in-out, in-out, in-out, and he stares at me again, as if I had to know what he wanted to say, and it is not clear that he knows where he is.

His face seems swollen, as if inflamed by cortisone, he has thick blond hair, and he constantly rubs further dirt into his red eyes with his dirty fingers. And then the others in the group, that tribe that lives together on this desperate strip underneath the freedom of Gauloise, come closer and try to join in the conversation. Just a girl with only one leg is left behind on the grass in the dark. Occasionally she tries to say something, but she does not reach us; a dog sits in front of the stump where her left leg used to be.

Augustin is annoyed. We ask the others to stay away for a while, and protect Augustin from distractions. Only Romana is allowed to stand next to him. Romana is his sister; she left home because she did not want him to be alone on the street. She is three years older and as illiterate as he is. They never went to any school, and the street didn't teach them anything. That's only a romantic tale.

Their language is like fishing in an empty river; they seem to throw out their thoughts, and only occasionally and by chance catch a word that grasps the meaning of what they want to express.

While we talk, there are always silhouettes coming out of the dark of the bushes, and someone appears right next to me and hugs me, mumbling some words I don't understand, pressing his or her dirty body and clothes against mine, eager to feel another body, it seems. It is not just one of those brief Western, upper-class embraces that you hardly feel. They really *hold on* to my body and press their heads against my breasts or shoulder and want to be stroked.

No, nobody stole any money out of my pocket, nobody grabbed my purse, and nobody went for my mobile phone.

It was a greeting. Nothing else. A wordless sign of approval.

The simultaneity—here the archaic living conditions, the self-destructive drug abuse, the tough attitude, the mature independence they acquired on the street, and there, in contrast, the soft touch, the confession of vulnerability and neediness—this was one of the most painful experiences of this journey.

Augustin talks about the nights they spent sleeping at the north train station, and how they were molested there, and when Romana wants to add something to his account, he turns his head around and yells at her, *"Taci"*—shut up, he yells as if she had stabbed him, *"Ta-ci,"* so loud and long that his voice sounds hoarse. And he turns back to us, as if nothing had happened, and he is lost and flustered. Angry with himself, he yells at her again. We repeat his last words, and he continues. Then we ask Romana something, and again, Augustin freaks out, and screams: *"Ta-ci."*

Suddenly, while looking at Augustin in disbelief, I remembered something: In his book *Anil's Ghost*, Michael Ondaatje writes about a plant in the desert. If you sprayed water onto the thin leaves of the plant, you could inhale the smell of creosote. The plant excretes this toxic quality when it rains—in order to keep away anything that would try to grow too near it, and so reserves its own small water supply.

Because It Is Clean

Florin lives near the Brancoveanu train station, on the out-skirts of Bucharest. A fair has settled next to the entrance of the metro, selling Arabic music and illusions, rides on the Ferris wheel, and disgraceful cotton candy. It is a hot summer's day, and Florin and his gang of street kids hang around in the park near the entrance. He has spent seven-teen of his twenty-five years on the street. The last time he saw his father, a couple of years ago, his father stood three yards away and did not recognize his son. For years Florin and his friends lived at the north train station. "Many foreigners came, and took children away: some gave them a warm meal, took them to the Hotel Stalingrad, right opposite the train station, abused them sexually, and spat them back out onto the street when they were finished, some foreigners took children for good."

The world of the street resembles a country without clear borders. Florin and his friends are experienced citi-zens of this country: they know the rules, the codes, the language, they invent rituals and protect themselves against decline as if generations before them had created this life-form, as if early death would not seize them long before any tradition could be established.

They protect one another and have stopped wander-ing. Unlike thousands of homeless children, Florin is not on the run anymore. They have settled in Brancoveanu.

He has lost the hope that his life will change one day, he has given up earlier illusions. He does not dream any-more of a home with a door one can lock, or of a job that lasts longer than a few hours and that brings more than a few diapers or a sandwich at the nearby shop, of a home where you don't notice the seasons and where the police are not allowed to enter without a warrant.

He has developed and perfected his survival skills. That's a lot.

The street does not automatically teach one how to survive. That's as stupid a myth as the illusion that blind people have particularly good ears, black people can dance better, and women are emotionally more intelligent.

No, sometimes kids on the street are simply overwhelmed, scared, helpless—and they stay that way.

In each vagabond community, the older kids try to teach the newcomers the basics of survival. Sometimes they succeed; sometimes the inexperienced remain in the lowest ranks of the group, useless and unprotected, pushed back and forth by the others, like an unwanted piece of furniture.

Every now and then Florin and his friend Laurentiu work as cleaners for the owner of the kiosk and the Ferris wheel. It is only casual work, but it allows them to buy some food. Florin has stopped sniffing paint thinner, and he cares about his clothes. "When you live on the street, you have to take care of yourself," Laurentiu says, "otherwise you die"—and he fondles his athletic body underneath his impeccably white T-shirt.

I notice—while walking with Laurentiu through the carnival (among those happy, well-fed kids)—the scars on his arm. They are thick, about ten inches long, ugly, white scars. The variety of their color and shape indicates their different ages. There are twenty horizontal lines, right next to one another, like a negative relief of sharks' gills. I have seen similar wounds on the arms of other kids on the street. So I ask Laurentiu what happened, but he only mumbles: "Oh, some old folly . . . " and avoids answering.

Like Florin, Laurentiu has a family of his own. He is no street kid anymore, he is the head of a family of two generations that live on the street. His wife is pregnant again, and "she will have her second abortion soon," Laurentiu says, without any attempt to give a further explanation or justification for this statement.

When I ask Florin where he lives now, Mihai translates "underground." I assume he means the metro station, but Florin says: "No, no, I live underground," and emphasizes it with an unmistakable gesture. I ask him to show me where, and we walk for a few yards to a gully. We climb down a small iron ladder, and we are inside his "home." It takes about thirty seconds until my eyes are accustomed to the darkness that swallows everything. It is hot and humid like a sauna, about 5 feet high, 2.6 feet wide, and miles long. To the right there is a monstrous hot water pipe. On top of it is Florin's "bed."

An apocalyptic sight. Complete darkness except for this one tunnel of light falling in from the gully, the humid heat from the pipes, and these tiny little beds, made out of banana boxes. There is a Mel C poster above one of the beds. Florin lives here with Daniela, his girlfriend, and Roberta, his eighteen-month-old baby! A few yards away, in the next cage, behind a cross-pipe, is Laurentiu's "house."

Florin is proud to have secured his family such a safe and warm home. During the winter the round steel tube offers enough warmth against the deadly frost on the pavements of the capital. During the summer the sticky heat is unbearable but the subterranean shafts give shelter and protection against police raids.

The gruesome campaign against stray dogs by Trainan Basescu, the mayor of Bucharest, has been terrifying the street kids for months. Instead of acting against urban decay and growing homelessness, the politician sent a special unit of his police force through the streets to clear them of allegedly rabid quadrupeds. Thousands of dogs are hunted, tied, and strangled or killed with a magnesium-phosphate injection into the heart.

There are supposed to be two hundred thousand dogs without owners, and Florin and his friends already ask themselves which victim of the street will be the mayor's next target—and whether Brigitte Bardot and all the other international activists would protest as passionately if the city were to be cleared of dirty two-legged vagabonds.

"It is safe here," says Florin, and then he tells me that they even have a shower. I ask him where, and he points into the darkness, "about a mile or two into the canal system." This is the moment when Mihai drops out. He refuses to join us on the way into those dark, small passages between the gigantic hot water pipes. Totally dependant on Florin, we go on a journey into this labyrinth.

We crawl about a half mile in unbearable heat through the darkness. Only Florin's flashlight dances like a dim glowworm in front of me. He walks ahead in the dark, but he carefully holds the flashlight to light my way. He moves smoothly, like an nocturnal animal in this underworld. Like a good conductor who is always a bit ahead of his musicians, he announces the turn of the hot water pipes and the low hanging cross beams in advance.

Had he abandoned me in here, I would have been lost.

After a while we reached a small wheel at one of the pipes. "This is shower," he says in his broken English, and smiles. I try to put on an impressed face and hope that the darkness covers my failure. Then he turns the wheel. Nothing happens. No running water. He apologizes and explains that the street workers cut the water supply this week. I thank him for showing me their bathroom, and we crawl back. When we finally arrive back in that little cage underneath the gully, he looks at me full of expectation and says: "It is clean in here, I told you."

Vocabulary

In Romania my vocabulary for odors reached its limits. The words seemed totally inappropriate for the kaleidoscope of fragrances: the smell in the canal system, in the ruins on the outskirts of Bucharest, in the Roma neighborhoods right next to the rubbish dumps in those areas "where the streets have no name" (the old U2 song), in the cheap brothels near the train station, underground, in the medical unit of the orphanage.

After a while one could distinguish minimal nuances and differences, for example in the perception of human emanations: dry sweat on the body smells different from dry sweat in clothes; there is this sweet-and-sour smell of an unwashed body with a little scent of strong alcohol, there is the smell of a dry, dirty body, and this scent of warm earth, there is the sour and slightly foul smell like a dog's wet fur after a rain shower, there is the bitter smell of this mix of heat, sweat, metal from the pipes, and urine, there is this sweet cheap perfume combined with the smell of humid sheets and sperm, there is this very peculiar smell of fresh detergent chemicals mixed with the sour smell from garbage.

Orphans

Romania in various respects qualifies as a perfect candidate for a country where children are abducted—whether for purposes of illegal adoptions or for sexual exploitation. The shadows of the era of Nicolae and Elena Ceauşescu, and the currents of the costly and painful transition to a modern capitalist society, have left one hundred thousand children abandoned. Elena Ceauşescu's family policy illegalized abortion and ordered fertility by state law. In dutiful response, between 1966 and 1967 alone the annual birthrate mounted from 273,687 to 527,764, a 92.8 percent increase in a single year. Forced examinations by gynecologists were supposed to guarantee that women would not use contraceptives illegally. Although the mothers could be forced to give birth to unwanted children, however, the babies could not be forced to survive (as an anonymous author wrote in an article in the *New York Review of Books* in 1986): the death rate of children increased at the same time by 145.6 percent. The results were sixty thousand unwanted

children in orphanages, and thirty thousand in foster care—
the latter is a concept that did not exist in Communist times
because it was considered too individualistic/privatized,
as opposed to state-run orphanages.

Homelessness and urban decline are not just children's
diseases in Romania's post-Communist era—but delayed
pathologies of the old regime: in March 1987, Nicolae
Ceauşescu's so-called urbanization program destroyed eight
thousand villages, predominantly in Transylvania. The inhabitants were moved into multistory buildings—allegedly
proud examples of Ceauşescu's agrarian-industrial vision.
But many of the predominantly Hungarian victims ended
up on the streets.

The turbulent years after Ceauşescu's fall brought with
them the mass dismissal of eighty-three thousand people
in the mining sector alone in 1999, and since 2001, un-
certain property rights (as a result of complicated restitu-
tion claims) have further destabilized the situation. The
dramatic decline of living conditions due to increasing
prices led to the inability of many families to afford their
own homes. Nobody knows how many children are living
on the street, like Augustin and Florin—they are not even
worth a statistic under those circumstances.

In a country with an inflation rate of 40 percent, an average income of one hundred dollars per month, and an
average of five children per family, children are often perceived merely as a burden.

On my first day in Romania, I was offered a child!

At night, we had gone to the park near the train station.
There were twenty or thirty Roma living in the park,

sharing it with another twenty street kids, apparently without any trouble. They had blankets on the ground, some used cartons as mattresses against the cold ground, and some had dug caves: they were rolled together like fox families. Vincent, the photographer who worked with me on this assignment, was talking to the kids and taking pictures at one end of the park, while I was wandering down a small path.

A small, maybe three-year-old Roma boy was pulling a yellow sweater behind him over the grass, and he looked up at me and I smiled at him.

His mother probably saw only this scene. But she thought she had detected enough interest to suggest a deal. "Ten dollars," she said. Then, when she noticed my confusion, she repeated more encouragingly, as if selling a particularly juicy ham: "Ten dollars," and had already taken the boy by his sleeve and moved him closer to me.

I only shook my head and did not know how to look so that this boy with his scratched knees would not think that I disliked him. How could I make him see that it was the business transaction that disgusted me—not him?

Only one week later my own disgust about the scene seemed completely hypocritical to me. What had seemed at the time like the only morally acceptable response retroactively appeared only cowardly and ruthless. Whereas at first it had seemed ethically impossible to buy a child, never mind taking it home to my nomadic life in Berlin, this first-world morality fell apart once confronted with the reality in the brothels, the police stations, the streets, and the underground of Bucharest.

For ten dollars I could have protected the child from what was now about to happen to him.

Who knows who would pay the price instead?

An orphanage in Romania is a streetcar named desire; it is a time capsule in which children's fate on the street is only administered. They are fed, yes, and they are not starved to death, as they used to be, and when they are ill, they receive medication, they can go to school, and maybe, if they are lucky and if they look cute, and if they are still young enough not to be considered "Romanian," but still "formable" according to the Pygmalion fantasies of Western childless couples, they can still be sold.

In order to be adopted by a Western couple, the child needs to be registered on a list with the national board for the adoption of children, and it needs to be registered with the orphanage, and it needs to be in a high-ranking position on that list. There were 4,352 legal international adoptions in Romania in 2000 alone. There are one hundred agencies/ associations worldwide that coordinate adoptions in Romania. Law enforcement officials guess that at least 15 percent of them also arrange illegal adoptions.

Of course, the association that is arranging international adoptions might pass on some generous "donation" that would help a child first *not* to be listed in any orphanage, then *appear* on the list of the national board right at the top, and then be handed over. The associations usually receive about five thousand deutsche marks for all the paperwork they do, that is, they *really* do. That includes secretarial work, visa work, coordination with the bureaucracies, and the like—and then they ask for donations, here and there, of a couple thousand dollars.

Currently, there are officially no adoptions whatsoever. After harsh criticism from a European Parliamentary Commission that "there was a systematic selling-out of Romanian children," and the threat that Romania would not be allowed to enter the European Union, the government stopped all adoptions, and is now preparing to reform the adoption procedures.

If you are not young, and cute, and sought by a Western family, you are stuck in an orphanage. If you don't run away from the abuse, or the boredom, or the beatings, you can attend school and continue to live at the orphanage until you are eighteen. But then you are kicked out of the house—whether you are still going to school or not, whether you have found a job or not, whether you have found a place to stay or not. That's the law, and that's reality.

Enough Time for a Lesson to Be Learned

The buildings are not standing beside but on the waste. There are stinking plastic bags, crumpled cans and coat hangers, and rotten upholstery spread on dried-up grass.

There are about six modern, five-story buildings of Stalinist beauty. All without heating or electricity. A place without an address.

Of the six completely run-down buildings, one is incarcerated, with a barbwire fence surrounding it—that's the unit of the "non-Gypsies."

142

They built this fence in order to demarcate their territory, to mark their difference from the Roma. They were
living in the worst ruins of the city of Bucharest, they
were literally living on and in the garbage of the capital,
they were living among hundreds of Roma families—and
the last effort in their struggle to survive was to draw
boundaries with the Roma, to build a fence in the middle
of everything falling apart.

Nobody seeks entry into their zone, nobody enters this
area voluntarily, there is nothing to steal, there is nothing
to protect behind this barbed wire but the faith in a hierarchy of the poor.

It is only demarcations that promise support in the
quicksand of social decline.

Probably nobody would have noticed that those of a
different ethnic background were living as forgotten among
the nameless Roma, maybe the Roma would not have been
visible as Roma, if they hadn't built the fence.

But now the fence indicates only how close they live to
the Roma and how much their fates are intertwined.

Instead of drawing lines, the barbed wire only high-
lights their common social fall. What was built as sym-
bolic power now displays only desperate impotence.

In the face of the perpetual attacks on the Roma during the 1990s, it would have been more appropriate for
the Roma to build a fence in order to protect themselves
against the "non-Gypsies."

Since the fall of Ceauşescu, the Roma have been victims of various waves of violence. Thousands fled to Western Europe, in particular to Germany. In 1992, the Federal Republic negotiated the repatriation of forty-two

thousand Romanians to the allegedly stable country. More than half of the refugees that were deported back to Romania were Roma families that have become targets of violent attacks in their home country.

Ahmet was slim, tall, and, perceived through the looking glass that reorganizes the diffused image of a person and that reflects the inner rather than the outer appearance, that veils or erases all material, circumstantial, superficial distractions, you could imagine him as a young intellectual in the surroundings of Cambridge or Oxford. He had these slow, gentle movements and gestures of someone whose hands and fingers are used to being careful and tender when turning thin pages of old books. Ahmet's father was Palestinian, his mother Israeli. The father was dead, the mother abandoned him when he was a baby and she left for Italy, where she is still living. "I visited my grandparents in Israel," Ahmet says. "They did not want to know about my life, about my interests, or about where I came from—all they wanted was a genetic test that proved that I was their grandson—actually all they wanted was a proof that I was *not* their grandson."

He was.

Still, he returned to Romania. Ahmet spent all his life in Romanian orphanages, he was a successful student at school, and he was still attending school. "But it is difficult now to commute to my old school." When he turned eighteen a couple of months ago, he was forced to leave his orphanage. That's the law. Nobody cared that he hadn't finished school yet, that he had no money to pay the rent for an apartment, that he had no passport and no job. "Basically, when you turn eighteen," Ahmet explains the vicious circle, "the end of your life begins. It is the number that indicates that from now on you are not even an orphan anymore, you'll be on the street, and you will never get off the street again—because who would employ anyone without an address?"

Even though it is far from his old school, and even though it takes him two hours each morning to get to the school, Ahmet moved into a small dirty room in this Roma neighborhood—it's the only place he could get. They are basically houses that do not belong to anybody anymore, or where nobody dares to collect the rent, or where there really is nothing left for which you could ask for rent. Ahmet lives together with two female friends of his, both orphans; they all knew one another from summer camp for orphans, and during the last summer they planned to face their future homeless life together. They share two small rooms, with no heating, a little oven; they have a tiny little table on the floor on which they display all their belongings: a pack of cigarettes, a chunk of goat's cheese, and a liter of milk for the fifteen-month-old daughter of one of Ahmet's friends.

"I do my homework for school outside on the pavement between the houses. I have more space, but I can only concentrate as long as I can bear the stench of the garbage. People think one would get used to it, but one doesn't. Well, maybe," he says, and looks down at his hands. "I guess I will have my whole life from now on to learn this lesson and get used to it."

Whose Definition, Whose Crime Is It Anyway?

"There are no illegal adoptions in Romania," says Colonel D., who is a member of the anti-organized-crime unit within the Ministry of the Interior, and he smiles. "There is no trafficking in Romania either. Officially they don't exist, but I spend twelve hours a day combating it."

The Romanian penal code does not recognize the crime "trafficking." So authorities crack down on prostitutes and pimps—since traffickers don't exist. "We have to be creative," says D., and he is already proud if they manage to charge a trafficker with the illegal forging of papers.

What does this mean?

If there is no crime of trafficking, there is no trafficker either.

And when there is no crime, nobody gets harmed.

No crime, no victim.

No victim, no violence.

It means: it's all voluntary.

Nobody forced the children to leave their homes, no one forced them to cross the borders, nobody lied to them, nobody hit them when they did not want to get into the car, nobody threw them into those apartments together with all the other girls, they were all by themselves and undressed voluntarily, and they themselves lined up like cattle in front of nobody's eyes, and they decided whose flesh would sell best, and they freely jumped into those cars that weren't driven by anybody, and they happily threw themselves into those sweet-and-sour-smelling, humid sheets somewhere in a run-down bar in Macedonia, and nobody beat them up on that first day, and nobody bumped their heads against the wall when they wanted to leave, and no one pulled them by their hair out of the bathroom when they were vomiting for no reason whatsoever, and they voluntarily fucked fifteen men per day, the same age as their fathers.

That's exactly what they did and that's what they wanted.

Since there is no trafficking, they are not victims—just prostitutes.

And prostitution *is* a crime, and prostitution *is* recognized by the penal code, and prostitution exists and they perform the illegal act of prostitution—and so they are criminals.

That's the law, that's reality, and that's how they are being treated.

Bogdan and the Manhunt on the Streets of Bucharest

At the police headquarters at 8 PM, the ten-man squad of the "emergency force" of the anti-organized-crime department is already waiting.

The terrifying group resembles an antiterrorist squad, ready to storm a hijacked plane, rather than a patrol for protection against human trafficking.

They wear black combat uniforms, guns and rubber batons, flak jackets with flashlights attached; they wear special, upholstered gloves in order to break windows easily, protective shields on their legs and elbows, and black, woolen camouflage masks.

It seems reasonable to introduce myself to these guys in order to make sure that they recognize me later.

147

The mission of the night is a raid on an illegal establishment in the city center.

Boyish laughter, spontaneous clumsy hugs and touches prepare everyone for the expected violence of the night. As if the energy would have to be electrified in the fibers of the well-trained bodies before it can explode later. Already here, in the cold fluorescent light of the police station, they practice sensual hype, and the eruption of violence is simulated.

I know that I won't be able to recognize them once they are in their camouflage, so I try to focus on details: Bogdan has glasses, so that should be easy; Laurin is a former basketball player and stands out because of his height; Dimitri has long black hair and a ponytail; Florin speaks English and will later stay by my side all the time. The rest of the men remain faceless. The roles in the brutal game are quickly distributed. Bogdan calmly explains what will happen. Dimitri will act as a rammer whose task is to destroy doors and windows as quickly as possible; Laurin is the chaser, running after fleeing pimps or "contactors"; Florin's job is to talk to the girls and find out if they have papers and if someone is still hiding somewhere.

We leave in three cars: one small civilian car, with the head of the squad giving instructions via walkie-talkie, and two small buses, with two men standing outside on the small platform beside the front doors, holding on to the car with only one hand, like mermaid sculptures at the front of a ship. The task is to first of all arrest the "contactors" on the street who broker the deal before taking the clients to the brothels, and then to catch everybody at the brothels by surprise. "By surprise" qualifies as a pretext for speeding, and so the cars chase down the streets of Bucharest at eighty miles per hour, and before they even stop, Laurin and Dimitri jump off the platforms and seize the two contactors—it takes about fifteen seconds, and four totally overwhelmed and shocked men find themselves in the back of one of the buses—and off we go to the brothel.

House no. 21 in Bihor Street in Bucharest consists of a small alley and two elongated buildings on either side, like stables, with rooms for the girls like stalls for horses. It takes Dimitri five seconds to crash through the wooden door—and Laurin another fifteen to catch the last customer in his underwear trying to escape via the backyard. It is hysterical chaos everywhere: some half-dressed girls try to hide in the last corner behind a fridge, dogs are barking in the night, one customer argues that he was only delivering propane and starts to stutter when he fails to show the propane tank he allegedly sold here in the middle of the night, some toddlers are running around between the high boots of policemen's legs, crying and in fear.

Nothing resembles the brothels in German red-light districts. It may sound absurd, but there is nothing "professional" about house no. 21. There were these two old couples living in one of the stalls/rooms, next to the girls' beds; when the squad destroyed their doors and broke into their rooms, one couple was sitting at the table (they had chicken soup without much chicken for dinner) and watching a *Star Trek* episode from the 1980s. They had nothing to do with the business right next door that was probably louder than the volume of their TV. The other couple had already gone to bed and stared at these men in black with small, red eyes. There were children everywhere, in the alley between the stables a tired soccer-ball was resting from a hard day's match, a green-and-yellow plastic crocodile was squeezed behind one of the doors, and everything was so familiar, that it seemed very far from the financial transaction: money in exchange for control over your body.

Everything was so poor with its sweet-and-sour smell of sweat, cheap perfume, and despair—I was standing among shivering girls and yelling policemen, I had one small child hiding between my legs, tightly holding onto my thigh with his small fingers, pressing his head against my legs, seeking protection, and I just could not understand how anybody could possibly get an erection rather than just a depression in that environment.

The whole military attack on this brothel was totally out of proportion—but Dimitri and his friends seem satisfied when they cram their hunting trophies into the buses and rush back to the headquarters: fifteen girls, half of them younger than eighteen, three from outside Romania, five clients without papers, three contactors, two pimps, and one unidentified guy without papers. They are kicked into the hall of the police station, and they have to line up. There are no chairs; there is no light, no water, and no carpet. Pimps, clients, and girls have to stay together—no distinctions are made among prostitutes and clients, grown-ups and children, victims and perpetrators. The police have twenty-four hours to hold them under arrest, and they want as many confessions as possible by the end of the night. That's all they care about.

Human trafficking does not exist in Romania, and so

the freezing figures in the hall of the police headquarters are being treated like criminals without exception and a fitting offense is created for each one.

When we are ready to leave, the head of the unit asks us if we want to spend the rest of the night with them.

"We are the street cleaners," Laurin explains. "We collect all the human garbage from the streets of Bucharest."

So far we had witnessed only the calm and gentle beginning. Now the real manhunt begins. Until four in the morning, they are chasing down the streets of Bucharest, arresting every girl who happens to be at the wrong place at the wrong time. There is no questioning, no conversation—whoever dares to run away from these scary-looking men is thrown to the floor when arrested or brought down with warning shots.

Dimitri and Laurin run after innocent street kids who happen to be up late at night and are standing at the entrance of a metro station.

For hours and hours, they chase pimps, contactors, and terrified girls, they urge each other on, push, thirsty for booty for themselves, driven by desire, by the obscure vision of clean streets, confirmed by the fear they produce with their appearance, their power, their facelessness behind the masks.

Somewhere close to a small park, the policemen see a prostitute standing on the pavement. They turn the car and chase the lightly dressed figure, who dives into the bushes. Laurin jumps out and runs after her into the darkness of the park. Suddenly we hear loud screaming. Two of the squad are escorting the girl back to the car, while two others are holding a Roma, apparently her pimp. His

151

hands are handcuffed and tied behind his back, impassively he stares at the knife that one of the masked men from our unit has just taken out of his pocket, and he remains silent when the masked policeman yells at him, "And what did you want to do with it?"

Then the first blow. "What did you want to do with it?" Once again. The next blow. There is no answer anymore that could prevent the escalation, no confession, no explanation, the question does not demand an answer, it is only the overture to the violence.

Over and over again, the faceless policeman beats the defenseless Roma in his face, his kidneys, his stomach.

Everything gets distorted, he strikes down the fear in his own body, he strikes down the threat of the knife that the other is no longer holding, he strikes as if the other could still attack. He strikes down his fear and his power, the hatred against Roma in each blow.

I stand next to it and just watch.

Paralyzed.

I wish I could say that I did something else. An old fear reemerged, filled my entire body like an anesthetic. I did nothing. I stood in shock, hearing the sighs and cries from the Roma, and the thudding rain of blows with gloved fists on the head and back—as if from another world, far away.

It took me at least two minutes until I overcame this inner cramp, the blockade, and I took the second policeman, the black figure standing next to me, by his arm and said: "Stop." Not loudly, I could just barely hear myself.

Everything was so slow, the shock about this outburst, the fear of the explosive violence in this massive body, the fear of the guy who was beside himself and who hit and hit, and who placed a gun to the neck of the Roma, who was screaming more and more desperately, as if there were anything the weeping, handcuffed boy could do to free himself.

"STOP." Finally, I regained my voice. "Stop." The masked man next to me stopped the excess. And the weeping pimp was taken to the waiting bus.

Would the policeman abuse a pimp of another ethnic background like this?

I tried to find out who it was, underneath that particular mask. The only remarkable detail of this unidentifiable figure was the flashlight in his vest that was sticking out of one of his front pockets—whereas his colleagues had the flashlight in their back pockets.

Back at the police station, everyone walks up to the headquarters. Vincent accompanies the unequal figures up the stairs, when we suddenly hear screaming and swearing from one of the cars.

Everyone gathers at the backseat of the bus, and the men pull out one of the young boys, who had cut his arms with a hidden knife he had carried. There is blood on the seats, unnecessary traces of the clean night: "They do this all the time," Laurin says. "The street kids do this because they are afraid and they want attention."

The boy, in the meantime, is being taken care of by Bogdan, who has taken off his mask and has gone to fetch a Band-Aid, and is now talking to the boy. I can see how he tries to calm him, and he gently takes care of the bleeding arm—in the front pocket of his vest the flashlight.

New York/Pakistan/
Afghanistan (Sept. 2001–Feb. 2002)

No soldiers in the scenery,
No thoughts of people now dead,
As they were fifty years ago,
Young and living in a live air,
Young and walking in the sunshine,
Bending in blue dresses to touch
something,
Today the mind is not part of the weather.
　　—Wallace Stevens

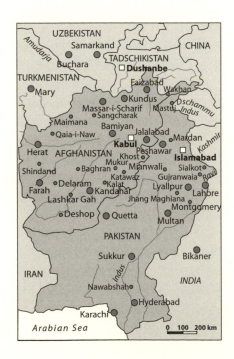

Dear friends,

Sometimes a certain homesickness takes hold even while being home, sometimes a journey does not come to an end after one's return, sometimes one changes perspectives so often that one loses a sense of orientation, sometimes it is easier to unpack one's suitcase than oneself.

I am a professional traveler. I am a wanderer and I know how to change my clothes, my habits, my composure, my language, my gestures. I am a stranger whose strangeness becomes invisible, a mute who listens to the pain of others. I move into foreign communities and discover a new world: I swallow different colors and odors, herbs, textures, and lights, I join wedding ceremonies and joyous celebrations, or funerals and farewells, I am invited to classrooms and maternity wards, I sleep in the tents of the refugee camps, or in the iron huts in the favelas, or in a car on the road, I witness fights and battles, I look at cracked bones, burned flesh, open intestines, and putrefied parts of legs, I am welcomed by strangers who open their hearts as few friends dare to do, I invite myself into unknown houses and ask for help and tea and patience and food as I would hardly dare toward friends, I accept gifts and generosities as if I could give anything in return. I give up the idea of symmetry, and I learn to say good-bye without exchanging addresses, without exchanging false promises of seeing each other again, and yet: without the fear of loss or death.

Then I return home, and then it is my turn to give: I write.

But since September 11th, I have not returned home. I came back to Berlin for a couple of days, and then I left for Pakistan, and then I came back to Berlin for some time, and then I left again for Pakistan, and then I went to Afghanistan, and then I returned, and then I went to Pakistan, and then to Kashmir . . . and throughout all those weeks and months, and throughout all those days and weeks that I was in Berlin, I never left Manhattan.

I thought I could come home, could unpack my suitcase and my memory, sneak back into the normalcy of a Western life in a metropolis, reunite with my friends, I thought that I would be as always at first—stuck in this twilight zone between the different places, communities, lives, that I would overcome it by sleeping lots, being on my own, getting rest and music and food, that I would have to wait for the dreams of violence and despair to come, and then I would finally be able to put the images and the assignment to rest. That's the usual procedure, that's the ritual, that's my learned and appreciated form of traveling and returning, of breathing in and out, of listening and writing, of going away and coming back.

It didn't work this time.

New York—A Lamentation

Most of my friends in my intellectual environment turned almost overnight into Islam experts, Central Asia experts, terrorism experts, anthrax experts. In the media, it seemed as if all bioethics and cloning specialists were reprogrammed as Islam specialists on 9/11 almost overnight,.

I, myself, was mostly speechless.

I don't think I have had a single reasonable thought or analysis in months. All ideological and historical explanations seemed distorted, the theoretical analyses of the theorists of conflict or the propagandists of a clash of civilizations premature.

Everyone tried to fit the shock of September 11th into handy theories, but these desperate attempts resembled the efforts of a freezing child under a blanket that is too short.

New York has become such a collective experience, the media have repeated the images so often that even the secondary viewers of the images believe they were authentic witnesses, whereas the primary witnesses sometimes question the truth of what they experienced.

September 11th is so overburdened with interpretations and commentaries; the day has been captured in thousands of photos, accounts, narratives, a perpetual media quotation in which certain images begin to dominate.

The small, individual scenes and encounters that lie beyond the official discourse are slowly forgotten. It is as if one could remember only what all the others have already reported.

But did you know that trauma can deafen memory?

In my memory there is no sound connected to the moment when the towers collapsed: I can recall the image, but there is no noise, no roaring crash.

In my memory it is quiet.

Acoustic and visual perceptions are disconnected. Out

of self-protectiveness I seem to have erased that perception that is the more painful one for someone acoustical
like me. The image of the collapsing towers is unreal, but
the noise would inscribe itself unbearably like the screams
of chalk on a school blackboard.

In the first few hours, we were all on the streets and the
towers were first burning and then collapsing, and all the
people were fleeing northward. We went in the opposite
direction, and nobody knew what was going on, we saw
groups of people around a radio that someone had placed
on a windowsill, and people were gathering around a car,
the owner had opened all four doors so that everyone could
hear the radio, and someone had placed a TV on the fire-
escape so that everyone could see the coverage of the unbelievable, the incomprehensible.

This way we found out that the Pentagon had been attacked, the White House evacuated, and so on . . . and
nobody knew what else was to come, and whether this
was a war, or a terrorist attack, and by whom, and whether
it was over or not, and so people listened to the radio as if
it could explain the world and make it meaningful and
sensible again.

It was déjà vu and evoked images from the refugee camp
in Tirana. Elegant New Yorkers suddenly resembled those
dirty Kosovo refugees in Albania, the way they were sitting in the mud of the camp, groups of ten or fifteen
around one small pocket radio, listening to the news, each
day, waiting eagerly for the news that finally Milosevic
would give in, would withdraw, would sign a peace deal,
would be killed.

160

The only difference in New York was that the people here did not share one language, and so the news from the speaker in the car was translated, it was handed over from one to another like fresh bread and each could break a piece, and so the word was transformed into Chinese, Spanish, Vietnamese.

"Estamos en una situación de guerra," a woman exclaimed and held her hands before her face, and even those who did not speak Spanish understood her.

While every New Yorker was shocked by the uniqueness, the incomparability of this event, of this disaster—I was mostly amazed by how similar they were and looked and how similarly they behaved to victims of violence in other places of the world.

Many commentators asked why there was such widespread solidarity with the victims of the World Trade Center attack. Why were people all over the world so fascinated by the images of this tragedy? Why more so than after the massacres of Srebrenica, Rwanda, or Chechnya?

Some critics suggested that the images of the World Trade Center attack had such an impact because it affected *us*, because it hit in the heart of *our* culture.

Actually, I don't think so. I think the images were repeated over and over again for two reasons: it was the only way to commemorate a collective death without corpses and because we could bear to look at the images. The victims of this crime were invisible, buried, burned, lost at the scene of violence. We could bear the sight because there were no recognizable corpses, no death, no blood, "only" the destruction of two buildings. So, how to mourn, how to commemorate, how to express one's loss? The images of the burning towers, of the tired rescue workers covered with dust, the collapse of the towers were shown over and over again.

Aleida and Jan Assman described in their book *The Body of the Deceased* the death cult in Ancient Egypt: when an Egyptian died, he was not immediately taken to his grave, but instead transferred to a space in which he was embalmed and mummified by specialists. It took no less than seventy days. This is what happened with the dead of the World Trade Center attack: they were not buried immediately, they were brought to a different space, our media— and we embalmed them, so that we could keep them alive, so that we could come to terms with their death, could find a form and an image with which to remember them.

The Day

It's 6:50 AM on a brilliant late summer morning in Manhattan, a wonderful day, as Gary Sarang, 27, steps into the elevator in the World Trade Center. Later, sitting in the offices of Morgan Stanley on the sixty-first floor of the South Tower, Sarang enjoys a bird's-eye view of the clear, blue morning. It's the second day of a financial training seminar being conducted by Morgan Stanley, for which Sarang, a practicing Sikh from Freemont, California, flew into the city on Sunday.

"It was 8:45, and we were just enjoying a coffee break, when we suddenly saw all this paper flying by outside the windows," says Gary, straightening his tall, black turban. "It was all this computer paper flying around, like in a parade—but it was just computer paper. First we thought it was some sort of practical joke, but then we saw the smoke coming from the other tower."

A minute later a man rushes into the office and instructs the seminar attendees to leave the building immediately. They remain calm. No one screams, no one panics, and everyone moves to the emergency exit stairwells and begins walking down from the sixty-first floor.

There is still a little time left before the next aircraft crashes into their building, the second tower of the World Trade Center. At 9:03 AM, the Boeing jet rips an enormous hole in the building, tearing to death many of its occupants.

"We had just reached the thirty-ninth floor or so. We'd been walking down those stairs for about fifteen or twenty minutes when we heard a loud bang. The entire building began to sway, and people started screaming and crying, falling over each other. The firemen were running up the stairs while we ran down. I was afraid. I'm usually not the kind of person who gets afraid. We thought the building was breaking apart. When I finally got outside, I saw people jumping from the tower. They just let themselves fall out of the windows. To their deaths. There was blood everywhere. It was the most horrible thing I have ever seen. I still can't believe that I made it out of the sixty-first floor."

Gary Sarang is now standing in line at a pay phone, waiting for other survivors desperately trying to reach their families to let them know they're alright. "My parents are in India and my family lives in California. I'm going to keep standing here until I've reached them."

"I lost my sense of time," says Joe Disorbo, 46, pointing to a band of white skin on his otherwise tanned left wrist, the spot where his watch used to be. "At some point between this morning and forever I lost my watch. I don't know where or when." Disorbo's right ear is bleeding. His shirt collar is covered in clumps of dried blood, mixed with ash and asbestos and dust.

Disorbo is an engineer who works for the Port Authority, New York's transportation agency that owns the World Trade Center. Its offices occupied two floors in the South Tower. Occasionally, Disorbo shakes himself. "I got to the office at 8:30. I went to get some coffee. Then it suddenly felt like an earthquake. When you looked out the window, all you saw was parts of buildings flying through the air. We wanted to clear the building quickly, but we were on the seventy-second floor. It took us forever to get to the mall level, and then there was this impact, this unbelievably loud noise, and the building shook, and we were still inside, and there was dust everywhere and we couldn't see anything. Everything was like it had been dipped in the same color, I'll never forget it, the kind of pasty white color you see after a volcanic eruption."

"I fell down at some point, but I don't remember falling. I just saw blood on my knees. I've been working in the building for thirteen years. I wasn't there for the first attack, in 1993, but now it's caught up with me."

He pauses, diving back in the depths of his memories, and finally says: "My coffee, it's probably still standing on my desk . . . but . . . my coffee, the coffee I just made. . . . I forgot it . . . it doesn't exist anymore, either."

A man who doesn't want to give his name, the dust and blood on his shirt and glasses bearing testimony to the last few hours, stands in the middle of Church Street down-town, just below Canal Street. "We were being chased by smoke and parts of buildings. It was like a war. We ran up Broadway and then we saw these unreal images. There were all these shoes, hundreds of shoes, all over the street, and there was computer paper everywhere, completely covered in ash. It was like a snowstorm without the cold. It wasn't cold. It was hot."

By 10 AM, downtown Manhattan looks like a city under siege. Police units are trying to evacuate the area, one block at a time. A blue-black wall of sweating, dust-cov-ered officers moves slowly, like a weary lava flow, in the direction of Chinatown. Mothers run crying through the streets, desperately trying to reach their children in day-care centers in the area south of Canal Street. Wall Street bankers with loosened ties and dead cell phones wander, confused, through the streets. Strangers embrace.

Artists in Soho seem to be the first to comprehend the catastrophe, and soon the first painters and illustrators are sitting in the middle of the street, holding their sketch-pads, with a clear view of the burning towers to the south, drawing this historic moment.

An angry young man is on the verge of attacking a falafel restaurant on West Broadway. For him it's a sym-bol of the Arab world, of the "Arabs," a target for his directionless fury. Frightened children stand behind the glass windowpane, staring at the man, while passersby hurry to the scene.

They grab the man by his trembling shoulders. "Stop it!" they shout. "It's just a restaurant, a place for hungry people to get something to eat. They're not even Palestinians." They hold onto the man, forcing him to read the red-and-yellow lettering on the window: "Israeli Falafel."

For hours, hundreds of people have been standing in line to give blood at the entrance to the St. Vincent's Hospital emergency room in the West Village, at the corner of Seventh Avenue and 13th Street. Jews wearing *kippot*, blacks, Latinos, a short man standing next to a well-dressed Wall Street banker—all are lined up in two rows behind two signs written in black magic marker on grayish brown cardboard. There are only two criteria today: O+; or A, B, and A/B. Someone has ordered a huge pizza, and the white cardboard box is passed down the line, each person breaking off a slice. Someone else has gone to buy a canister of drinking water. It's a hot day, and New York seems to steam under the midday sun, in the face of terror. But no one screams, and there are no cars on the streets. Occasionally, a taxi carrying someone worried about a family member rushes southward past a steady stream of fire and emergency vehicles—carrying its passenger as far as possible toward the still-flaming inferno, but closer and closer to what can only be bad news.

"Every one of us knows someone who works in the WTC," says Neil, 31, whose blood group, O+, is in great demand. "Every one of us has lost someone—we've all lost something today."

Down on Canal Street, Officer Joe Ryder of the Brooklyn Police does his best to calm people down. "We saw the news on TV at the station," he says. "And then we took off. Thirty people. But then we lost each other in this chaos. I don't know where the other guys are. We just lost each other. We were really supposed to be here for crowd control. But there is no clear division of labor anymore. Everyone helps out where they can. We got here shortly before the second explosion. I was down there on White Street, at the corner of Church Street. The next thing I remember, there was this loud bang. It was like a nuclear war down there."

Denzel Sancho, 35, walks aimlessly through the crowd. His shirt is open and his tie hangs low from his neck. Denzel can barely speak. He seems to have forgotten how to put words together in the correct order, and so he just spits them out, lets you try to sort them out yourself. "My wife, Susan, she's been down there since eight. That's too long now. And she works there, in a beauty shop. She gets to work at eight. It's only a block, only a block from the tower, and she's been down there too long already. I can't find her, I just can't find her. She should've been here a long time ago."

The First Night

South of Canal Street, the entire tip of Manhattan around the World Trade Center has been evacuated. People walk up the street, northward, away from the catastrophe zone, carrying everything they need for the next few days on their backs, some even carrying their cats in bags. There are police officers on every corner. The National Guard has arrived by now, and soldiers stand guard, keeping people out of restricted areas.

There are no cars on the streets, except the occasional police car speeding by, its red-and-white flashing lights silently illuminating the night.

In the most heavily damaged southern section of the Lower East Side, a few homeless people and petty thieves stand at the corner of St. James's Street and Madison. The only remaining light comes from Dream Deli, a grocery store; otherwise, the surrounding buildings are immersed in the complete blackness of a power outage.

"They almost beat a young Arab to death," says Jose Rivera, 34, but there is nothing in his tone to suggest that he somehow finds this unsettling. "A whole gang of people attacked the guy at the corner of 116th and Third Avenue. He was just walking out of his shop when ten men attacked him. He was still conscious when the police got him out of there."

A ghostly silence hangs over the East River, underneath the Brooklyn Bridge. Not even dogs venture out into the street. High-rises and office buildings are dark. The only traffic on the Brooklyn Bridge consists of the occasional cars with agents in civilian clothes, windows darkened, rushing silently across the East River into Manhattan. The market stands on the pier at South Street Seaport, normally a tourist attraction, are empty and desolate, only the smell of fish suggesting the bustle of early morning business on the pier before the catastrophe struck.

Then, at 12:30 AM, the pier is suddenly bathed in orange light. A convoy of thirty-five garbage trucks from the New York City Housing Authority has arrived to pick up the garbage.

Farther down the East River, South Street Pier is filled with semis, forklifts, and pickup trucks, all battling with time and the unexpected trauma of one's own vulnerability.

A cloud of smoke still hangs over the East River, rising from the crater that once housed a symbol of New York's skyline. The trail of smoke, this sign of destruction, has now flattened somewhat, become more yellowish, as it floats across the river toward Brooklyn Heights to deposit its toxic layer of dust.

It's almost dawn in the area around Wall Street, just a few blocks from the column of smoke and the epicenter of the tragedy, where everything is bathed in the glaring white light of spotlights. Fire trucks are everywhere. A lone policeman sits in the empty Fulton Street subway station, motionless for minutes at a time, his head resting on his hands, too exhausted to stand up or to weep.

The streets, the cars, the people—everything seems covered in a grayish coat of fresh powder snow. Each step, each police car raises clouds of dust that gradually settles on hair, eyelashes, roofs, and cars.

No one walks around here without mouth protection or even a protective suit. The journalists are gone. Only a few lost residents wander through the night. The ground is covered with papers from what was once one of the world's nerve centers of power. Thousands of singed memos, their browned edges reminiscent of discolored condolence letters, lie in streets coated with dust and asbestos. E-mail printouts, business documents, contracts—the banal reminders of normalcy—lie here on this street, in this city where nothing is normal anymore.

Pakistan—and Its Blind Spots

The war in Afghanistan began last night. The photographer Markus Matzel and I have just arrived in Peshawar. The refugee camp Cherat is located a few miles outside Peshawar, the capital of the North-West Frontier Province of Pakistan—an area that shares a 680-mile-long border with Afghanistan, that centers in the valley of Peshawar with its water from the Kabul and the Swat rivers, and the Kaghan, Indus, Swat, Dir, and Chitral rivers in its northern part. The North-West Frontier Province is populated by Pashtuns (sometimes called Pathans), who form one of the world's largest tribal societies (about sixteen million).

The Pashtuns living in the hills have never been subdued: the Mughals, Afghans, Sikhs, British, and Russians have all failed to defeat them. The British rulers left the Pashtuns to govern themselves in their so-called tribal areas, which were (and are) an uncontrolled zone, a no-go area, and a buffer zone between the North-West Frontier Province around Peshawar and Afghanistan.

In 1893, when the border with Afghanistan was demarcated, what is now known as the Durand line (after the poor British foreign secretary to India, Sir Mortimer Durand, who had to make up a line, a border, a frontier as if there were natural reasons for it), the Pashtun homeland was cut in two. The border divided one community into two nation-states, but the tribesmen could move back and forth freely—a privilege that is at the root of the current intense smuggling business of arms and opium between Afghanistan and Pakistan.

New York/Pakistan/Afghanistan

Around two million refugees from Afghanistan have crossed the border over the course of the last twenty years. Despite Pakistan's secret service's active involvement in the various battles for power in Afghanistan, and because of Pakistan's previously close ties to the Taliban regime, despite (or because of) its historic ethnic interwovenness with the Afghan people, these refugees are hated in Pakistan.

The government in Islamabad has no interest in any reports from the refugee camps; they do not want the world to pity these people because they do not want the world to expect Pakistan to host more, and there will be more, because the American bombing has just begun, and there are millions of hungry and scared Afghans on the run. So, foreign journalists are forbidden to enter the camps.

In our hotel in Peshawar, badly disguised undercover agents from the secret police watch our every step. At the reception desk, I hand over my passport to the manager. He does not look at me and he refuses to talk to me—the properly veiled Western woman—about the room and the price. He addresses Markus as if we were married and he had thereby acquired all property rights over me. We submit to this assumption and pretend to be a couple. But this scene offers me a first insight into how women become invisible here.

In Islamabad, the previous day, we had met a young woman from the Afghan organization Rawa, and we had discussed with her Rawa's underground work of teaching young girls and women and providing medical help for women. After a couple of hours, she asked me if we wanted to get into a refugee camp.

We agreed to meet in Peshawar in the early hours of

171

the morning, me covered under a long veil. They promised to find a way to smuggle me and Markus into a camp. Since Markus has what one used to call a punk hairdo, white-blond dyed hair standing obstinately in all directions, he has to have his head covered by a turban. With lots of conspiratorial effort, we meet a contact person in the hotel, and he guides us to the hotel's garage, making sure that no one follows our strange group. It works—and undiscovered we get out into the morning.

Only the children at the brickworks are up at this hour, carrying the bricks to the fire—they are hardened just like the porous, soft material that they carry, which is later sold for one thousand rupees per thousand bricks. One is lucky and has a tired donkey to help with the heavy load. The donkey is bleeding on his back where the rug is too short and the bricks chafe, and I wonder where the child bleeds. The cruelty of child labor looks almost picturesque in this scenery, immersed in "Eos, the early light with rosy fingers" (as Homer called it). And without interruption or control we drive into the camp.

Cherat—The Sandy Surface of Despair

Officially, we have never been to this camp. Not only because we are prohibited from entering it, but also because officially it does not exist. Cherat is a fifteen-year-old illegal camp and it hosts seven thousand people in small clay huts that substitute for the tents of its early years.

There are three small shops in the camp that sell rice and cookies and shampoo. There is a butcher who has four

172

parts of a lamb—at least that's what I hope it is—hanging on a wooden stake, covered with flies and sweating in the sun. There are no roads in this camp, there is simply space between the huts, and faces are floating in small green-blue rivulets like an arterial system through the entire camp. Men sit on the main square and watch the sky.

There are no B-52s during the day, only the kites of children who were forbidden to play with these "symbols of evil" under the Taliban regime.

"I don't hate foreigners," says Mariam, who is sitting on the floor of a small hut without a door, surrounded by veiled and barefoot women and five black Omega sewing machines. She teaches how to make shawls, scarves, burkas. "I don't hate foreigners, it is just they never did us any good." Whether Russians, Arabs, Pakistani-Taliban, or now Americans, it has always been foreign powers that battled over Afghanistan, over oil, power, and territory and always against the civilians. "For twenty-five years our sons are killed, our daughters raped, our husbands jailed, our country destroyed—first by the Russians, then by the Jihadis, then the Taliban. Why should I now trust the Americans who are bombing us?"

Mariam's pain has no personal addressee; she associates suffering with actions, not with particular actors. In that sense she is much further along than the international community and our contemporary political theory. She is upset about what was done to her, not by who did it—because it has always been the same over and over again. She had been here before, in Pakistan, in the refugee camp, in this homelessness, this despair, this fear. In 1986, she fled because of the Russian invasion and left her home in

173

the Farah province in Afghanistan and came to Pakistan, waiting for better times. When the Northern Alliance reconquered Afghanistan, she had hope and she trusted them. She believed they could provide a safer life, and she took her five children and returned to Fatah. "I saw what the Jihadis did to the women," she says, and the other women turn the hand-wheels of their Omegas and hold their breath. Mariam need not say more. In the course of the following days, I will hear this over and over again: "we know what they did," "we have seen what they did," "we haven't forgotten what they did."

In 1994, four men came to Mariam's house at 9 PM. They claimed that her husband, a teacher and shopkeeper, was a thief. They beat him with their guns, and they beat Mariam till she lost consciousness. When she woke up, her husband was dead—and she fled again. So, here she is, in Cherat, with so little money that she could keep only two children with her; the others she sent to an orphanage in Lahore, in northeast Pakistan.

She has no reservoir of trust anymore, and yet, she greets me with warmth and she offers a small cup filled with raisins and nuts and a glass of tea. She holds my hands, and she makes everyone laugh because she loses her composure and the distance that is required toward a guest. She yells at me, and she looks into my eyes, and asks, and demands, and begs, and she shakes me, as if we could thereby bring the world back to order. "You have language, you can write, *tell* them."

There are generations of pain in this camp. Like sediment, it has piled up on the ground, it has shaped and colored the inner landscape of these refugees.

174

Each regime has driven them out of Afghanistan: the Russians, the Northern Alliance, the Taliban. They fear them all. An end to the Taliban regime is welcomed by all of the women I spoke to in Cherat. But does that reinstall hope? Will these women return? Will they embrace a new government under the Northern Alliance?

"Under the Taliban regime we had to wear the burka for religious reasons. If we didn't we would get killed," says Mariam, like many others. "Under the Jihadis we had to wear the burka for security reasons. If we didn't we would get raped. What's the difference?" They will not return if a new government under the Northern Alliance is established in Afghanistan.

In the camp's hospital sits forty-year-old Abdul Quayum. He tries to clean up his desk and bring some order to his life. For ten years he was a guerrilla fighter in Afghanistan; the Russians arrested him because the student of Negrahar Medical University had distributed an underground newspaper on the streets of Kabul. They kept him in prison for six months.

"They beat me, well . . . hard . . . with . . . instruments . . . with electro . . . shock is how you call it in English, isn't it?" He stops to think. "It does not really . . . g-r-a-s-p . . . that experience . . . *shock*." He was fighting and working as a doctor with the resistance, with each resistance, against each oppressive regime. Now he is here, in the camp, and all he fights is the malaria, the tuberculosis, and the depression of the refugees stuck in Cherat. There he is—with all his strength, and his courage, and his athletic body—and it all seems so useless here. So he moves his stereoscope and the pencils on this desk before he asks the next patient to come in.

We are invited to spend the night in the camp, and we feel very honored and stay. We share a plate of rice and three potatoes with our hosts, and sleep on the floor in one of the huts. The next day we are treated differently, as if we have become friends, and we are allowed into all of the huts and tents. We start to really talk about ourselves, and how we live, and how we love, and we begin to share who we really are, and we begin to ask about who they are under the veils, under the beards, under the layers of sorrow that seem to erase all individuality. In our world, the pain individuates us; here, it seems to cover and abrade all distinctions into one sandy surface of despair.

At the end of our stay, Mariam comes to say good-bye: "Afghan people all have their grief," she says and strokes my hair. "You cannot listen to all . . . nobody can bear it all," and she touches my forehead. "One by one is enough. You have to be careful."

The Pill—or Lying with Tacit Understanding

A Dutch friend of Markus's was working with her boyfriend in Peshawar and desperately needed a supply of contraceptives but could not expect any help in the rather traditional Peshawar. So she asked Markus whether I could go on her behalf to a gynecologist in Islamabad and ask for the pill—and then later bring it to her in Peshawar.

With a certain awkwardness we explained to our Christian driver, Elyas, that I had to see a doctor, and he took us to an elegant private estate in a rich neighborhood in Islamabad.

176

A veiled lady in her fifties listened first to Elyas and then invited me into the house with a welcoming gesture. She asked me in fluent English what my complaints were.

I didn't know whether laws in Pakistan prohibited medical contraceptives, nor which religion this doctor belonged to, nor whether her faith might forbid her to hand out contraceptives.

Hesitantly, I began to explain to her that I came on behalf of a friend of mine who had been working for months already with her partner in Peshawar, and now had to stay longer than expected. The medication she had brought along was running out, and she needed the pill.

"I suppose," the doctor underneath the veil interrupted me, "that your friend is *married*, isn't she?" And she nodded to indicate that I had to answer her question affirmatively if I expected any help.

I faltered briefly and then lied dutifully: "Yes . . . married . . . certainly."

She got up and disappeared. After a minute she returned and gave me an envelope with a monthly ration of the pill (even if I don't really know a lot about this, it was clear even to me that it was totally stupid to take any medication for a complete stranger) and a sheet of paper with a name and a phone number. In Peshawar there were a couple of women, doctors, who would take care of women.

"If your friend visits this doctor and sends her greetings from me, then she can examine her and maybe prescribe her something else than this pill. This is the only one I have here currently."

I thanked her, and then she suddenly invited me to have tea with her family. She opened a double door in the wall behind her, and unexpectedly the room opened up to a spacious, beautiful living room.

Fast, almost invisible servants brought tea and milk and cookies and cake and samosas, and her husband and daughters greeted me in excellent English. We sat around the table and they talked about their lives in Pakistan and the ironic turns of world history that had them banned as outlaws until yesterday, and suddenly today they were America's best friends.

They were funny and warm-hearted, sophisticated and unbelievably generous to me, who knew so much less about their world than they about mine.

After a while, I remembered that Markus and Elyas were still waiting for me in the car outside and were probably worried by now.

I thanked them and said good-bye. Only then did I realize how shabbily I had behaved. I had lied to this wonderfully helpful lady and doctor, and that is just not done. So on the way to the door, I said to her, "By the way: I would like to apologize to you. I have lied to you. The friend for whom you gave me the medication—she is *not* married."

She took my arm, smiled, and said, "I know. And, of course, there *is* no such friend. It does not matter."

And she brought me to the door.

She had not believed me from the beginning; she had assumed that this conversation between knowing women had been nothing but lies: mine rooted in shame, hers in subversion against existing laws. In countries such as this, women command a language of their own to communicate secretly—otherwise they could not survive. Acknowledging this code, it did not make sense to explain to my doctor that the pills *really* were not meant for me, but for a friend.

Afghanistan—or Pandora's Box

The border to no-man's-land has no turnpike. Four Northern Alliance tanks are standing between the corroded gasoline pumps at the little gas station near the center of Maidan-Shar, where the soldiers of General Zemerai are waiting in the sun. They've stood at this lost outpost for seven days, the liberated Kabul to their backs and the armed Taliban in the hills in front. "We fought long to get here," says General Zemerai, "but it is not over yet." There was fighting in the past few days: four people were killed, three injured, the population was evacuated. Only a few of the old have remained, at the side of their unkempt goats.

This abandoned town is located on the strategic trade route from Kabul to Bamian and Herat. You would guess that it is the remaining Taliban in Maidan-Shar and the surrounding hills who were fighting against the "liberators" of the Northern Alliance. This is what I believed when I heard of the fighting in Kabul. And yet, this is a feud between the cousins Ghulam Mohammad and Abdul Ahmet—neither of whom belongs to the Northern Alliance. Ghulam and Abdul have fought for years and years—hundreds of people have died in the course of their feud. "There were only attacks and counterattacks, there were never any talks between the two sides," says one of the

179

town's elders. Both were mujahideen—but fighting for different factions.

This was never an ethnic conflict, and it isn't now. The parties and factions they belonged to are irrelevant today, and mostly they fight about what they always fought about: territory. And territory means not only power and honor, but money, particularly if it includes water resources or an important trade route, such as the road between Kabul and Herat. Nothing has changed in that respect. The Northern Alliance does not move beyond the gas station, so once we have passed that, we are without protection in "Taliban" land. We are stopped on the small, sandy path over the hills of Maidan at a checkpoint (it is totally unclear with what authority or in whose name we are being stopped, but the Kalashnikovs forbid any negotiation). We try to show the armed militias our credentials from the Ministry of the Interior in Kabul, but they are illiterate and they don't care.

While we are waiting for them to let us go, a truck with local refugees and travelers passes by and gets stopped. The "soldiers" climb into the truck and check each passenger. They take money, a tape recorder, and whatever else they desire. Suddenly, they yell and display two bullets that they claim to have found in the pockets of a poor ethnic Hazara boy—an old trick by bandits to blackmail a traveler. They pretend to have found bullets or arms, and threaten to take him to the police, only in order to receive some bribe—and then let the innocent boy go.

Finally we pass the checkpoint and drive two miles farther into Taliban territory. In the square in front of the Salman-Fars school, a bunch of Northern Alliance soldiers with brand new camouflage uniforms are sitting next to dozens of antitank grenade launchers on their pickup trucks. They wait, just like the thirty Taliban fighters who are sitting on a carpet in the sun, as far away from the Northern Alliance fighters as possible—Kalashnikovs shouldered, quiet and serious. Both sides are waiting for their leaders to come out of the classroom.

Ghulam Mohammad, the Talib, is debating with the representative from Kabul, the Tadjik Maulana Abdul Rahman. We enter the classroom, and Ghulam explains that he is ready to agree to all concessions, he is ready to broker any deal with the Northern Alliance in Kabul—as long as his old enemy, archrival, and cousin, Abdul Ahmad, does not profit from it.

Ghulam has been a Jihadi before; he switched sides to become a Taliban when it was convenient, and now it is time for him to make sure that the new power in Afghanistan does not reduce his power. Convictions or ethnicity or religion should not get in his way. The Northern Alliance soldier Maulana makes a deal: Ghulam can keep his territory, he can keep the control over the roads, he can even keep his heavy weapons—as long as he does not fight the Northern Alliance. Whether Talib, enemy, or criminal—the Northern Alliance does not care.

Ethnicity is not the prime source of friendship or hatred here. They don't battle over religion or ethnicity—that is a Western fantasy. One kills or dies out of stubbornness, ambition, and greed.

The Northern Alliance has no interest in upsetting the old order or balance of power. The new rulers in Kabul have no interest in calling into question the old system of

181

feudal powers and rituals and tribal rights. Their units control the capital—but outside Kabul there is anarchy.

An anarchy, though, with a structure: there is a fine, changing, moving, porous patchwork of territories that are run and controlled by different groups and factions, who have the authority to control, patrol, rob, or kill you at will.

"Nothing is safe in this country now. We told the international community that this would happen," says Eberhard Bauer, the director of the German aid organization Welthungerhilfe in Kabul. "Pandora's Box was opened . . . and we have to see how to cope with this nightmare now."

When we return, Abdul Ahmad is waiting at the gas station with his men. He does not know yet of the deal that his enemy, Ghulam, has just negotiated with the Northern Alliance. General Zemerai's men have begun to polish the tanks again: "You never know when they'll begin to fight again."

The Veil—or Who Decides on the Meaning of a Garment?

I never wanted to travel to a country where women had to wear a veil. The thought of the veil, whether a headscarf or a chador or a burka, terrified me. My fear had nothing to do with a feminist rejection of the veil per se, nor with radical atheism or contempt for any faith or confessional symbolism.

I cannot argue against the veil as long as the democratic value of autonomy is respected and everyone can decide individually and freely whether to obey the religious suggestion from Sura 33 of the Qur'an. I cannot expect other faithful to assimilate to our forms of expression, just because the Christian religion suggests a culture of inwardness that does not need any external signs.

Still, the idea that I *had* to cover myself under a veil terrified me.

I took the old vicuña poncho of my grandfather from Argentina with me on my first trip to Pakistan. It was totally inappropriate because the garment was too thick and looked completely different from the thin, fine fabric the Pakistani women were wearing. Apart from that, the poncho was clearly coded male because it resembled the gray and brown woolen blankets the men were using for prayer purposes and as coats.

Female Afghanistan had hardly changed since the fall of the Taliban, at least visually. Even when the public was always shown these smiling, liberated women during the first days—I at least could never find one single woman on the streets of Kabul without a burka. Not one.

A burka covers a woman completely. You cannot even guess the contours of the body underneath. You cannot tell her age, the size or shape of her breasts. You cannot see the tightness of the muscles of her arms, nor the softness of her skin. Nothing.

At first sight, these women lose their individuality under the burka.

But then, after a while, you notice the shoes! There lay all the distinctions; class, age, everything is visible in the shoes: red, blue, yellow, pink, elegant, poor, dirty, clean, polished, dusty. The whole range of life is reflected in those few inches.

There are countless women living on the streets of Kabul. They are often widows who lost their husbands and sons in the endless wars and battles, and they are not allowed to work, so all that is left for earning their living is begging or prostitution.

The homeless widows on the streets not only have old shoes, but their burkas are worn out as well, the color is fading, life on the streets has turned the blue into an ugly gray-brown-green, and they smell, and the widows are so desperate, and so poor and helpless, and covered underneath their burkas, that they have lost all their shame, and so they come in groups of five or six, and they run behind you and stop you, and they arrest you with their bodies, and you are squeezed in their midst, and they touch you, and they beg, and they want money, and they really want it, and they become aggressive and pull at your sleeves, and it feels like an unwanted, nasty, multiheaded, horrible insect, and you get scared, and you feel molested as if by an insect, and you notice that you treat these poor women as if they were an insect, awful, horrible, and you are disgusted with yourself for feeling so disgusted by them. And you feel ashamed, and you feel shame for those who have lost their shame on the streets, and they are so faceless, and you cannot look into their eyes behind these polyester bars, and you flee into your car, and you try to shut the door, and their hands are inside the car, and you are worried that you will hurt their hands, and yet the desire to get rid of them is stronger, and the fear of their proximity is stronger than the worry of hurting them, and then you finally close the door, and then they bang against

184

the windows with their dirty hands, and you wish you could die.

Maybe I should say that I had given some money. Right away. The first one. It didn't matter.

On my second trip, in Afghanistan, I bought a local, simple brown-gray chador, a thick blanket, rather than a shawl (which is used by Afghan men for everything: as a jacket, a blanket, a prayer rug).

Quite often I found myself in the middle of a group of Northern Alliance soldiers, and I was talking with them, and when they felt more comfortable and less shy, they would ask, "Do you wear such a veil at home also?" I replied, "No," and then they asked, "But why are you wearing it here?" I did *not* say, "Because I am scared of you people who are famous for mass rape." Instead I said, "Because I am a foreigner in this country, and it is a sign of courtesy." They were on the one hand pleased by my answer, and yet utterly confused and irritated. "But you are fighting this war against this veil also," they said. "Why are you wearing this then?" It was clear that they were wondering: if it were really that bad, that evil, that repressive a garment, how could this foreigner then wear it?

The Western logic confused them, rightfully so: one can reasonably argue against the obligation to wear the veil, not against the veil itself.

My veil seemed strange to them.

Of course, I would have felt less uncomfortable and alienated without the monstrous veil, but how much was I obliged to risk just to send that political message?

What the Western media often neglects to mention is

that the burka has many meanings and uses: it covers, it protects, it hides, it collectivizes, it desexualizes, it unsocializes; it has a cultural code, a class code, a religious code, a political code. It is used as an instrument of repression of women. But the abuse of women begins earlier; there are many more techniques of structural exclusion and disrespect besides this garment.

"The burka is the least of our problems," a woman in the refugee camp in Cherat said to me.

This is not to underestimate or relativize the laws that order the wearing of the burka, but it should be pointed out that the liberation of the Afghan woman does not solely depend on the disappearance of the burka.

Osama: The Suicide Bomber in a Kabul Prison

After the attacks, everyone tried to track down the histories of the terrorists of 9/11, people wanted to know: Who were they? How religious were they? Who trained them to become fanatics? What incited them? Was it personal experiences? Personal trauma? Political shocks? And how could they live among us? How could they look so normal? How could they study with us?

According to most media, the biggest surprise seemed to be that they were immigrants well integrated into our societies, who had a middle-class chance. They were not outcasts, outsiders, asocial asylum seekers, but well-educated, integrated students. This surprise seems to suggest that "normal" people would not commit such a crime—that integrated immigrants would not do this. We suggest that these people were leading a somewhat schizophrenic life: here, the assimilated immigrant, there the fanatic Muslim, here the friendly neighbor, there the cruel terrorist.

We try to incorporate their deed into our rational, analytic framework. We trace the history of fundamentalism, we trace the premodern segments of Islam, and we analyze the social dissonances in the Arab world. We look at the disastrous social conditions in Islamic countries that result from some form of global capitalism.

And for some analysts this leads to thinking that this terrorism is intrinsic to a certain type of unreformed Islam. Others think that this terrorism is intrinsic to a certain type of (our) globalization. Accordingly, the first blame Islam and its leaders, and the second blame ourselves and our unjust capitalism.

But despite all these attempts to find an explanation there always remains a moment of inaccessibility. We can uncover in part the ground in which such deeds grow, but the decisive moment of the conscious decision of a human being to kill thousands, remains in the shadow of reason—inexplicable.

With some luck, we managed to get access to Kabul's security prison. Eighty-six inmates are locked up here; thirty-five of them are Pakistani nationals, five are so-called Arabs. There are always six or more together in cells in the basement of the building, without heating or beds. They have a few blankets from the International Red Cross, some of them have copies of the Qur'an, they are allowed to have tea in their cells, and they keep the sugar for the tea or any other personal belongings in plastic bags, hanging high up above their heads on the wall so that they don't get wet on the cold floor. They have not seen a judge yet, let alone a lawyer. They have not seen the light in weeks, only the few yards of the hallway that leads to the dirty toilets on the first floor.

We are allowed to enter one of the cells and talk to the inmates: there are six men squeezed into this cell. There are three plank beds for the men. Five of them are sitting on gray woolen blankets; one man is lying under one of the plank beds, face to the wall; the others ignore him. After a while we figure out that he is the only foreigner in this cell. Foreigners, in particular Arabs, were apparently hated in Afghanistan, and now since the end of the Taliban regime, the easiest way to deal with the past of their country is to blame all evil on Osama bin Laden and his Arab forces and the Pakistanis who created the "monster Taliban." It is a form of dishonest cleansing of one's past to suggest that all evil came from abroad.

The Afghan prisoners do the same: they pretend that they were arrested only because of some fist-fighting— pretend that they were normal petty criminals and had nothing to do with the Taliban. I ask "the Arab" they have banished underneath the plank beds to talk to me, but he does not speak any Dari or Urdu and I lack a translator for Arab. Someone suggests another inmate who could translate, and five minutes later Osama turns up. He is a thirty-two-year-old, good-looking, slender Jordanian with impeccable English. He is friendly and helpful. Osama was arrested while on a suicide mission to kill as many Americans as possible.

For the next two hours, I talk to this gentle young man. He does not mind talking about his motives or about his

188

background. He confesses everything he wanted to do, and gives reasons for his motives and aims. He is willing and able to debate passages from the Qur'an with me, the history of the Middle East conflict, as well as Bush's rhetoric. Did he seem strange to me? Mad? Ill? Irrational? Fanatic? Evil? No, he seemed just like you and me, except that he would blow himself up to kill Americans.

Was there a long history of fanatic teaching of ideological training at the root of his mission? No, he just grew up in Jordan, in Amman. He did not get radicalized in a mosque, or by a particular fundamentalist group.

On October 4, 2001, he took three hundred dollars and flew on a Gulf Airlines flight from Amman to Karachi. He did not inform his parents or friends, he left simply because he wanted to help "the Muslims" in Afghanistan fight the foreign invaders, fight "the Americans." He spent one month in Karachi before he met someone called Abdul in a mosque. Abdul promised that he would bring Osama to Afghanistan, to a training camp where he could train for a suicide mission. After receiving five thousand rupees from Abdul, Osama traveled via Peshawar, in the north of Pakistan. He arrived in Kabul a few days before it fell. "I would have done anything," he says. "If they had said I should stay and cook, I would have done it, if they had said I should kill myself with a bomb, I would have done that."

But when he arrived in Kabul his guide, Abdul turned out to be a liar, and there were no contact people in Kabul, and there was no training camp, and the Muslims in Afghanistan weren't waiting for an outsider. Then Kabul fell, and Osama left for Jalalabad—one of the last strongholds of the Taliban in those days—and he was arrested. "If only I had known that they hate foreigners here in Afghanistan! Nobody had told me that."

Osama gives plenty of political reasons for his mission: the Middle East conflict, the killing of "all the Muslims" in the occupied territories, the destruction of the Palestinians, and the ignorance of the Western world toward this crime. He is upset about the bombing of Iraq, and he attacks the United States for fighting the Muslims, and Bush's announcement of the "Crusade" only seems to prove his point.

When I ask him why he is talking so openly about all this, he answers calmly, "Why should I be afraid? I had decided to sacrifice my life for the Muslim cause; there is nothing that I could fear anymore." When I ask him about the contradiction of being a faithful Muslim and wanting to commit suicide, something that the Qur'an clearly condemns, he answers, "No, the Qur'an condemns only suicide for people who are bored with their lives, who don't have any respect for the gift of life, and who throw it away out of egoism or sadness. But I love life, and I enjoy its beauties, and I don't just throw it away, I give it up for something more sublime. That is not prohibited, that is a great deed."

There is no way to distinguish between the religious and the secular-political motives for his decision to become a martyr. It seems to be an ill-informed distinction because a fanatic is, by definition, someone who cannot disentangle politics from religion or religion from politics. There is always an aesthetization at the core of each fanaticism, the desire to bring the disordered, disenfranchised, disenchanted, confused world into a smooth shape and order.

190

If we look at some of the most secular political terrorists' ideologies, they often have features of a religious sect.
They often have a symbolically closed logic and program,
they have creeds, and their forms of recruitment seem to
reproduce the worst and most ridiculous forms of clerical
practices. And if we look at religious terrorists, they have
political justifications, and only a religious promise of life
in another world, they name historical-political events as
their religious awakening, and they crave a different setting, justice for the people in this political world.

Borderland—or Kafka in Pakistan

On my third trip to Pakistan, I wanted to write on the
newly erupting conflict/war between India and Pakistan.
The photographer Sebastian Bolesch and I travel along
the border between India and Pakistan to the part of Kashmir that belongs to Pakistan. We begin in the southeast,
in the border towns close to Lahore.

We find cattle farmers who own a few cows and two
sheep, and they sit down with us and give us tea with fresh,
creamy milk, and we talk. They tell us about their history
of losses, of the systematic policy of the Indian army of
shooting cattle, of how the Indians invaded the area a
couple of years ago and killed everything, and how they
are repeating it now. They walk with us to their fields,
fields they cannot use anymore because the Pakistan army
has turned them into minefields.

Memories of past attacks by the Indians are both a curse
and salvation: they prevent all hope for peace, and yet

they also save them from obliteration. Without memory nobody would flee. Without memory of the dead, of the looted farms, without memory of the lost herds, no refugees would be on the roads north of Sialkot. Fear is passed on from generation to generation in this area. For some, the old and enduring fear of the past remains nothing but the inherited obstacle to any new and different future. For others, real experience joins that fear—because sometimes foreign bullets are still faster than one's own instincts.

Back at the hotel, I find a report in a local paper of four wounded men in a rural area close to the border who got shelled by Indian artillery. The next morning at 6 AM we drive for three hours to the hospital where they were taken. We enter the hospital and wait in the reception area for a half hour until someone guides us to the director. He refuses to take my card and refuses to listen; he asks for orders from Islamabad. No charm offensive works, no gentleness, nothing. When we leave, he keeps the translator and threatens him for having brought us.

We drive to another building with another general, who lets us wait twenty minutes and then admits that he is not in charge. We drive to another building to find the local commander, who offers us tea and samosas, and we have to talk with him about the world at large. After a half hour, he listens to our request to talk to the wounded and he says that he will try to help. Another fifteen minutes later, a soldier takes us to another building, and a security officer sits down with us. He gives us tea and milk and cookies and samosas and spring rolls, and we talk about Bosnia and Germany for an hour. The sun is already going down by the time we finally make our request. He says that he has to talk to his superior, and after another half hour, he says we can go, and we go. We are all shattered: my entire store of charm, anger, yelling, and flirting is empty.

We arrive back at the same hospital where we had begun a couple of hours before. After all that military stupidity and Kafkaesque bureaucracy, and after all the yelling and the repression and the struggling, we are finally in the middle of this smell of death and disinfection. Everything we had been dealing with is wiped away in a second. There is only sighing from the woman in that last bed on the left-hand side, and her mumbling and weeping. There is a young man who lost his right foot five hours ago, because he stepped on a mine. The doctors told him that they could save it, but he is now looking down at his bloody body, and it seems like a stranger's to him. Nobody has told him yet that on this same day his brother-in-law died in an attack. Sebastian, wonderful Sebastian, has put his camera away, and he just stands behind me and is very present, and yet not so present that anyone would find him disturbing.

We forget the time in there, and we just listen, and we move from one bed and one injury and pain and despair to the next. We arrive at the bed of an old man. The sign above his bed says that he is called Mohammed Shafi, and before I can even say anything, he lifts up his body a little toward me, and raises his right hand and draws some lines in the air, and just bursts out crying, and he has the voice of a child when he weeps "aaaaaa—ah—ah . . . aaaaa—ah—ah." It is always the same rhythm, his weeping, and it cuts right through, because it is not the weeping of a child about an immediate pain in a demarcated, clear wound, or

193

a loss, or a lack, or a direct pain. No, this is the weeping over the injustice of it all, this is the weeping over the experience of a long life full of suffering and pain, the weeping over the lack of attention, over the ignorance of a world, our world, our common world in which crimes happen every day. He weeps and weeps, because finally someone pays attention and cares. Mohammed stutters: "They will kill us," and his chest moves up and down, this chest which two projectiles destroyed, and from which a flexible tube sticks out that has taken the blood and pus that is running down into the bottle that stands underneath his bed right in front of my feet. "All of us" and his chest moves up, down, "they will kill all of us," up, down. "They are standing as close as you do now," up, down, "and they shoot us." He is not ashamed of his tears; he is too old and too tormented to be embarrassed.

The next day we want to go into the region where Mohammed Shafi was shot. It is a small area of Pakistan territory, nothing but farmland that is under perpetual attack from Indian shelling. (Meanwhile in Islamabad, Colin Powell reassures the world of his great diplomatic success in brokering a truce between India and Pakistan.)

We leave in the afternoon because Sebastian wants to take pictures at sunset. We drive on the roads where only refugees drive—in the opposite direction to ours. We talk to them, and I ride with some of them on their tractors, squeezed in among their household goods, mattresses, and children. We drive for hours through this spooky area, where we meet fewer and fewer people. Everyone warns us not to drive on; only a few cattle farmers go with us because they have left their herds in that area. Every now

194

and then there is a half mile or so that is within the range of some Indian post on the other side of the front line, and it is demarcated and announced with an absurd sign—"BE FAST. DRIVE QUICK. AREA UNDER INDIAN ATTACK"—so that you know when to be afraid of pain or death. Quite convenient, I think. Quite absurd, Sebastian thinks. Of course, it is potentially fatal because the sign falsely suggests that you could get killed only where there are such signs.

After passing evacuated town after town, after passing soldiers digging trenches along the road, we see frantic refugees leaving this territory. Finally, we arrive at the last town where the old man was from. We have to walk two hundred yards in an open field, directly under the eyes of the snipers in the three Indian watchtowers overlooking this place. We arrive and find only soldiers, and one old woman, too old to hope for something better than her sudden death in this town where she was born. We find one farmer with his donkeys and lambs in front of his house. "Don't just stand here," he whispers, as if the Indians could shoot with their ears. "Come down here, behind the wall, one does not stand in this town."

Then we drive back home, through the night, and we have to stop at each army post because people want to have tea with us and hear from us about the world that has forgotten them.

Being German—or Promisingly Anti-Semitic

On the way to our car, in one of the towns, we get stopped by an old man who wants to talk to us. He is the elder of

195

the town, and he gives orders to some men to bring us chairs and offer us tea and cookies, and he wants to know what we think of "NYC," and what we think of "the Jews." Sebastian turns away, and I know that he wants to leave these anti-Semites, but I also see that slowly the young men come closer and sit down on the floor in front of this house, and we decide to stay, and then we talk and talk for hours, about all there is to talk about.

This is an area where hardly anybody reads papers or owns a television, and not many foreigners pass by. It is an oral culture and we are one of the few chances they get to talk and listen and hear different points of view.

Nearly everyone I met in Pakistan believed that the World Trade Center was attacked by "the Jews"; nearly everyone I met in Pakistan came out with this story about "4,000 Jews not going to work in the WTC on the morning of the 11th." "So, why didn't they?" "Because they knew." It is always the "Jews," the "Mossad." They have never heard about the connections between the pilots and the financial network associated with bin Laden, they have never heard anything about the biographies of the perpetrators, nothing.

Amazingly, the conspiracy theory about the Mossad or the CIA as the secret actors behind the attacks rests not only on the strong belief that those organizations would be mean enough to commit such a crime, but also on the doubt that any Muslim organization could be intelligent enough or well enough equipped or sophisticated enough to coordinate and execute such a task. Amazingly, there seems to be at the root of this conspiracy theory less hatred against the Others' omnipotence than frustration about their own impotence.

Still, nearly everyone I met in Pakistan was "anti-American." I guess that's what we would call it. What does that mean? The tricky thing about this "anti-Americanism" is that it tends to conflate Israelis with Jews, Jews with Americans, and Americans with the CIA and the Mossad.

Critique of certain policies of the state of Israel goes along with a racist attack on "the Jews" in general, and each attack on American politics is combined with some wild conspiracy theory. And when you argue with them, you always try to disentangle the rational from the racist, and you try to agree with some of the criticisms, and sometimes that helps them to also admit some mistakes or errors inside "their" group. I should add that nobody applauded the WTC attack, but they all felt like victims of the American war of revenge, since Bush had announced not just a war against terrorism but a "crusade."

People here may not have televisions, but they *all* know that Bush called his mission a "crusade." I don't know if there has ever been a single term in history that has caused as much damage as this mistake.

Generally, they approach me and talk to me because being German sounds promisingly anti-Semitic to them, and so you can only decide whether or not you are up to this conversation now, because once you enter it, you have to be serious and make a real effort and really argue.

But if you don't even try, these people will think that you shy away because of guilt, or shame, or an inability to talk, or lack of interest, or arrogance.

And so Sebastian and I sit down, and we talk, and we struggle to understand the other, try to erase prejudices, explain what remains questionable in our culture. We discuss under the curious eyes of all neighbors the Middle East conflict, and Afghanistan, and Bush's rhetoric.

And when we are finished, a group of about twenty-five men are sitting around us, and only the old man and I have been speaking, and various translators spread our words to the others.

I don't know if I convinced them with any argument I put forward in those hours on the terrace—but at the end of the day, I knew that at least for once they had met a Westerner, a non-Muslim, who sat down with them, had tea and listened to them, argued and agreed and disagreed and shared all those hours till the sun went down.

War Zones: On Death and Normalcy

Some of my friends and some of the media representatives have asked over and over again why we go to regions of crisis.

Why do we want to visit death and violence?

Why do we always return to such places?

Why do we carelessly risk our lives?

When eight of my colleagues were killed in the course of the first ten days in Afghanistan, some asked: What did they do wrong? Why did they take that road? Why did they travel on that road? Why were they in the company of these people? How could they be so reckless? Were they driven by ambition? By voyeurism? By pressure from their headquarters?

I go to countries at war for a whole set of complex reasons, motivations, and drives. Some of them I know, some I don't. Some are so intertwined with who I am that it is difficult to disentangle them enough for a brief, clear explanation. Some are banal, some egocentric, some political.

Mostly, I go on these trips because the knowledge of victims of war and injustice haunts me.

Of course, the victim of today quite often becomes the perpetrator of tomorrow, the despair of today quite often nurtures the brutality of tomorrow.

It's about the genealogy of exclusion and war—and about giving a voice to the victims.

Quite often, abuse and violence mark the victims not only physically: not only are individuals beaten or raped, but the trauma also steals their ability to speak or to express themselves intelligibly.

Repression and violence against individuals or groups not only aims to destroy the people, but also seeks to erase all traces of the criminal deed. Language is at the beginning of all traces and traceability. It is a systematic method of repression to destroy a person's ability to give an intelligible account of what was done to her.

I travel to war zones because the experience of violence often leads to the inability to give an account of the injustice endured, to the speechlessness of the victim, to their being forgotten. But that only increases the injury.

In war everything is present simultaneously: there is the normalcy of a peaceful life, there is laughter and sen-

suality, there are people out on the streets, there are ba-
zaars and food markets open, and there are wedding ceremonies and children with kites. There are feasts, and
there is love, and there is no sound or sight of war. "No
soldiers in the scenery, no thoughts of people now dead,"
writes the poet Wallace Stevens.

People come home and they tell of death and cruelty in
places that were peaceful until yesterday. And they take
you to their homes in the ghettos, in the favelas, in the
outskirts, at the border, in the countryside, and they move
back and forth between areas and zones.

The fighting also moves back and forth and it changes
its locations, and shape, and timing, and appearances and
forms.

And at some point, you are not an outsider anymore because you cannot stand outside the violence in such areas—
it is everywhere and has penetrated all segments of society and its topography.

People lie in hospitals or you meet them in farmhouses.
And you hear that there is a lonely old woman in this village at the front, and she does not want to move, she has
seen all the suffering and she does not want to run away
from war anymore. And her son wants to visit her and
asks whether you want to accompany him.

And of course you go.

Of course, I have no interest in getting killed. Of course,
I try to be careful. But one cannot calculate where death
awaits. Not even in our Western world.

Life is not in our hands.

It is not that I have no respect for life, or no gratitude
for the privilege of living in a peaceful society.

I appreciate this gift, in particular because I know that it is not my entitlement, just coincidence, and because I know that it can be taken from me, anytime, anywhere.

Nobody pressures me to go to such regions—definitely not my foreign news department. Quite the opposite: out of concern for my safety, they would probably prefer to prevent each dangerous assignment, if I would not insist.

I also travel because there is so much beauty and joy, in particular, in such areas of conflict. There is such generosity and hospitality. There is an intensity that allows us to achieve the impossible: to overcome mutual strangeness.

It was a long journey, but I have returned home at last. I have unpacked my suitcase, and slowly I can reach for the experiences and images in the depths of memory.

In German there are etymological connections between the word for *mourning* and the words for *slow, to calm down, to become lazy,* for *bloody,* or *gruesome,* but also *to water, to pour, to trickle through.*

It seems to grasp my own slowness, my inability to come to terms with all I saw, my difficulty in giving it words, to find an analytic frame in which to situate the events—but it also describes the feeling of being filled with sadness and despair, and how it trickled through my being and life.

"You have language, you can write," is what Mariam in the refugee camp in Cherat, Pakistan, said to me.

Nobody I ever met on my assignments in the regions of crisis of the world has ever asked me for direct, practical help. Nobody ever believed that I, as a journalist, could change his or her situation in the prisons, in the hospitals, in the refugee camps, at the front lines.

But over and over again people have asked me, "Will

you write this down?" and "Will you tell people what's
going on here?"

The opportunity to have a witness, who listens to and
writes about the victims, who gives the incredibility of
violence a name, who carries them out of the zone of silence, the ignorance of stigmatizations—this testimony
confirms that they live in the same world as "we."

That is why Mohammed Shafi wept so bitterly when he
saw me in the hospital in Sialkot—because a witness, a
human being from the unharmed world, listened to him
and "made" him human again.

"You have language, you can write," is what Mariam
said to me.

But mourning had dried out my language for quite a
while.

"Tell them," said Mariam, and in the beginning I mostly
wrote for her.

And probably she knew already then that it wouldn't
necessarily be for her alone—but that the writing would
be Ariadne's thread out of my own labyrinth of sadness in
which I had gotten lost over the past few months.

Colombia (October 2002)

Part of the mechanism of domination
is that one is forbidden to recognize
the suffering which that domination
produces.

—*Theodor W. Adorno*

Dear friends,
I know everyone is concerned with Bush's war against terrorism—but there is war in Colombia, too.
   Every day.
   For forty years.

A milky, humid fog covers the small alleys and steps of the hilly neighborhood of Comuna 13 on the periphery of Medellin. The red brick houses stand closely crammed as if seeking protection from one another. The flat, wrinkled corrugated iron roofs reflect the morning light a thousand-fold. No enemy is visible in this sea of dusty streets and buildings. Nowhere. Everything rests in deceitful peace.
   Jimmy Díaz and his comrades are preparing for battle. The young fighter is standing at the highest point of the neighborhood, a high-caliber automatic rifle over his right shoulder, smoking a last cigarette. Brand new tanks are maneuvering between hundreds of soldiers from the Fourth Brigade, and the penetrating stench of diesel envelopes the entire crossing. Doctors and nurses are sitting on the terrace of the Café Marvel, drinking *maracujá* juice through straws, waiting like vultures in search of carrion—before the battle has even begun.
   "We will get them out of there. Dead or alive," President Alvaro Uribe Vélez has announced on television this morning, and Jimmy Díaz, the policeman from the anti-

Colombia

terrorism squad, will execute the order against the *insurgentes*, the rebels, in Comuna 13, in West Medellin. Uribe has sent three thousand soldiers and policemen, with helicopters and artillery, for Operation Oríon to fight the notorious rebels and criminals. War is the best weapon against civil war, Uribe has declared, and Jimmy Díaz believes him. That's why this morning he is fighting the guerrillas, the militia, and his own fear. "Fear is natural," says Jimmy, with the face of a milksop and the voice of a war veteran. "It only warns you that death is close." Whether he is quoting the war heroes he has seen in the movies or his own experiences in previous battles have inspired such words remains unclear.

Fanny Ruiz does not trust Jimmy Díaz, she does not trust President Uribe, and she does not trust the army that is waiting at the top of the hill and is about to storm her neighborhood at any minute. It has already been a couple of months now since the civil war moved from the mountains to the cities and has been raging in the alleys in front of her little shop. For her, a mother of nine, the deployment of troops promises nothing but further havoc. The Bible rests on a wooden music stand in the corner of the living room. A red, twisted thread marks the words, the prayer that should help her through the day: Psalm 103, Hymn of Mercy: "The Lord gives justice and right to all who suffer injustice." Fanny still keeps her faith in those words.

"This used to be a nice neighborhood," she says, "but nowadays we only live in fear of the violence—whether from the guerrillas, the criminals, or the state, it makes no difference to us." She pushes the children into the corner behind the fridge in the kitchen. As far away as possible

206

from the street where Operation Oríon rages. As many walls as possible between the bullets of the Kalashnikovs, the hand grenades, the shells, and her children. "Nobody evacuated us," she says. "We don't count in their plans." She moves a small, wooden footstool to the sink, and begins to pray silently, only her lips moving: "The Lord gives justice . . . "

Colombia

Colombia is at war with itself. The country that used to be called The Golden, *El Dorado*, has tropical rainforests and the high mountains of the Cordillera, it has deserts and fertile land, it is rich in natural resources: it has gold and oil and emeralds, it is the world's third-largest exporter of coffee and bananas—and yet it is systematically destroying itself: socially divided between, on the one hand, an oligarchic elite of cattle farmers and coffee and banana exporters and, on the other, the vast majority of the people, who own nothing. Twenty-two million Colombians live in poverty, 11 percent of the entire population in complete misery, 27 percent of all households in the countryside live without access to water, 18.2 percent are jobless (according to the official statistics), and all of them are defenseless against the violence of an all-encompassing civil war with ever-changing front lines: the Marxist-Leninist guerrilla groups FARC, ELN, and CAP; groups of drug lords; and the militant, right-wing paramilitaries called *autodefensas* are fighting for power.

The intellectual battles over political visions and utopias

have slowly vanished over the years; increasingly, the combatants have mimetically adapted to one another in their crimes.

Violence moves across Colombia like a caravan (led in turn by drug lords, left-wing rebels, or the paramilitaries). Wherever it stops, its terror leaves behind ravaged regions and uprooted people.

Two hundred thousand people have died in this war, eight thousand in the last year alone (there are competing statistics according to different sources, some suggest three thousand, some ten thousand). There are two million *desplazados*, displaced persons. According to the conservative Colombian newspaper *El Tiempo*, four to six refugees arrive in Bogotá every hour—searching for a loaf of bread and the end of the bloodshed.

Bogotá and the Haunting Details of War

On Simon Bolivar Square, right behind the yellow palace of President Uribe, a lonely ice-cream man is making his rounds between pigeons and bleakness. A school group is crossing the square around the statue of the Latin American liberation hero. Only the small yellow, red, and blue ribbons in the schoolchildren's hair insinuate a touch of past glamour. The misery of the war arrived in the capital long ago. Not a single tourist strays here. The beggars are standing in front of the Senate House in their worn-out elegant suits from better days and refer to their academic backgrounds. They don't sell umbrellas, but rather walking sticks for the impoverished disabled war veterans.

These few hundred yards of the old center of Bogotá constitute the only area resembling a city. The rest of Bogotá is a somehow "spaceless" place; there is no stable set of streets or alleys connected with one another without any obstacle. The entire city is destroyed, cut into small slices of houses by gigantic inner-city highways. Hardly a square mile without a monstrous freeway of steel and cement cutting through it, there are almost no naturally grown units of houses and compounds of gardens anymore, hardly any real communities of neighbors sharing a *barrio* with the butcher's shop, the grocery, the bakery, the stationery, the carpenter's shop, and the Internet café.

A gigantic monster perpetually moving his ugly body across the city, suppressing and penetrating all living communities and neighborhoods and destroying the space to breath. Hannah Arendt had not envisioned this kind of totalitarian technique to repress people's ability to associate.

This is not a megalo-city—the word Western media tend to use to palliate the bursting, violent, vibrant, struggling cities of the developing world. Rather, it is anarchy; there is an instrumental logic, a multifaceted perspective and confusion, there is subversion at the borders of the borders, systematic destruction, an inability to find zones untouched by the machinery—this is an architectural metaphor of a country at civil war with itself.

It conjures up the image of one of those boxes that magicians use to make people disappear: they introduce one sword after another, until finally the entire box is penetrated by those sharp, shining swords, leaving absolutely no space for anything inside the box.

That's what the freeway system does to the city, the only difference being that the body still *is* in the box.

The streets in Bogotá have no names. They have numbers, and the houses have additional numbers, and the units inside the buildings have numbers, and the crossroads have numbers, too. That does not sound terribly sexy, but at least it should generate a relatively clear system of coordinates, one would think. But you take a taxi and say: "Carrera 18, no. 31, 125 a, crossroad Carretera 3" . . . and when you arrive there, or where you think it should be, then Carrera 18 does not have a corner with Carretera 3, and there is suddenly Carrera 18 II, and even 18II doesn't have a number 31.

Subversive cultures and communities have grown beneath the bridges of the freeways; there are nomads, and they move with their bags and families and children and sometimes animals, following the movements of the construction sites and the freeways.

It is the details in this country, noticed only briefly from the corner of one's eye, sometimes almost unconsciously, that disturb the most.

It is not the scenes of war and combat, not the hospitals with this peculiar scent of death and disinfection, not the screams of the wounded, not the dirt in the refugee camps, not the sound of exploding hand grenades, not the hopelessness of children in the zones of terror—it is very, very small details that imprint themselves in the membranes of one's soul.

Colombia

Details like this one: There was a homeless man in the street in Bogotá; maybe he wasn't homeless, just poor. He was walking on the pavement on the left-hand side of the street, actually he was limping. He was walking next to his buddy. In his right hand he held an empty soft-drink bottle that was moving with his arm in rhythm with his syncopated steps and seemed to pull his body forward. He was wearing dirty black jeans and short green jogging pants over them. A strange combination. He was limping, and so I looked down at his leg, this leg that he wanted to burden as little as possible and yet that moved so slowly that it twisted the axis of his entire body and its movement, and gave it an angular momentum to the right. It had a gravity pulling it toward the pavement and to the side.

And then I saw why: there were five or six metal nails, about five to eight inches long, sticking out of his leg. Actually, they were sticking out of his trousers. It had become one indistinguishable material: leg, skin, nails, trousers—it was all one. How could he undress? How he could take off those trousers? How could he wash himself with this construction on his leg? It was hard just to imagine how he could *move* without agonizing pain.

How had the doctors done this? Did they nail through the trousers? Did they press the nails, one by one, through the worn-out jeans? Were the jeans already dirty then? Was his leg clean when he had the surgery? How did he sleep on the streets with this leg? Would he have the money to have the surgery to get them out again? How would they get rid of the jeans then? Would the skin be attached to the fabric of the trousers by then?

In a country that cannot afford proper health care for its

211

people, there are probably worse images of poverty, there are probably stronger symbols of insensibility, and we certainly witnessed more brutal scenes in Colombia, more sorrow, more desperation—and yet the sight of this leg has inscribed itself in my memory, into the inner archive of images of human suffering.

Uribe, Money, and the War against Terrorism

The newly elected president, Alvaro Uribe, the former governor of the rich province of Antioquia, won the election with a single, simple slogan: "War against War!"— Order and security in the entire country.

If he meant it seriously, Uribe would have to fight on three fronts: against the two different guerrilla groups, the ELN and the FARC, which are interested in negotiations only if they offer social reforms in Colombia; against the international drug Mafia, which moves freely in the impenetrable areas of the Colombian mountains and jungle; and against the illegal troops of the paramilitaries, right-wing militias that began as *autodefensas*, private armies created to protect the properties of the oligarchic elite when the state proved unable to do so. What began as private troops to "help" the state authorities have now established an authority of their own and are totally out of control.

Now Uribe is preparing for the final battle that is supposed to bring peace. Civil rights and budget issues are no obstacles for the hard-liner. Right after his inauguration, Uribe declared a state of emergency, freedom of the press rights were castrated, freedom of movement limited, the defense budget doubled, and a special "war tax" introduced that would give him an extra eight hundred million dollars to increase his army equipment. There is not going to be the option of negotiations with this man—at least not for the guerrillas.

Additionally, Uribe received millions of dollars from the U.S. administration. Human Rights Watch writes:

> On January 10, 2002, United States President George W. Bush signed Public Law (P.L.) 107-115, which authorized $380.5 million in aid to Colombia. The bulk of this aid is for Colombia's military. Weeks later, President Bush requested from the U.S. Congress an emergency supplemental package that included $35 million more for Colombia. That legislation, signed on August 2, also authorized the United States to fund, equip and train Colombia's armed forces to combat illegal armed groups as well as drug traffickers.
>
> Support for human rights motivated the U.S. Congress to condition security assistance on clear and convincing progress by Colombia's government in stopping abuses by its forces. . . .
>
> Before making a decision on Colombia's compliance with U.S. law, the Secretary of State must consult with human rights organizations. Amnesty International, Human Rights Watch, and the Washington Office on Latin America (WOLA) met with State Department officials on February 1, 2002, to present evidence that Colombia had not met any of the three conditions.

Nevertheless, Secretary Colin Powell certified Colombia on May 1, thereby releasing 60 percent of the funds available.

So funds from the United States that were originally supposed to support the "war against drugs" are now relabeled as supporting the "war against terror."

Since nowadays almost every armed conflict is considered terrorism and every armed combatant is considered a terrorist, it seems natural to turn antidrug officers of the U.S. Drug Enforcement Administration into CIA personnel—and to fight a war against everyone in Colombia under the heading "war against terror."

Whereas the infamous human rights record of Colombia's army (and judicial system) never seemed to be an obstacle for Uribe, since it did not really concern the United States, the latest U.S. indictment against the notorious head of the right-wing paramilitaries, Carlos Castaño, has put the Colombian president under pressure.

Castaño is famous for the most cruel and repulsive crimes against rebels and civilians. In his autobiography, *Mi Confesión*, he openly admitted to the massacres of hundreds of people, gouging out eyes, cutting off limbs—but he always denied his involvement in the drug business. Even though practically *all* the parties of the civil war are in one way or another—whether actively or passively—profiting from the drug trade, Castaño always criticized his fellow combatants for "collaborating with evil." And yet, the American indictment against the man with whom the American embassy in Bogotá maintained friendly relations

for years does not charge him with human rights violations and murder—but rather with drug trafficking.

If Uribe wants to please his American benefactors and arrest Castaño, he would have to fight the illegal hero's fighters for the first time: a militia of ten thousand soldiers.

Uribe's biography, though, suggests partiality toward
Castaño. As the eldest of five children, the thin-lipped,
bespectacled Uribe grew up in Colombia's archconserva-
tive province of Antioquia, the heart of the elite of big
landowners and banana farmers. In 1983, FARC rebels
shot his father (a businessman with close ties to one of the
major drug lords, Fabio Ochoa) and started Uribe's ideological proximity to the illegal *autodefensas*, which were
created in Antioquia to crack down on the left-wing guerrillas. "My family belongs to those 50 percent of Colombia's population that became victims of the violence,"
Uribe says. He does not say if it is revenge that is guiding
him in his mission against the guerrillas.

This was the original task of the trip: to find out how
seriously Uribe is battling the paramilitaries, how seriously
he is attempting to arrest Castaño, how credible the rumors are that Uribe would rather see Castaño killed than
extradited to the United States, where he might talk about
the government's involvement in the paramilitaries' bloody
war or drug trafficking, how cruel Uribe's war against war
has turned out to be—and, if possible, to interview Castaño in the mountains close to Montería, where allegedly
he is hiding. Since Castaño is famous for his openness and
vanity, there was a chance, depending on how safe he felt
under the new circumstances, that he might grant us an

interview. Before our departure for Colombia, we had contacted a "social foundation" working in the city of Montería, which basically functions as a front organization for the paramilitaries. And they had told us to come.

Catch-22 and the State of Exception 1

After I arrived—as agreed before the trip—I called the German embassy and tried to arrange a meeting. Colombia is famous not only for its endless civil war, in which nobody can expect mercy or protection, but also for the kidnapping of foreigners.

The civil servant at the embassy was open and friendly—even though the embassy clearly had no influence on whether we would manage to maneuver safely through the war. But at least they should know who they should be looking for in case of a kidnapping.

Three hours after I arrived, I also sent a fax to the Colombian Ministry of the Interior to inform them that the photographer Thomas Müller and I would be working in Colombia for approximately fourteen days; I gave them our passport numbers, the duration of our stay, our hotel, and so on, and asked for credentials.

Then I went out to meet a few opposition writers and activists and strolled around the city of Bogotá.

Twelve hours later, the Ministry of the Interior called.

A female voice asked me what I intended to do in Colombia and where I wanted to travel. I answered truthfully that we had not yet decided where to travel. The woman from the Ministry of the Interior pointed out that I was not allowed to travel to the *zonas de rehabilitacion*, areas under the official control of the FARC, the left-wing guerrillas. I would have to ask the Ministry of the Interior for permission. I said that I knew all the new laws and legislation, and that I had no interest in traveling to Putumayo (the area controlled by the FARC). She did not seem satisfied. She asked whether I knew that there was a state of emergency and that there were areas of "disorder" to which I could not travel either.

I asked how I could find out which areas were considered ordered and which problematic so that I would not unintentionally transgress their orders.

She replied, "That changes."

I was confused and did not yet understand the genre of the conversation. I kept on trying to fulfill her demands, I made offers, I acted as if this were a test I *could* pass.

In Kafka's "Before the Law," at one point the man tries to bribe the doorkeeper, and the doorkeeper answers: "I only accept your gifts, so that you don't have to think you neglected something."

I asked how it was then possible to *not* transgress laws. Pretty funny, I thought.

She did not answer my question, did not even laugh, but said, "Well, and you know, there is always the possibility that you might encounter visa problems."

"What visa problems?"

She said, "Well, I don't know what kind of visa you have, but there is always the risk that you might get expelled if there is something wrong with your visa."

Cheerfully victorious, I replied, "You know, I cannot have a visa problem because I don't *have* a visa."

Now she exclaimed with feigned surprise: "What? You don't have a visa?"

It was absurd. I had asked the Colombian embassy before my departure whether I needed a visa as a journalist, and they had said no. Upon my arrival, I had told the immigration officer at the airport that I was a journalist and had entered the country in order to write about Colombia. I had followed all the existing rules and had not lied to anyone. And now the Ministry of the Interior was playing this game with me, a game that you can never win because they are the masters of the rules and they change them constantly, and they are always faster than you, and it was not even about actually proving to me that I had transgressed them, it was about getting across to me that I was in danger, that no rules or laws or precisely correct and careful behavior could protect me.

Extralegal Zones

We travel to Uribe's own province, the beautiful Uraba region, with its fertile soil and vast banana plantations. This is the heart of *his* country; he finds his strongest support here.

The Yacaren finca lies a bit off-track from the main road of the city of Apartado. The workers are sweating in the midday heat. They are bending over washtubs filled with chemicals, and cleaning green Del Monte bananas. The foreman and his secretary are lying in the hut at the entrance of the finca—and having fun with one another . . . while Ramiro Llona and his team are harvesting bananas at Lot 10. We are advised not to walk through the jungle of banana lanes all by ourselves. Rebels used to hunt on the farms, we are told. The paramilitaries have fended them off, we are told. It is quiet now, we are told. But we should not walk here. Ramiro Llona and his team have to, and so we go and look for them.

We follow the wire with its steel hooks, deeper and deeper into the banana forest. Lot 10 stretches for fifty-four yards either side a wire pulley, along which the bananas will be hauled back to the entrance of the finca. We are not sure whether we will be able to find Ramiro. It is miles and miles of banana trees, a labyrinth of green and blue (of the plastic bags covering the spikes of fruits), no sunlight reaches through the leaves, a sea of humidity weighs on your lungs and runs in little streams down your body.

After a half-hour's walk, we find them. A group of five.

You can see their experience in the smoothness of their movements: it takes only one, or a maximum of two strokes with the machete to cut the bunch of bananas from the tree; they fall directly into the black rubber basket on the shoulders of the second worker, who carries the precious load to Ramiro, who ties them to the hook on the wire pulley, one after the other, until finally he hauls them hundreds of yards back to the entrance. "No police protected us here," he says. "We used to be on our own. Now it is quiet. The paras fought the FARC, they withdrew, for now. One never knows how long the quiet will last."

The muddy road to Banadex, the neighboring 148-hectare plantation, which grows Chiquita bananas, used to be guerrilla territory. Up until a couple of weeks ago, the war between the rebels and the right-wing paramilitaries was raging in these fields. Many landowners have

219

fled to the cities. Nobody knows when they will return. Until then experienced managers run the farms. People like C., a technical manager at the Banadex farm. We are not allowed to take pictures, and before getting a tour we are given a lesson by the director on the major improvements in social rights that Banadex has established for its workers and Chiquita Banana's major achievements in quality standards. C.'s boss sounds as if he were talking about similar products when talking about his employees and his bananas. C. then shows us the farm and introduces us to the science of perfect bananas and imperfect peace: "He who owns arms, owns the law in Colombia," he says while testing the size of the fruit with the *calibrador*, judging whether the banana fulfils the norm for a real Chiquita. "If you want to stay alive, you have to remain neutral."

Everyone here supports Uribe and his war against the war. The president should use violence to stop the violence, we are told—only the heroes of the paramilitaries should remain untouched. No complaints about the brutality of the paramilitaries, the illegality of the troops, the arbitrariness with which they punish "traitors," "rebels," *insurgentes*.

"They brought at least a preliminary peace to this region," says Modesto Restrepo Zapata. The construction draughtsman is leaning against the bar in the pool hall in Apartado. It is pouring with rain in Apartado tonight. The men pour alcohol, while the women pour into the church service. The metallic voice of the priest from the speaker permeates the masses standing in front of the church and reaches the pool hall, where it mixes with the tunes of the old chansonnier Oscar Agulelo. A few drunken laborers hack away at three pool tables. Every once in a while one of them reels to the urinal that is hanging on the wall and relieves himself in front of everybody. The pretty waitress winds her way through the bar to Restrepo, allows him to paw her, and places another glass of booze in front of him. "In a war of ideologies, people have to die," Restrepo says, and draws the lines to Uribe's mission with surprising sobriety. "The state cannot do it. They are too inefficient."

Parallel societies and authorities have grown in the space left by the state. There are no rights or guarantees by any government in these extralegal zones, there are hardly any official police, there is a shifting stateless state, moving with the paramilitaries' military victories, a zone of exception with the promise of normality, illegal, illusional, and yet free of combat—for a while.

There is no resistance to this kind of extralegality, no protest against the arbitrary rule of the paras. Maybe because everyone knows that the paramilitaries of course act as the illegal arm—some say "bastard"—of the state, their authority may be illegal but it is permitted by the government in Bogotá.

In our Western societies we often talk of "negative freedom" as a democratic value. We mean the absence of state intervention into our private matters—only in countries such as Colombia does one understand what a luxurious conception of freedom that is. In all-encompassing social instability, without any institutional security, perpetually threatened by the moving front lines of the war, subverted by corrupt authorities who do not exercise authority, only violence—in a disintegrated society where only the oligarchy holds a stable position, nobody calls for "negative freedom."

For the eternal refugees, for the victims caught between the ideological fronts, for all those for whom the war does not pay off, for whom the violence has no political meaning, for those eternal refugees, the enemies of war have simply become accomplices in the perverse logic of justified killing.

There are generations, two at least, that have known nothing in their lives but war. They have grown up with the violence, they were socialized with death and destruction, they were educated in the laws of lawlessness. Suffering and loss have silenced their expectations.

It is often said that "people are embittered" by pain. But the metaphor seems misguided. Their diminishing anger and ability to resist their mistreatment—this does not take root in a sense of bitterness, but rather in numbness. The terror of eternal war has not left them with burning anger—but has left a dull, heavy, suffocating numbness.

Years of traveling have expanded my vocabulary of trauma, taught me lessons in the phenomenology of *gravity of violence*. I have to perpetually learn and invent a language to decipher the broken scripture that war leaves on the membranes of the soul.

An endless process of learning.

Turbo and the Fluidity of the Enemy

Not everybody is able to defend her- or himself or finance a private militia. Not everybody is able to distinguish between the fighting parties and circumvent coming under false suspicion. The fronts have turned porous, the images of the foe are blurred and melted.

When the victors change, the civilians rescue themselves by changing convictions.

Refugees such as Eugenio Palacio have no choice. Palacio no longer even recalls how long the fighting had been going on in his home in the Choco province when the paramilitaries dislodged them by force. Eugenio is sitting on a green-and-white plastic chair in front of a few lousy wooden huts in the refugee camp of Turbo on Colombia's Caribbean coast. A tropical thunderstorm is brewing on the horizon. It does not bother him, neither the noise of the children nor the grunting of the gray-brown pigs that are sniffing around him. "Those who did not obey were shot," he recalls. That easily. Forty families were washed away by the war like jetsam, farther and farther away from their homes, until they were stranded here and were allowed to build a new provisional home in this mud, all set to go, always ready to jump, if violence should catch up with them here. For now, they feel safe. It does not frighten them that their old enemies, the paramilitaries, are their new protectors now. "It is like a state of its own here," Eugenio says—and he means it as a compliment.

Time has its own speed in this refugee camp. Actually, it is not even a camp. It is only an empty space, at the end of the small town of Turbo, at the end of the paved roads, beyond the invisible border that separates the locals from the refugees. No matter how long they live here, even after ten years, the refugees remain refugees, they never acquire a different status, they always remain at the mercy of local authorities who are no authorities.

Time has its own meaning here. To spend time without anything happening is not a cause for boredom but for relief. A morning, an afternoon, a night without threat, without blackmail, without bloodbath, without killings . . . moments of reprieve, an exception to the expected, a moment to rest.

We walk around in the mud, on this little path between the huts. There are little rivulets running in front of the wooden homes, there are chickens and a few pigs running around, children are sitting in front of the huts, watching the stranger walk by, inviting us in, telling us of their lives in times when they actually had a life.

Nobody has a job in Turbo.

If the boys want to go out at night, they walk—that's their entertainment. No music, no bar, no pool, no disco. They walk a few blocks; maybe they even walk outside the "camp," beyond the invisible line to the houses of the locals, not much richer than they are, but locals, people with roots, with a history connecting them to this place, a history that might protect them, next time the violence breaks out. Maybe. Maybe not even them.

Time seems to pass slowly, but as long as it *passes*—it is a relief.

Montería and the Rain

In Montería we go to the paramilitaries' foundation.

The contact man, Manuel, sits in an empty office.

No attempt has been made to cover up the real purpose of this "foundation"—there are neither files nor of-

224

fice equipment that might at least look like the work of a social organization.

Manuel sits in front of an empty desk, in an empty office, the hands of a farmer folded on his gigantic belly.

He seems to be straight out of an old Sergio Leone western.

Absolutely no unnecessary efforts are to be made. No inviting gestures, no cordial questions or answers.

I search for flies or snakes in the office that he could *shoot at* while talking to us.

Did I say "talking"? He is only mumbling in a language that consists of no more than two words per sentence.

All he said was that he needed to make contact, and there was a meeting in the mountains right now. It would be no problem. He would let us know as soon as he knew *when* we could get going.

We checked into a hotel in Montería and waited.

The next day, we return to the foundation office. The two model secretaries put their hair in order, ask us to sit down, and offer us a *cafecito*—only to then tell us that Manuel is gone. When he would return, they do not know. They ask us to call again in the afternoon. We go back to the hotel and wait. A few hours later, it turns out that the director of the foundation is a new man.

Could we meet with him?

No.

He is not in the office either, so we talk with him on the phone. He claims to be angry, and seems to be in the same position we are: dependent on Manuel.

We wait again. A few hours later, we return to the office and find out that Manuel has run away with all the money—and apparently one of the secretaries. Whether he ever informed Castaño as planned, we do not know.

The new man in charge is smooth, friendly, talkative—and totally incompetent.

One has to fear that he is *so* naive that he believes that he *really* runs a social foundation.

After a half hour of talking, I already miss our Sergio Leone Manuel and begin to whistle "Once Upon a Time in the West."

We return to the hotel, and as if this entire excursion to Montería hadn't been—journalistically—disastrous and inefficient enough, the tropical rain begins.

The sky has turned pitch black, and it is pouring thick, voluminous, warm rain. Within fifteen minutes, Montería is transformed into a paralyzed city. The streets turn into rivers, the pavements are deserted, and not even dogs leave the house.

We are stuck.

Catch-22 and the State of Exception 2

In Montería we heard about a group of natives who had fled the fighting between paramilitaries and guerrillas and had been stranded about an hour's drive from Montería. Since Manuel had disappeared and Castaño seemed to be changing headquarters in the jungle, we could not do anything, and so we took a car and drove to the village where the stranded Indians were.

We wanted to learn from the Indians about the way they were expelled. But it was not possible simply to interview individuals. Not even the chief was authorized to decide for the tribe.

There had to be a collective decision procedure. We, the strangers, had to introduce ourselves and to explain why we had come to visit them and what we wanted. So the chief called an assembly of the entire community.

They gathered in the main hall, women and men sitting on different sides. A table with the elders and the chief stood at the front; Thomas and I sat on chairs next to them so that everyone could see us.

The women were dressed in beautiful, colorful dresses, some with stunning makeup. The men were dressed in "normal" modern clothes, only some with old Indian jewelry.

With the help of a translator, I gave a speech to the entire community and explained my background, my roots, my interest, and my concern for them, and I asked the entire group for permission to ask questions.

Then the group deliberated on whether my speech was *convincing*, whether they would care to talk with me.

Finally, they gave their vote to the chief, who then confirmed to me that *yes*, I could talk with them.

I was allowed to ask them questions through my translator, and whoever felt called to respond stood up and recounted the individual and collective narrative of their expulsion by the guerrillas from the land they had cultivated and lived on *for generations*.

Later, when we were shown the camp and the houses/tents of the indigenous people, we encountered two soldiers. We greeted them—but they did not seem to care about us. We were in a safe area, no official declaration

227

had been made concerning this territory, and we had not transgressed any orders.

But on the way back, we suddenly got stopped on the road. A military transport blocked the street; two more cars stood by the side of the road. A soldier asked for our passports. A second car moved behind our car, so that we were trapped between two military vehicles. The soldiers got out of the car and took positions around us.

I tried to call someone from the office, but the cell phone did not work.

Finally, the commander came and asked us to get out of the car. He asked us what we were doing. We said we were journalists and had interviewed the native refugees, that's all.

He then said that we had to accompany them. The soldiers around us had their rifles pointing at us. We got back into the car and followed one of the military vehicles to the headquarters of the secret service in the next town.

The guy from the secret service began with a simple opening: we had entered a zone of *desorden*, he said, an area of heavy fighting.

He lied.

That was easy to fend off: the refugees had gone there because it was *free* of fighting; the newspaper had reported on it and there was no mention of any battles or of the zone being declared a no-go area.

Then he came up with another strategy: how come we had no visa?

I said that we had asked the embassy in Berlin, and I had informed the immigration officer at the airport and the Ministry of the Interior upon my arrival that I was a journalist. He asked us to wait and left the room with our passports.

A half hour later he returned and said that I had lied at immigration and had declared that I was coming as a tourist.

Unbelievable . . . at first I had to laugh because his lie was so obvious.

But Thomas pointed out that this was not funny anymore and that we were in real trouble.

Thank God, I pulled out the copy of the fax I had sent to the Ministry of the Interior from my pocket, *with* the sheet that registers the time the fax had been sent.

I gave it to the secret service guy and asked him why on earth I should lie when entering this country if I was ready to inform the Ministry of the Interior and ask for credentials two hours later.

He was still not convinced. Finally, I recalled that I had called the spokesman of the army battalion in this province before my departure, and had told him that we'd be in this area. I gave the secret service guy the mobile phone number and asked him to call the army—and it worked.

The press office confirmed that yes, we had called the spokesman, and had announced that we'd be traveling in this region and that we planned to come and see him in Medellin.

When we were about to leave at last, the boss of our guy came and wanted to show off his power, and the whole interrogation began anew. A nightmare. After about three hours, we were finally let go, but asked to leave on the next plane to Medellin.

. . .

We knew that there had already been fighting between the paramilitaries and the guerrillas for a couple of months, battles over streets and neighborhoods—without any army involvement. But recently the paramilitaries seemed to be unable to control the rebels, and rumors suggested that the state might soon intervene to help out the losing paras.

We didn't know until the next day *how* soon "soon" would be.

Comuna 13, Medellin 2

When we arrived in Medellin, Operation Oríon had already begun.

Helicopters and air fighters were patrolling, tanks were entering the zone at the periphery of Medellin. A few hours after the war in Comuna 13 had begun, a bomb exploded in the financial center of Medellin, right in the "elegant" area of Medellin. A fifteen-story skyscraper was destroyed, the broken glass hit trees and bodies fifty yards away. Revenge for the army's attack on the rebels in Comuna 13? Or a private battle between businessmen? Nobody knows. The same morning, the governor of the province was kidnapped.

No area and no person is safe in this civil war. No matter where we go, or who we are—we cannot protect ourselves here.

We decide not to go into Comuna 13 by ourselves while the battle is going on.

230

We wait till General Montoya announces, "We have Comuna 13 under control." Thirty people are dead by the time he makes this announcement; the bodies are carried out one after another. On TV he proudly presents weapons and explosives confiscated during the night as proof of the violent threat inside the notorious neighborhood. We are told the area was reconquered by the state. There is a local radio journalist (no foreign journalists are anywhere) who decides to enter the *barrio*. After all the threats from the previous days, we are cautious. We decide to drive to the army headquarters and ask for official permission to enter the area. We return to the entrance of the Comuna with the permission. Our driver takes us to the marketplace, right next to the church and the three tanks that are guarding this strategic point. The neighborhood lies ahead of us, nestling in the hills. A group of young kids, none older than fourteen, are leaning against the wall of the barbershop, their hands cuffed behind their backs with sharp plastic cords, their faces bruised and bloody. An army bus stops at the barbershop, and a *capuchero*, a police informant, dressed in a camouflage uniform with a woolen hat, is taken out of the bus. Escorted by a group of heavily armed soldiers, he walks by the boys, who cast down their eyes, and then enters the barbershop to deliver his betrayal.

Comuna 13 lies before us like an impenetrable labyrinth of streets and steps. I don't feel comfortable entering the zone alone. The neighborhood is inhabited not only by indifferent civilians, not only by left-wing guerrillas, but also by plain criminals for whom a Western journalist is just grist for their mill. We leave our driver at the market, and ask a police unit that is just about to leave for a patrol through the *barrio* if we may join them. They agree, but ask us to walk behind them; no pictures are to be taken of their faces.

We agree, even though walking with a police patrol presents its own risk. There is no neutrality in our entering the zone, given our company, and yet there is no neutrality in any case, if you are prone to being kidnapped—not as journalists but as welcome extra money. Our interest is in investigating the crimes committed by the army during the attack the previous night (it also makes sense to talk to the police because quite often they are so free of any doubts concerning their own legitimation that they openly admit to all kinds of crimes), and yet we are worried about entering the neighborhood without their help.

Still, our decision remains ambiguous.

We follow them at some distance, slowly, and enter the Comuna.

The street quickly turns into a small alley, not more than two or three yards wide, the houses right next to it, small paths and steps leading uphill or right and left of the alley deeper into the neighborhood. We are already out of sight of the marketplace, our driver, and the soldiers there.

Some people are standing in front of their doors, breathing quietly after a night and day of battle, their physiognomy and movements displaying the particular nervousness of animals in the woods before a storm begins: a shy oversensitivity that could be lifesaving. When they see the patrol, they vanish; curtains in the windows are moved by invisible hands.

Suddenly, the head of our unit tells us to stop and wait.

Intuitively, we squat down, close to a wall of a house on our right, from which vantage point we see our police unit turn a corner to the right—and disappear.

It takes about a minute, a long minute, for trust to fade and doubt to arise.

The policemen don't return; we are abandoned, alone in this area, far away from the marketplace and the car.

Thomas and I debate what to do: return to the car by ourselves or move on toward the corner and see where the policemen have gone. We opt for the latter. We walk up to the corner. There is a steep hill in front, a small alley to the left, and to our backs a long, winding alley leading down to the market where we can see the silhouette of a tank. No policemen in the scenery. We are told that the men took the left turn and entered the tiny alley—but we cannot see them anymore.

I enter the alley, and suddenly hesitate.

It is quiet, neither sight nor sound of war.

And yet.

It seems *wrong* to walk further into this unknown territory, a few hours after the battle, still in its afterbirth, without protection and without the knowledge of the geography of anger and violence in these alleys.

I grew up in a small town west of Hamburg, an old fisherman's town on the river Elbe, close to the North Sea. It is one hill overgrown with thousands of small steps, a real labyrinth of steep, winding steps and tiny houses. It would be impossible for a stranger to enter the heart of my hometown and not get lost. It took me years of daily explorations with my dog to really *know* and understand all of it.

233

Nowadays, after fifteen years abroad, when I return to my hometown, I no longer dare to really try each alley. I stick to a few remembered paths and steps and don't dare experiment. Nowadays, I walk around like one of those dreadful tourists who come to my town on Saturdays and Sundays and stay on the two main terraces leading down to the water.

It must have been this socialization in my hometown, the respect for labyrinths it taught me, that warned me the moment I was about to enter the alley in Comuna 13. "Epistemological comforts of home," Russel Hardin called this— but "home" is a concept bigger than the place you come from, "home" is recognizable abroad, too, and it helps you find your way in strange places.

I stopped, turned around to Thomas, and said: "I think we are about to do something extraordinarily stupid. This has disaster written all over it." We paused and forced ourselves to carefully evaluate the situation. We stepped out of the alley again, and waited at the corner. The police were gone, and we had three options: first, enter the alley and search for "our" unit; second, walk down the long, poorly visible path, in the direction of the market; or third, walk uphill.

I opted for uphill.

I felt terribly uncomfortable to be lost in the midst of this jungle of steps and houses, unable to understand the territory or its military logistics. I longed to be positioned somewhere where I could *see* the neighborhood, seize its cartography, measure its dangers, sound its risks. Being in the central depth made me nervous.

Thomas strongly disagreed: uphill was definitely wrong, he thought.

He was right.

But it didn't make a difference anymore. Before we could decide anything, the war erupted again.

About five yards above us, so *uphill*, a group of rebels began shooting from one of the houses next to the steps, and within seconds, the army returned fire. We were *right* on the front line. No way out. The civilians who could ran into their houses and closed the doors; the small alley to our left was full of *insurgentes*, uphill the rebels were shooting with Kalashnikovs and throwing hand grenades, downhill the soldiers from the marketplace were firing back with bigger-caliber weapons. "Our" police unit was lost somewhere in the middle. We jumped to the left, trying to seek protection at a wall, to have at least one side— our backs—safe. But we are totally lost. Nowhere to run, nowhere to hide.

Right in the center of the killing.

Comuna 13 turns into flight and injury. They kill from a distance, the injured and dead are invisible to the perpetrators; in the previously calm streets and alleys, war arbitrarily seizes its victims: children who were simply on their way home from playing with some neighbors get killed, one three-year-old is shot in the eye, and nobody knows what to do with the wounded, how to help them.

No doctors or nurses around or nearby, no cars available in this labyrinth of steps to transport them to the nearest hospital.

We cannot see the entire battle, the perpetrators, the

victims; everything takes place in hidden corners, alleys, behind walls and shutters.

Some wounded are left on the street; a mother tries to drag her screaming toddler out of the line of fire.

Qui lacriment, desunt—"He who weeps is not here," Ovid says in *Metamorphoses* when describing the endless deaths, the countless corpses in the streets after the plague. Nobody who cries is here.

S/he who cries mourns someone else, but everybody who is here is threatened by death itself.

Suddenly, the door six feet ahead of us, on the other side of the path, opens and a hand waves us in. We run over and jump in.

It is Fanny Ruiz and her husband, Martín.

Martín crouches on the floor in his little kiosk between dry soup powder and potatoes; Fanny shows us the way through the darkness of the corridor. There are two children, Daniela and Luis, and one boy who belongs to the neighbors, who, like us, is stranded. We crawl along the inner wall and finally sit down on the floor, always below the level of the lethal windows.

Thomas is wonderfully calm and distracts the children by showing them his camera and the big funny lenses.

The war is raging outside.

We follow the course of the battle by ear; we hear its dynamics, the movement of the fighters—acoustic cartographers of war: the unmistakable dry, flat sound of an AK-47, like stones skipping on the calm surface of a lake, endlessly, over and over again. A sound in diametric opposition to its effect: very light, on a high note, a tone apparently without resonance or expansion.

It is the rebels who use the AK-47, and they are in the house right next door, Fanny confirms. The alley that we avoided is full of "criminals" who use all kinds of weapons, the sound of the bigger-caliber guns comes from down-hill, and the soldiers on the tanks are firing rounds into the neighborhood. And then there are those moving sounds, like hectic fireflies whirring around as if without orientation, the sound of police units, coming closer to the multi-focal danger of the rebels, and then quieter again, farther away, withdrawn after yet another unsuccessful attempt to storm the cells of the *insurgentes*.

We are leaning against the wall. Silently.

Fanny prays, and occasionally gets out of her meditative state and begins weeping. She throws her head into her hands and cries; the kids stare at her.

Luis is six, and over the course of the first hour he comes to understand that the strangers in his house are just like him, vulnerable potential targets for bullets and hand grenades—that Thomas's camera equipment additionally turns us into potential objects of kidnapping, he does not understand.

After he loses his shyness, Luis comes out of the kitchen to sit next to me on the floor in the corridor. But he is restless, he wants to play and talk, just like any boy of his age, and yet unlike boys of his age he already has the experienced movements of someone acquainted with civil war. He knows the codes and meanings, the sounds and distances, he knows the changing *topography of life* during war times: a wall is not just a wall, but there are circles, layers of walls, and only the innermost circle may offer some protection; a window is not just a window, but ac-

237

cess to death; a door is to be locked to keep bandits from entering but to be opened to offer life-saving shelter for innocents running around, helplessly, in the streets. He knows that silence is not always speechless, sometimes it is telling, and he knows that words may have no addressee: his father's silence speaks of his fear; his mother's words address a God who seems to have abandoned Comuna 13 a long time ago.

There are moments of extreme isolation during those hours in which we hide on the floor of the corridor or in the kitchen, next to the fridge, there are moments when we all feel terribly lonely, somehow cut off from the others and the rest of the world. And then there are moments of wonderful togetherness, of closeness among strangers who spend these crucial hours together, who are bound together by the danger.

We sit in the kitchen and we begin to talk—about war, of course, and about life in the face of death, how it is to perpetually stare at despair. Fanny asks me, "And you? At home, where you come from? Isn't it the same? Don't you have a government waging war against you?" We sit between the pots of beans and bottles of olive oil and the food for the cat, and we hear the shooting and the screams and the grenades only a few yards away and we talk about giving birth to a child (clearly without much input from me on that one), and losing a child, about losing loved ones through violence, and the conversation is meandering between knowing silence and curious dialogue.

Et iam reverentia nulla est—"No shame, no reticence is left," Ovid writes. Being with Fanny and her family means exactly that: no shame is left, there is an amazing familiarity, no need to pay attention to one another, to make any conventional effort, no rules or norms of formality restrict us.

We are just together in this mess, and each follows his or her needs or fears, if someone decided to sleep, or weep, or yell, or play—there is no hierarchy of emotions, no order of appropriateness of responses.

In the summer of 1944, James Reeves wrote letters from the front lines of the Second World War (from France and Belgium) to his partner, Carson McCullers, in Newack, New York. Repeatedly he mentions the *rhythm* of war, he describes those moments of sudden silence, of apparent peace, of quiet, of resting and waiting and preparing for the next round—and then these eruptions, when the violence breaks out again, initialized by one shot and answered by a thousand roaring weapons.

We are also torn between hope and paralysis, each time the firing stops, briefly, we wonder if the battle has ceased, and each time it bursts out again a few minutes later.

Battles may require you to run and hide, to move fast, to carry the wounded, to attend to the injured, to help the old, and to offer solace to the desperate or hysterical; sometimes you are allowed to *act*.

But sometimes you can do nothing but wait.

It is not only the danger that threatens, not only the arms that transform you into a victim—it is also this paralyzing inability to *do* something, this passive state you are forced into. You just sit on the floor and wait until the shooting reaches you or disappears. It is not only the humiliating disrespect of those who fire the ammunition into their midst that undermines the self-respect of victims of war.

He who is unable to act, who is speechless and useless behind a wall, seems worthless not only to those who fire at him with hand grenades and rifles—but also to himself.

There are moments when you develop a desire to just run outside and yell and express anger and frustration and somehow show some *resistance* to being nothing but an arbitrary object of some mercenaries.

After some time, Fanny goes to bed. She cannot bear to stand or sit or crawl around, so she withdraws into a small room at the end of the building and lies down. Martín crouches down in his kiosk, somewhat tumbled down, silent, only every now and then he jumps up because of a loud knocking at the steel door—someone breathless, soaked with sweat, coming in from the street to seek protection. Slowly, the group inside the house grows, but some attempt to run farther, from house to house, to reach home. We know that the knowledge of our presence in this house is spreading with those fleeing people, and we know that the longer we stay here, the greater the risk for ourselves *and* for Fanny and Martín.

We move closer to the window, and try to get a connection with our mobile phone and call our driver—but his phone is apparently turned off. We try to call *Der Spiegel*'s Latin America correspondent in Rio de Janeiro—and leave a message on his answering machine with the basic coordinates of our location and the phone number of our driver. In case we get kidnapped, they should at least have a chance to know *where* we disappeared.

Colombia

When the army begins to use tear gas, Daniela loses her temper and tranquility and cries out loud so that her entire body shakes and shivers. There are waves of calm and panic; she is clearly no longer in control of the meandering rhythm of fear and despair. Martín feeds the coughing, puking cat with milk. The tear gas almost kills her, while we are using towels and shawls held to our faces to filter the air we breathe. Luis has gone silent, seeking comfort between my legs and arms; he sits on the floor and watches his family in despair as if from a distant place.

After hours and hours, night begins to fall, and we decide to run no matter what.

Out

The next moment of silence, we go out into the alley and run down the hill. We can see the soldiers on the tanks, and only hope that they will recognize Thomas's camera and refrain from shooting. When we finally make it to the marketplace, our driver is still there. He has been in the heart of the battle, the army has repeatedly told him to get lost, but he has stayed and not moved at all until we return.

The soldiers in the marketplace are in sheer panic; apparently, they have been firing at patrolling police units and their own men and rebels and civilians. There are dead and injured on all sides.

"With Colombia's geography, the state can never win this war. Not against the guerrillas, and not against the paramilitaries. This is a war without victor," Dario Villamizar, the director of a Latin American human rights association, had told me a week earlier when I was still in Bogotá.

Now I know what he meant.

Fernando Hincapiel Agudelo gets to know the losers of the war every day. He is the director of the emergency unit at Medellin's general hospital.

Hincapiel knows the tides of Colombia's violence. For twenty years he has been taking care of the wounded. Whether victims or perpetrators—he does not know, he does not care. "I know all kinds of war. The drug war of and against Pablo Escobar, then the war between the paramilitaries and the guerrillas, and now the army joins in." The wounds have not changed: leg or stomach shots, splinter wounds, disjointed limbs, injuries from explosives, beatings, grenades—an endless stream of wounded and dead. Hincapiel does not count or distinguish according to uniform or ideology—only in terms of injuries.

"I treat them all," he says.

We never found out what happened to our police unit, whether they survived the labyrinth or not. It seems unlikely.

General Montoya of the Fourth Brigade is standing at the entrance of Comuna 13 at the top of the hill and proudly announces that he has everything under control. Now there are only shattered fighters in front of Café Marvel, doctors and nurses carry victims covered with blood. The Policia National leads away a bunch of rebels along a long rope. Jimmy Díaz is ready to go home. Five of his friends have died today in this war against the war. "It was a good day," he says. He is young, and yet he is already satisfied if he just survives.

242

Late at night we finally return to the hotel.

The shock of the violence arrives with a twelve-hour delay. The next morning, Thomas and I are paralyzed. We go to Medellin's morgue to double-check the numbers and the statistics of death that the army and official television had announced.

Afterward, we give up—and decide to leave Medellin.

We had failed to meet with Carlos Castaño—but as for understanding Uribe's war against war—well, *that* we did. Operation Oríon was a telling example of how cruel, brutal, undistinguished, senseless, biased—and inefficient—Uribe's war is.

Return

One friend commented: Wasn't that terribly careless of you? One friend said: Why on earth did you have to go to Medellin? One friend said: Next time you should protect yourself better.

Of course, all of them care about me and the underlying motive was affection.

Nevertheless, such comments are based on two unfounded assumptions about the war and its witness. They suggest that one could protect oneself in areas of war, one could calculate the risks.

But are all victims of violence in a civil war careless? Were those local civilians who died in a war simply incautious?

Everyone qualifies as a candidate for death in times of war.

The myth of a clean war between the armies of two

nation-states, where only soldiers fight and die, had already been destroyed long before the days of the war on terrorism. This discourse of the alleged new epoch of totally different wars is a farce. Civilians already were being slaughtered or bombed in the Second World War, in Vietnam, and in the civil wars in Spain and Central America.

Sometimes I wonder if these exclamations about the *unnecessary* risk one takes are not only rooted in an understandable ignorance of war—but also in the disbelief that one would voluntarily share the fate of *strangers*, far away, in a country at war. Why would one do this?

I don't have an answer. I can only guess.

There are colleagues who want to write because they want to read themselves, there are those who want only to win prizes, there are those who want to tell a story, those who want to stir up public opinion.

What I know is what I already wrote: I want to be a witness *with* the people who suffer injustice.

But I am appalled by war. *Every time.*

It does not diminish.

I don't get used to it.

I am not fascinated by pain and despair. I am *sickened* by it.

The moment I began to find these journeys *bearable*, I would leave this job.

Northern Iraq/Iraq
(April 2002 and March–April 2003)

War is no longer
declared, only
continued. The monstrous
has become everyday.

—*Ingeborg Bachmann*

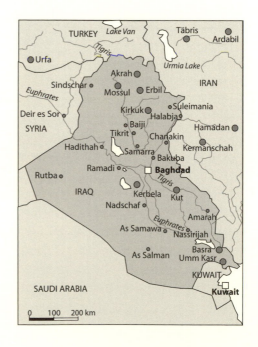

Dear friends,

I have not touched the notebooks of my trips to northern Iraq in months. They are black leather booklets, with a thread that marks the current page and that wanders with time toward the end of the book. There is a little pocket on the inner side of the back that contains business cards, old passport photos, and sometimes some sand. A green and white label on the front indicates the country, the date, and the number of the notebook for each trip.

I had not looked at them in months. They were piled up, one next to the other, on a bookshelf, the writing on the stickers already washed out from pulling the notebooks out of backpacks or jackets.

It's been more than a year since we traveled into the war, and yet so far I could not write about it.

When I open the notebooks today, I immediately recognize the logic of life in those times.

Each book begins with a list: names, telephone numbers, profession/function. The handwriting is still orderly and proper on the first few pages, the black letters do not transgress the lines yet, and everything is readable. Later, the characters move across the pages in the rhythm of the ups and downs of a car on unpaved roads. Dirt and humidity have erased some letters, names of villages and individuals appear in the handwriting of a stranger who helped me spell them correctly.

However chaotic the last pages of one book, the next notebook always opens with the same proper list of names and phone numbers. The most important ones first. Names of those who became friends during those long weeks and months. The number of those whom one could call day or night, in need of help or advice or simply something to eat.

Some of the people, whose names are on the first page of my notebooks have not lived to see the end of the war; others have not survived the beginning of the proclaimed peace.

When two suicide bombers walked into the headquarters of the two Kurdish parties, the Kurdistan Democratic Party (KDP) and the Patriotic Union of Kurdistan (PUK), in Erbil in January, and killed themselves and 170 others, many acquaintances and one real friend were among them.

The trip was long ago, the war was officially declared to be over, but another rages on, and it is only now that I try to return to my thoughts and write to you about it.

The Trips

Together with my friend and photographer Sebastian Bolesch, I traveled twice into Kurdish northern Iraq. In April 2002, long before the American intervention, we wanted to write about the situation in the semi-autonomous region in northern Iraq; on the longing of the Kurds for a war that would free them finally from Saddam Hussein and would allow the return of one million deported and displaced Kurds to their homes and land in Iraq.

In March 2003 we traveled again to northern Iraq.

248

We were greeted like friends.

The Kurds registered quite well which international reporters had developed an interest in their fate only after
the American interest awakened. And they hadn't forgotten those who had made the troublesome journey to their
forgotten region long before the American troops arrived.

We lived in a small, dirty room on the fifth floor of the
rather run-down Hotel Tower, right below the old fortress
of the antique city of Erbil. The toilet in our bathroom
flooded the floor with each use, but we had water to wash
ourselves. Our dirty laundry and Sebastian's cameras and
lenses lay around our beds; the room had no desk, but a
small TV where we could watch Al Jazeera and *BBC World
News*. Our windows faced the wrong direction, and so in
order to file articles or images via satellite phone, we had
to carry all our technical equipment up five floors to the
roof: computer, phone, satellite dish, adapter, cables.

The only functioning sockets were located in a tiny den
for the laundry. So I had to place the computer in that
dungeonlike room. On washing days, the soapsuds ran
out of a rubber tube directly onto the floor. To avoid an
electric shock and the destruction of my laptop, I built a
little chain of islands of plastic washtubs so that my cable
could travel safely from the plug to my computer, which
was enthroned on an iron bucket.

Occasionally I wondered whether I was more likely to
get killed on this roof than at the front lines.

There was a restaurant on the second floor of our hotel
that had one specialty on offer: chicken. Cooked with rice,
grilled with rice, cooked with bread, or grilled with bread.
All other dishes were presented in such a way that the

original animal was no longer recognizable, either in taste or visually.

Every now and then a rather obese rat would cheerfully run between our chairs over the floor of the restaurant.

From here we traveled across northern Iraq, to the Turkish border, to the green line that separates Kurdish northern Iraq from the Iraq of Saddam Hussein, to the territory in the southeast that is controlled by Islamic fundamentalists, to the refugee camps where the victims of Saddam Hussein's "Arabization" policy had been scraping along for years.

Ten days after we arrived, the war began.

We stayed with our translator, Ahmed Hemen, throughout the entire war. Our drivers changed. We witnessed the air bombardments, the slow advancement of the Peshmerga forces, the tenacious skirmishes and battles for streets and strategically important positions; we were stuck in the trenches and holes along the unclear, broken front; we were in Kirkuk when the city fell and in Mosul when the looters raged—and together we witnessed the transition from the last battles of the war to the first fights of the peace.

On Journalistic Misjudgments

Journalism is an almost impossible profession.

We want to be messengers with news about events and people in our neighborhood or in distant places.

And as accurate witnesses or social critics we depend on the appearance of truthfulness.

250

Our stories contain descriptions and perceptions that are presented as objective truths. We, the authors, remain more or less invisible and our subjective perspective is made indiscernible.

But this alleged objectivity of the journalist conceals its risks: we suggest not only neutrality, but also infallibility. It obstructs the view of all the errors that we, all of us, unintentionally commit when we observe or write.

Facts can be verified by careful archivists or fact-checkers.

But sense perception and personal judgments cannot be verified by any editor.

The assessment of a source whom we interview, a witness to whom we listen, remains ultimately subjective. Whether we consider someone credible or doubtful, whether the tears seem honest or fake to us, whether we take the stuttering of a source as a sign of his fear or of his dishonesty—it does not follow any systematic methodology, but usually is guided by sheer intuition.

All of us can err. Myself included, of course.

Memory can fail us, we can ignore crucial aspects and care too much about minor aspects, and we can believe and follow false informants.

Certainly, those who have studied various books and articles about the place and its history can situate current events in a historic and cultural context; those who search for different witnesses for the same event can reduce mistakes or biases; those who ask for comments from conflicting parties can try to balance one person's judgment.

But objective? Infallible?

Nevertheless, the acknowledgment of possible sources

of error is by no means a free ride for cheerful fiction or manipulative propaganda.

Those who endanger the reputation of the media through their carelessness eventually harm the victims of war and violence whose stories nobody believes anymore, because nobody trusts us, the messengers, anymore.

In the spring of 2002, the journalist Jeffrey Goldberg of the *New Yorker* interviewed a man in the security prison at Suleimania. A few weeks later, he presented a scoop to a surprised public and a probably absolutely delighted American administration: the prisoner in northern Iraq was the chief witness to the connection between Saddam Hussein and Osama bin Laden.

Up until then, no secret service in the world had been able to deliver convincing evidence that Saddam Hussein was an ally of Islamic fundamentalists of the region, let alone of al-Qaeda. Nobody had been able to prove an alliance between the Sunni dictator from Baghdad and the Wahabist fundamentalist bin Laden.

There had been increasing signs that the American administration desired a military intervention in Iraq, but they were lacking reasons and justifications that could persuade the public of the urgency of such a war. Iraq could not be connected with the attacks of 9/11 and bin Laden continued to live and mock the war against terrorism.

At this moment the *New Yorker* published Jeffrey Goldberg's story "The Great Terror" in its March 25th issue. The reaction in the public sphere was to praise the text as a masterpiece of investigative journalism. Intelligence agencies were subsequently criticized: how could it be that a single journalist was able to find evidence of the axis of terror, evidence that they had all been searching for?

On page after page, we are presented with a brilliantly researched, substantial article on the persecution of the Kurds by Saddam Hussein's regime; countless witnesses and quotations evidence the author's extensive interviews in northern Iraq; emphatically he gives voice to the Kurdish victims of the brutal dictator from Baghdad; and finally, he describes the battles between the Kurds and Answar-al-Islam, a heavily armed and radical Islamic fundamentalist group, in the southern portion of northern Iraq, which controls an area near Biara.

Very impressive. There is nothing, at first sight, that would give any reason for mistrust or suspicion.

But then there are these two passages in the article under the subheads "The Prisoners" and "The al Qaeda Link."

In the first section, the author talks about a visit to a prison in Suleimania. He wanted to interview members of the terrorist group.

Names and obscure characters are introduced to the reader, factions of parties and splinter groups of Answar-al-Islam are presented, sources from Iraqi intelligence agencies appear, and suddenly there is—amidst all these political prisoners—Mohammed Mansour Shabab (who is later called "Jawad"). The man to whom the title "The al Qaeda Link" refers.

And then the author tells us what Shabab told him:

How in 1996 Shabab met a man named Othman, how he sold weapons to Othman and how Othman invited him to come to Afghanistan. He talks about his second journey to Afghanistan, his visit to Kandahar.

Soon, Shabab's account turns wild: how he was doped with a sleeping pill one night, and brought by car to the mountains, to Osama bin Laden's tent.

We learn about Shabab's meetings with al-Qaeda officers, about Shabab's killing of Iranians, about his trips to Iraq and the headquarters of Saddam Hussein confidants in Tikrit, about the weapons and suspicious refrigerator motors that Shabab smuggles between the Iraqi dictator and the Afghan fighters.

The author does not seem to have any doubts about Shabab's credibility. He does not detect any contradictions.

Instead Goldberg offers another source to add credibility to Shabab's account: he refers to informants who also claim that the Iraqi regime had regularly smuggled weapons to al-Qaeda via Dubai to Pakistan, and then on to Afghanistan. Who exactly these informants are, the reader is not told. "Sources from the Iraqi opposition," it says.

The article's thesis depends primarily on the statements of Shabab. And the author trusts his informant.

A few weeks later, in April 2002, Sebastian Bolesch and I are sitting in front of the chief witness to the link of terrorism between Saddam Hussein and Osama bin Laden. I have no idea whether "Mohammed Mansour Shabab" is really his name, as he claims. I cannot verify whether he was really born in 1973, as he claims.

He is Iranian, he says; he has worked as a drug trafficker, he says; he has killed 420 people, he says, with his own hands.

254

He is sitting on a sofa right in front of us, and talks joyfully about killing.

The director of the prison had warned us beforehand.

An unsupervised conversation with this prisoner would not be possible. He was an unpredictable, brutal murderer, the director had said, and our safety could not be guaranteed. Shabab was a threat to anybody, at any moment, and one could not talk to him without protection, the director had argued.

In order to prove his point, he had shown us a series of photos from the detainee's file. In the photos you could see "Shabab" going about his business of killing.

In the first one he could be seen with a knife cutting off a man's ear.

Then, in a second picture, he rams the knife right into the victim's head.

The pictures were from a film that the Kurdish police had found in "Shabab's" luggage, the director said.

From a journalistic point of view, an interview under the supervision of the prison authorities would be worthless, we told the director; the prisoner could not talk openly in their presence. We asked for a separate room without supervision.

We would be risking our lives, we were told, and nobody had talked to this prisoner without police or guards present. According to the director, then, there had never been an unguarded conversation between the prisoner and a journalist.

When we threatened to leave since there was no possibility of a correctly done, fair interview, the director offered to give us a separate room and place an armed guard in front of the door who could come in and help in case of a sudden attack by "Shabab."

So, at last, we are facing "Shabab."

Was he willing to talk to us?

He smiles.

He seems to like the attention, even if he does not seem to believe that we are really from the media. Secret service seems more likely to him.

And then he begins to describe how he smuggled heroin from Afghanistan into Iran, and weapons from Iran into Afghanistan. He jumps in his narrative, sometimes he confuses times and names, he praises his own crimes, and he stares with a slightly crazed gaze at us, the door, and the floor.

I repeatedly invoke the scary images of the man sitting in front of me and his violence, and I anticipate an attempt to flee from him or an attack.

We are sitting in this cold room, on the edge of our iron chairs, ready to jump at any moment.

After three minutes, Sebastian interrupts the conversation.

This is senseless, he says; the informant is not only strange, but evidently ill.

"This is a psychopath," Sebastian exclaims. "You not only cannot quote this guy, you cannot even interview him. He is nuts." I do not trust anybody's judgment as much as I trust this photographer who has traveled through crisis regions around the globe for the last ten years. "Let's go," Sebastian says.

I do not want to end this interview. The statements of this man had been too important for the argument about the connection between Saddam Hussein and al-Qaeda.

We continue.

He talks about "Osman"—who was called "Othman" in Goldberg's article.

He had killed in the name of the Iraqi intelligence service, "Shabab" explains.

In the *New Yorker* article, he had killed mostly in the name of Othman and al-Qaeda.

He personally had killed 420 people, "Shabab" says.

"I enjoy killing," he says, and watches us with a perfidious lust for scaring people.

He had met bin Laden, "Shabab" says.

Where?

In Kandahar.

Where exactly?

He had had to wear a hood, he answers.

In Goldberg's article he had received a sleeping pill when he was taken to bin Laden's tent. Now he had been blindfolded with a hood.

Suddenly he spits at our translator and threatens him.

He was a traitor, "Shabab" tells him, because he was collaborating with foreign powers. He would receive his punishment.

Again Sebastian asks me to stop the interview. He would not need further evidence that this prisoner was nothing but an impostor, a crazy storyteller. A murderer, clearly, a violent psychopath, but not a credible source for *any* article.

The translator hustles me to leave.

We try to continue the interview for another twenty minutes in which "Shabab" produces more and more absurd stories. He becomes angry because we do not buy his account "like that other journalist" who had been here a couple of weeks ago, and "who had not questioned his descriptions."

Finally I give up.

We call the guard in front of our door, who guides "Shabab" with a rifle back to his cell.

We cannot believe it.

This was the chief witness?

How could somebody be duped by this madman?

How could Goldberg present the turbid anecdotes of a psychopath and self-exposer to the world as credible?

We try to exonerate our colleague: Maybe "Shabab" had seemed calmer and more concentrated on the day that Goldberg had met him? Maybe his account had been more coherent then? Maybe Goldberg's translator had palliated the story?

Maybe Goldberg's subjective impression had simply been different?

That alone would not be careless.

We continue to investigate for the following few days.

We organize a trip to the south of northern Iraq, to the frontlines between the Kurdish soldiers, the Peshmerga, and the warriors of Answar-al-Islam.

In Goldberg's article "Shabab" had appeared in the context of the prisoners of Answar-al-Islam, but "Shabab" himself had not said that he had any connection with the group.

258

The Kurdish officer Ramadan Dekone gives us an idea
of the perpetual battle with the Islamic fundamentalists;
he tells us about the military strategy and the topography
of the war zone. We are standing on a hill, surveying the
area, surrounded by his soldiers. Dekone points eastward:
the terrorists not only were able to withdraw to the mountain region, but they could also flee at any time across the
border to Iran. "These terrorist groups are no real enemy
to us," Dekone declares proudly, "but Iran, that is a serious enemy, and they are fighting with the help of Iran."

We ask: Are there any connections between Answar-al-
Islam and the fighters from Afghanistan?

Yes, certainly.

And any connections to Saddam Hussein and Iraq?

No. They receive ammunition and supplies, TNT and
mines, from Iran. Not Iraq.

"Just have a look," Dekone says. "It's already geographically self-evident. They are operating in the shadow of
Iran, directly at the border."

The Kurds fear and hate Saddam Hussein. A connection
between America's number one enemy, bin Laden, and
their own enemy, Saddam Hussein, would serve them well.

They would have a strategic interest in offering the
Americans reasons and justifications for an intervention.

The heavily armed warriors of Answar-al-Islam are a
real, serious threat to them; the brutality of the Islamic
fighters is evident. Confiscated videos of the group have
indicated furthermore that there are Arabic-speaking fighters among the group.

So, a link between Answar and Iraq would be welcomed

by the Kurds, and they would be most happy to present it to the Western press.

And yet: nobody claims that link.

We hear witnesses and arguments only for an alliance between al-Qaeda, Answar-al-Islam, and Iran.

Maybe our colleague had never encountered any voices countering his thesis.

Goldberg? Yes, he had been here, Dekone claims, a few weeks ago.

I do not know what motivated Goldberg to write his article on "The Great Terror."

Maybe he really believed "Shabab."

Maybe he just wanted to believe him.

I sent Jeffrey Goldberg these comments, and asked for his reflection on this source from hindsight, in the spring of 2006, and gave him the opportunity to correct or explain his judgment. Goldberg replied in an email to me: "If I'm to be your scapegoat for the war in Iraq, so be it—I know from experience it's not too easy to change the minds of ideologues, but please don't misrepresent certain fundamentals."

Goldberg then goes on to explain that his section on the prisoner came late in that long piece and was mostly ignored by the administration and the press.

It is surprising to me that Goldberg now wants to downplay this particular part of his story and the impact it had. Talking about his own article at the time, in March 2002, he sounded different:

> There has been a certain amount of discussion this week
> in Washington about one particular point I raised,

260

which concerns allegations that Saddam is more closely tied to al-Qaida than we had previously thought. I had actually gone to Iraqi Kurdistan in late January not expecting to learn anything new about terrorism (post–Sept. 11 terrorism, that is, not state terror against the Kurds). But when I was in Kurdistan, I started to hear stories about an al-Qaida-style terror group formerly known as the Jund al-Islam, or Soldiers of Islam, which recently changed its name (for the most naked of PR reasons, I believe) to the Ansar al-Islam, or Supporters of Islam. . . .

But what I learned—and I'm not going to give away the whole story here—is that Saddam's intelligence agency may jointly control this group with al-Qaida. If this is true, well, the implications are quite serious, which is why people in Washington who don't want the United States to do anything about Iraq have been (unsuccessfully) trying to discredit this aspect of my article. (www.slate.com/id/2063437/entry/2063447/)

So, the article has caused a "certain amount of discussion in Washington," and Goldberg himself suggests that the particular passage on the link between Saddam Hussein and al-Qaeda was a crucial one.

In his email to me, he then writes: "That said, I obviously had a different experience with this prisoner than you did. He seemed fanatical but not crazy to me." Goldberg argues that individuals who seem insane and violent can commit complex crimes—and refers to "prisoners in Israeli jails and Jordanian jails."

I agree with him. The fact that someone is violent and

261

insane does not stop him from acting violently and insanely, even on a complex level.

But the question here is not only whether "Shabab" ever committed crimes (the authorities have photographic evidence of that), but whether he was the link between al-Qaeda and Saddam Hussein as he claimed. And whether this story, which was contradictory in itself and contradicted by other sources and information available, could be found trustworthy. "Shabab," at least in the conversation I had with him, was unable to give any substantive information to support his claims, whether a description of the landscape near Kandahar (where he claimed to have been) or a description of the interior of the houses of Saddam Hussein's confidants in Tikrit (where he also claimed to have been). He basically seemed to lack the knowledge that he would have needed to have were he the link between al-Qaeda and Saddam Hussein. I also could not obtain any other material documentation from police records or other sources that supported his account.

Goldberg goes on to describe that during his interview with "Shabab" the prisoner behaved well, even when he, Goldberg, challenged aspects of his story. He agrees that different translators might have given different impressions to each of us, that maybe the prisoner had been on medication when he saw him. "On the other hand, I'm an experienced reporter, as are you, and any reporter who tells you he or she has never been fooled by a source or a subject is undoubtedly lying." At the end of his response, he writes: "I'm happy to admit to manifold imperfections as a journalist. Believe me, I've made mistakes. The several paragraphs on this prisoner might well be mistaken."

At the same time, Goldberg insists, "you don't tell me that you've proven my story wrong."

I myself have been fooled by sources. I have trusted false informants or found a liar credible. What may be worse: I probably have mistrusted someone whose account was true. And the sense of guilt and anger toward myself, like that toward the person who misled me, has remained ever since. Why is it that these misjudgments haunt us so much? Why is it that we hold on to our own statements, beliefs, convictions for so long—sometimes for too long?

Probably writers feel particularly unsettled by the fact that we can be fooled because we depend so heavily on words. We live on them. We live on the belief that we can read and understand another's words, that we can read between the lines, decipher all kinds of broken and distorted scripture or narrative. We believe in our capacity to detect what remains unexpressed, repressed, silenced—and we give it words. Yet again. And, more often than not, we take a position, we criticize, we intervene, we challenge.

The idea that we, the masters of words and language, can misread, misjudge, be misguided still seems haunting to us. Despite all knowledge of psychoanalysis or methods of deconstruction. No matter how critically we assess the ideas of "truth," "objectivity," and "neutrality," we nevertheless engage them, we claim them temporarily.

And that is exactly the reason why we need to admit our own vulnerability to misjudgment, why we need to reflect on our work and the foundations that shape and limit it.

It is not our mistakes that endanger our credibility, but our unwillingness to handle them critically. Closeness

263

and distance to the objects of our stories can be equally distorting, trust and skepticism toward our sources can be equally misguiding. We can only reflect on potential biases or motivations, fears and hopes that constitute and subvert us at the same time.

We will not always succeed, but we cannot stop trying. Particularly in times of war.

That is what we owe to its victims. Soldiers or civilians.

Of Just and Unjust War

For one year we had followed the chronicle of an announced war. We had watched the spectacle in the Security Council, where Colin Powell acted as if it hadn't been decided long before the meeting that the United States would wage war against Saddam Hussein.

With or without weapons of mass destruction. With or without evidence. With or without authorization by a UN resolution. With or without the support of the international community.

It had been a flagrant spectacle.

Fifteen years after Saddam Hussein had bombarded Kurdish villages near Halabja with gas, fifteen years after thousands of civilians had suffocated harrowingly and had painfully died of combustion, twelve years after the Americans had called for rebellion against Saddam Hussein only to then stand by watching passively while Saddam Hussein brutally cracked down on the Shiite and Kurdish insurgents, killing fifty thousand of them and expelling one million—the Security Council conferred on Iraq.

264

While the American secretary of state presented those blurred images of alleged weapons of mass destruction and mobile laboratories, I asked myself why these meetings were taking place now.

In my fantasy, I imagined this same meeting fifteen years earlier. I imagined the debates at the UN headquarters at the East River, how the crimes against the Kurds would be presented as reasons for an intervention, for a just war to end the "Arabization" campaign and the crimes against the Kurds, the people without a state.

Would the governments of Russia, France, and Germany have opted against such a military intervention? Would there have been worldwide demonstrations against such a war?

But there had not been such sessions; nobody had acted to stop those crimes against humanity when they occurred.

The no-fly zone along the thirty-sixth parallel was established years later, and the embargo mostly punished civilians, not the corrupt class of Baathists or Saddam Hussein.

But now, suddenly, there was an alleged need for action.

I could imagine how the Kurds Sebastian and I had met in April 2002 were staring at their TVs in great expectation, how they longed for this war, just as I imagined Iraqi civilians staring at their TVs in disbelief and fear.

"I know we are an easy target," wrote Nuuha al-Radi, an Iraqi artist, in her *Baghdad Diary*, during the first Gulf War. "I know we are a thorn in everybody's flesh. But . . . we are also a people."

During the slow-motion overture to an unavoidable

war we prepared ourselves for our journey through Iran to northern Iraq. We arrived in Erbil on March 9th.

The New Year

The hero of past battles is quiet. Mustafa Nasraddin climbs the loamy hill of Quosh Tepe near Erbil with fast steps, his turban over his forehead, a rifle over his shoulder, the wound on his left arm covered by the traditional uniform of the Peshmerga. He ignores the green flags on the graves at the bottom of the hill. His soldiers are standing in a half circle at the top, their Kalashnikovs in front of their bodies, the hand grenades in their belts. The enemy positions of Saddam Hussein's army are only a few miles away from here. There is no regular border between Kurdish northern Iraq and Saddam Hussein's Iraq.

The fighters have piled up truck tires and pieces of wood in various layers and are holding gasoline-soaked torches. They all wait for the signal from their commander.

It is Newroz, the Kurdish New Year, and they are celebrating the story of the blacksmith Kawa, their first resistance fighter. Kawa freed his people 2,600 years ago from the despotic King Duhok. Now they are fighting for liberation again, and Nasraddin's unit longs for a speech from their taciturn commander. They want him to give them courage for this war that they hope will be the last one; they want him to place them in the long history of Kurdish resistance against tyranny and oppression.

The Americans have begun their assault against Saddam Hussein in the south of Iraq the previous night, and the men on the hill of Quosh Tepe in Kurdish northern Iraq already desire the end of the feared leader in Baghdad.

They are chosen soldiers in the elite unit Spi Kirkuk. Only Kurdish deportees from the lost city of Kirkuk are allowed to serve in this brigade. Only fighters who were expelled from the "Kurdish Jerusalem" are accepted into Nasraddin's unit. They do not have anything but rocket-propelled grenades and Kalashnikovs, but Spi Kirkuk is supposed to spearhead the reconquest of Kirkuk. They are only twenty-five miles away from their hometown, which Saddam "Arabized" like so many other towns and villages on the other side of the green line.

Nasraddin hesitates and looks at the faces full of expectation around him. He chose every one of them himself for this unit, every one of them experienced individually the collective fate of the Kurds: war and desolation, deportation and exile. Each of them has lost siblings or parents, his house and his home.

They experience each moment and each day as a mirror of historic events. Just as they understand each individual as an example of the collective, since they see in each particular life what is common to all—so they see in each moment a reflection of the long Kurdish history.

Nasraddin knows that his soldiers do not celebrate only the blacksmith Kawa at New Year's, but also themselves and the indefinite cycle of war and oppression in which they find themselves.

Myth and history become blurred on these holidays—and that is what nurtures their hope and their anger.

They were the eternal losers in the game of the Great Powers of the region of old Mesopotamia during the twentieth century.

"Kurdistan" remained a meaningless promise to the victors of the First World War, a specter to the hostile neighboring states with Kurdish populations, and an unattainable dream for the Kurds.

Kurdistan remained a country without location on the world map, the Kurds a nation without territorial sovereignty. Until today.

For the four million Kurds in northern Iraq, the history of the past century repeated itself as a sad series of disappointments. Even though the contract of Sèvres (1920) that decided on the dissolution of the Ottoman Empire at the end of the First World War promised the Kurds an independent state, even though Woodrow Wilson promised them the right to self-determination and far-reaching autonomy—they were soon forgotten.

Kurd dosti nia, says an often-quoted proverb: "the Kurds have no friends." And the collective memory of the Kurds recalls countless examples of betrayal by an international community that seemed blind to the injustices and crimes committed against the Kurds.

"We had either a state of emergency or genocide or war in our region," said Dschauhar Namik, the general secretary of the KDP in Erbil, "It is time that we are free at last."

I have to say: despite what is being written in the papers, I have not *once* heard a Kurd asking for an independent state. Not once. Not a politician, not a military official, not a soldier, not a peasant. Not one person seems to call for an independent state of Kurdistan anymore. They all seem to understand that this was a utopia that nobody is going to help them achieve. All they want is freedom from oppression. Everyone I talked to before and during the war talked about a democratic, federal state of Iraq, with a Kurdish province, and with a constitution that guaranteed minority rights for Assyrians, Turkmens, and so on.

The war of the Americans against Saddam, for whatever reasons it is being fought, offers the chance of an end to persecution and liberation from oppression.

That is why Nasraddin begins to tell the story of Kawa and the killing of the tyrant in the year 612 BC and of the fire that Kawa kindled after his successful deed.

"The fire shines as a symbol of the liberation of the Kurds on that day; next week will spark a fire in Kirkuk. *Inshallah!*"

He brings the torch close to the wood and the flames flare against the evening sky.

They sing "Srwddi Newroz," the song of New Year's, "the New Year is a year of victory."

Of Those Who Went Out to Unlearn Fear

His name is famous, his image omnipresent, but nobody knows his face. Umed Khawar can be portrayed only from behind. His limbs are cramped and bent, his left leg pulled in. His exhausted, dying body supported by his left arm, he crawls across the street on all fours. His head under the turban is turned away; protectively he holds a bundle to his body.

269

Every child in Kurdistan knows the story of Umed, the baker from Halabja. He had always wanted a son. His wife gave him seven daughters. The first son who had been born to them died in 1985.

The second son, Shwan, was finally born at the end of 1987—and lived. The picture shows Umed as he harbors this long-awaited son in the hollow of his upper body.

It illustrates a historic day: March 16, 1988. Clouds of smoke in the picture testify to the bombings by Saddam Hussein's army, and Umed Khawar drags his suffocating son Shwan through the contaminated streets of Halabja. The fatal smell of apples lies in the air, and Umed is not able to keep the seductive-smelling poison gas from his beloved child.

Dying, faceless, with his dead son in his arms, Umed became the icon of Kurdish martyrdom.

Two days ago the war began, and since then the image of Umed has been shown again and again on television. Everybody expects Saddam's retaliatory attacks against the Kurdish civilian population, and so the traumatic memory of the corpses of Halabja is combined with practical advice for the present.

Along with the famous images of the deformed victims, Kurdish news programs broadcast tips every hour on how the frightened population can protect itself against death from the air: doors and windows should be sealed; food should be wrapped in plastic.

Even the superior strength of the American allies cannot calm the fear that has grown over generations.

The shelves of the bazaar have been swept bare. For

hours already there has been no rice, flatbread, or oil. Restaurants and tearooms haven't even bothered to open; the local weekly newspaper has stopped operations because the printer won't print anymore. And besides, there are hardly any readers left in a city whose inhabitants are fleeing. Every few minutes, the crash of blinds falling in front of shop windows announces the next departure. Since daybreak the overloaded convoys have streamed by the thousands like lava from the ancient city of Erbil to the rain-soaked fields and mountains of the surrounding area. There, too, there is no protection—but at least there is the illusion of being beyond the reach of Iraqi missiles.

Whoever stays behind stands in line at Siadi's, the carpet dealer at the bazaar in Erbil. The fear of Saddam Hussein can be measured in meters. Siadi lays an iron ruler against the roll of plastic film. With nimble hands he unwinds meter upon meter of the rolled-up strip from the rod. The gaunt chickens in the wooden cages on the neighboring stand flutter, easily startled, at the swish of the plastic. A long line of veiled women already stretches from his little corner store to the next street corner. They each hold a wad of red-and-blue dinars ready, which they will give to Siadi. He has already sold twenty thousand meters today. Three dinars per meter. "We import it from Iraq," he says: "First Saddam sells us the plastic—and then he attacks us."

In the rain-drenched fields in the mountains, families squat around small fires and try to stay warm. The women and children were able to spend the first stormy night in the tent. The men waited outside, blankets and sheets of plastic around their shoulders.

In the morning, children with numb fingers look for small stones, which they can use to stabilize the tarpaulins. There is flatbread and a glass of tea is passed around. Without sugar. It is necessary to save. Nobody knows how long they will have to wait here. Nobody knows whether the provisions will last. But they are all prepared for the worst. They are not able to take hope from the past. Experience teaches them fear. They would gladly be confident; they would gladly believe this is finally the last flight, the last exile, the last war.

Between the Fronts

The war has begun, but the second front in the north is a long time coming. The Turkish government has refused passage to the American infantry. For this reason, until now the war against Saddam has been waged chiefly from the south. In northern Iraq, U.S. Special Forces units are operating in utmost secrecy. Only sometimes, when a convoy of Kurdish army vehicles tear over the rural roads, does one get a quick view of a few lighter Jeeps with slightly more athletic, taller types in the backseat. They're racing toward the south. By the time the American parachute units land, by the time the second front is truly opened, the terrorist hideouts in the southwestern part of northern Iraq should be eradicated. Kurds and the invisible Americans bombard the fortress of Answar-al-Islam day in and day out.

Her confidence was not sufficient for sheep and goats.

A herd simply needs a pasture. A secure place. You can

breed and sell such animals. But you can't take them along. No, Massoma Hama Ali shakes her head. They must be able to flee. At a moment's notice. So they can't accumulate any dead weight. They must always be prepared. As in the past twenty-five years. Twelve times their house was destroyed, twelve times they had to leave their homeland, and their existence was ruined.

Like last night, when the explosions in Khurmal shook the earth.

The alliance of U.S. Special Forces and Kurdish Peshmerga attacked the camps of the Islamists in the southeast of northern Iraq. Strangely enough, Answar-al-Islam, the terrorist jihad organization, was spared. Instead, the bombs fell on the troops of the Islamic Foundation, which until now was indeed hated by the Kurds, but officially tolerated.

"It is always the same sound of war that causes us to flee," she says, and with the corner of her skirt she wipes the runny nose of her filthy daughter, sitting on her lap. It is supposed to be an American war against terrorism. But for Massoma, it is simply a recurrence of the same old story: Kurdish displacement and exile.

They have taken shelter in the deserted shack on the farm of Khanqa, away from the road between Suleimania and Halabja. A small stone wall shields the misery. Behind the closed doors, they live on the bare floor in the open air. There is no furniture, no carpet, no blankets. Outside in the courtyard it is warmer than inside the shack, and so Massoma sits among her ten children in the spring sunlight. The whole night long, she hauled her daughters and sons, one after the other, farther and farther, until

273

they were beyond the checkpoint of Sayed Sadaq, which marks the border of the new war zone, and through the thousands of Kurdish soldiers sent to the front to fight against the Islamists in their own land.

For more than a year already, her family has lived in continual fear in the southeast of northern Iraq. Not of the fundamentalist Islamic Association centered around Ali Baphir, not even of the heavily armed terrorists of Answar-al-Islam, whose bearded fighters came into her village again and again in order to ask for food and blankets. "Our homeland became a bloody battlefield between Answar and the Patriotic Union of Kurdistan," complains Massoma. It doesn't matter to her who assumes power, who wins the war. "But if the Americans destroy our homes now, then they must also rebuild them."

The Homeless Terrorist

He can't take real steps. Without actually raising his feet, Nzar Ahmed Mohammed Shukar shuffles across the floor. The faded blue-gray canvas sneakers have been without shoelaces only since yesterday, and Shukar hasn't gotten used to walking without losing his unlaced footwear yet.

Two armed guards lead the deserter from Answar-al-Islam into the interrogation room of the prison in Suleimania. Shukar sits down, slouched, on the sofa right next to the door and is silent. His first night in the cell has left traces. His black, curly hair hangs tousled on his forehead. His fingernails have begun to turn blue from the

274

cold. Shukar moves his hands in slow motion over the flickering heat of the gas burner in front of him.

"I'm going to lose my mind," stutters Shukar and takes a drag on a cigarette. "I'm dying of worry because I don't even know if my mother is still alive."

For six months, the twenty-two-year-old served the jihad fighters of the terrorist organization Answar-al-Islam in their stronghold near Biara. He is half-Kurd, half-Arab, his mother lives in Iraq, his father and brother in Kurdish northern Iraq. He set out to seek the true faith. "I believed they were truthful." Virgins with beautiful eyes had been promised to him by the religious leaders of Answar-al-Islam—if he would fight against blasphemy, and that meant against Massud Barzani, the hated Kurdish leader in the northwest of northern Iraq; then against the PUK, the thoroughly secular party of Jalal Talabani; and then against all other infidels. "I had a clear vision of my fight for Allah," says Shukar.

However, since the previous October, Shukar and the other young Answar fighters have already had to prepare themselves for a possible war with the Americans. Several *katibas*, brigades from Answar-al-Islam, blasted caves with TNT in the Shram mountains behind Biara. Regularly, he and his unit had to live in the five- to six-yard-long caves for two to three days in a row. "We normal fighters were soon completely intimidated and demoralized," says Shukar. Every *katiba* received a religious preacher and a military instructor. A merciless regime: questions were not allowed; whoever wanted to flee was tormented by the *gwmamer*, the torturer, in front of the others, with electric shocks and blows to the soles of their feet, Shukar recounts.

No exception was made for the youths among them. Answar-al-Islam united clueless teenagers with al-Qaeda fighters trained in Afghanistan, fanatics from Syria and Turkey along with those from northern Iraq. "Nobody really knew where the weapons came from," says Shukar, "but it was clear that al-Qaeda supported us."

Soon Shukar regretted not having listened to the warnings of his very different brother, Diar. The brothers stood across from each other in enemy armies on different sides of the front in northern Iraq. While Shukar was drawn to the fundamentalists of Answar-al-Islam, Diar enlisted in the secular Peshmerga of the PUK, which fights against Answar.

Once, in October of last year, they had secretly met. His brother had offered him a pistol—he was supposed to murder one of the leaders of Answar. At that time his own jihad fighters already seemed to Shukar to be "terrorists like Saddam."

"I saw the corpses of dead PUK soldiers," says Shukar and lowers his voice. "True Islam does not do something like that. God, the Almighty, did not call us to murder like that." However, he was not able to flee at that time. Only now, in the confusion of war and bombings, was it possible for Shukar to disappear.

He would like to live freely, whether as Kurd or Arab doesn't matter to him. "I want to look for my mother," says Shukar. "My older brother is married. He has a wife and a peaceful life. And I? I have nothing."

He fled four days ago; for four days he has not been able

to pray anymore. He lost his faith under the rule of the jihad fighters.

The Kurdish authorities have promised him a letter, with which he may soon leave.

He wants to go home.

Even if he no longer knows where that is.

The American Landing

During the night the first American parachute units landed in northern Iraq. The second front with Peshmerga and American soldiers can be opened. We drive into the mountains behind Salahaddin. A wide area is cordoned off around the American camp near the provisional landing field of Bashur, Kurdish checkpoints have been set up to keep unpleasant media representatives away from the Americans.

We are waiting on a hill, undecided how we should proceed, when a patrol of three tired paratroopers in boots come toward us through the softened fields. We can scarcely believe that the soldiers, who usually shy away from any contact with the press, are voluntarily seeking out a conversation with us, but they are heading directly toward us.

During a short conversation in fluent English, the misunderstanding is cleared up. The clueless soldiers approached our small group only because they took us "for well-dressed Kurds."

"And we wanted to speak with the people we are freeing."

Absurd.

They just landed during the night. Frozen and hungry, they stand by our Jeep and tell of their first night in the war. We offer them some of our provisions from the car.

No, no, they couldn't accept that.

Flatbread with fresh cheese.

They look at one another inquisitively. In their minds they are reeling off the rules about danger from foreigners. Never accept anything that could be poisoned.

Sebastian sees through their hastily acquired hesitation and gets a small can of sardines from our crate, which he opens in front of them.

They dig in.

Thankful and yet a little ashamed.

We wouldn't write that they had asked for food, right?

A bit later we succeed in getting as far as the entrance to the American camp.

Dirty and frozen paratroopers from the 173rd Airborne Brigade sit in the back of Kurdish trucks and attend to the traces of the previous night before they are brought to their operation base. With knives they scrape the mud out of their boot soles. "We didn't really know exactly where we were going," says First Sergeant Bryant, who shaves the stubble from his chin with an electric razor and squints at the glare. "They simply opened the door of the plane and shouted: Jump, jump."

Only on the ground did the soldiers find out where they had landed.

It's a miracle they didn't shoot every single Kurd who had been so ardently awaiting their arrival.

Air War

The machines with the deadly freight can't be seen. Only a light, delayed humming and rumbling in the sky points to the imminent attack.

We are standing at the green line, the invisible border between Iraq and northern Iraq. A few hundred yards away from us, on the other side, stands the first Iraqi post, and several miles away, on the hills, the Iraqi soldiers are waiting in their positions for the next American bombs. A gruesome spectacle.

From a safe distance, surrounded by Kurdish Peshmerga, we observe how the fighter planes of the American-British alliance fly away over northern Iraq and how, right in front of our eyes on the other side, soil, buildings, and people are blown to pieces.

Hour after hour, the Kurdish soldier Ibrahim observes the explosions on the crest of the hill in front of Chamchamal. Twenty-four miles from Kirkuk, the Kurdish border officials crouch, leaning against the wall of their guardhouse, between rifles and blankets that have been tied together. Two dogs lie in the grass and squint sleepily. A few stones are lying in the middle of the street. The border has been closed since the beginning of the war. The black-gray fountains caused by the impact of the bombs shoot yard-high out of the soil around the Iraqi positions.

And nothing.

No reaction.

None of the much-touted Al-Samud missiles have as yet come from the heavens to punish the Kurds for their coalition with the enemy attackers.

279

In the evenings, at sunset, Ibrahim stands at the deserted checkpoint and stares across at the uniformed enemies with the same passport. He observes the silhouettes of the last Iraqis at their lost posts. They seem to him to be prisoners in their own land, subjected to American bombs and to Iraqi officers who force them into a hopeless battle. "We hear it all the way over here when they shoot at deserters on the other side," says Ibrahim, a note of sympathy in his voice.

We can follow attack upon attack unendangered. The earth quakes, even miles away the window panes vibrate, the dull thunder from the front comes across.

Night after night, Sebastian and I sit in our room and feel the waves of the war. Sometimes we climb the five flights of stairs up to the roof of the hotel. Between clotheslines with half-clean boxers and T-shirts and countless colossal satellite dishes from the various television stations, we stare toward the west. In the pitch-black night, we can follow the bombardment of Mosul; yellow-white lights flicker in the distance like lightning.

Long after midnight, we drive to the green zone, which separates victims from onlookers.

The villages lie silent in the clear night, no cars cross our path. The moon lights the scenery between the Iraqi positions and the Kurdish region. On this starlit night, everything is bathed in a light gray shine.

We make a perfect target for Iraqi snipers. Therefore, one mile before the last Kurdish post, on the bridge of Kalak, we turn off the headlights and motor of our car; we roll another couple of hundred yards. Then we go on foot, as much as possible in the shady darkness or under the cover of abandoned buildings. It is icy cold but unbelievably calm as we go to the last Kurds who are still awake.

They have become cautious here. The small old town of Kalak on the great Sab River has been evacuated, the position on the bridge darkened. Frogs croak. A few mangy mutts, yapping, make noise. Otherwise only the bombs thundering down upon Mosul and the surrounding area rip through the silence in intervals.

In front of a small military barrack, Peshmerga are sitting on the steps. They are happy about a visit in the loneliness of the night and ask us in.

"The landing of the Americans will perhaps provoke the Iraqis to acts of revenge," says Abu Asar, "so that's why we're careful." The Kurdish fighter sits barefoot with his comrades on the stone floor of the hut. To ward off hunger, they have flatbread with scallions and some cold chicken. Kurdish northern Iraq, too, is plagued by the UN sanctions. Food is scarce. They have only one glass left and pass the sweetened tea around the circle. There is no radio or television, so Kassim Nasar, a young fighter, sings old folk tunes from Erbil. Leaning against the wall, he begins—with folded hands—a *lawuk*, a ballad, which wafts wistfully through the night. Everyone in the circle listens to him in silence. They think of the Iraqis on the other side of the river, for there they also sing in the evenings. "Sometimes we can hear them. They are giving us a secret sign with their singing," says Nasser. "They want to say to us: We too will celebrate, when you and the Americans win. Don't shoot us."

Asymmetries—or a Lesson in Tolerance

Every conversation we had with Kurds on our trip led early on to the question of the war.

Whether we were sitting among exiles in the draughty tents of the refugee camps, among the fighting Peshmerga from Mustafa Nasraddin's Spi Kirkuk unit, with the vegetable dealer at the bazaar in Erbil, from whom I bought fresh cucumbers week after week, or with his cousin at the next stand, who poured liquid cream cheese into bags for me, whether we sat at the richly set table of the advisors to the Kurdish leader Massud Barzani in their secure residential area on the mountain of Salahaddin or on the floor of the huts of impoverished Kurds, who could offer us only a glass of tea: everyone asked us about the war.

Would we support them? Why were the Germans against this military action of all things? Were we perhaps not aware of Saddam's crimes? How could we side with the dictator?

Again and again we disappointed our Kurdish interlocutors with our criticism of the American administration's actions; we tried to explain that our doubts about the war were in no way motivated by solidarity with the Hussein regime in Baghdad. Of course we could understand that they wished for this attack, of course it was clear that the Kurds finally wanted to see this very dictator, who had driven them out and gassed them by the thousands, punished.

But why then were we not for this war?

They had lost their homes, their farms, their siblings

282

had been driven out or murdered, they had spent years in exile in Germany or Austria, their laments had remained unheard, their suffering had been ignored, they had followed the American call to resistance against Saddam Hussein at the end of the first Gulf War, and they had been brutally massacred right in front of the eyes of the international community, without any one of the instigators coming to their aid. Many of their politicians had studied at elite universities in England and the United States, had earned diplomas from Harvard and Oxford, they had ruled themselves as well as possible in their de facto independent province in the shadow of Saddam Hussein—and I should turn away from a war that finally promised them liberation from the despot in Baghdad?

How easy it was for me to take an honorable antiwar position from my desk in Berlin, with a European passport in the drawer that allows me free travel, with an apartment from which nobody drives me away, in a region in which no sanctions hinder the flow of goods, a life without the everyday experience of war. How easy it was for me to insist on legitimacy of procedure, on the importance of the international bodies, which must not simply be ignored, on the regulations of the Geneva Conventions, on the dubiousness of the intelligence regarding the alleged weapons of mass destruction—but in the eyes of my Kurdish companions, all these were flimsy intellectual dodges.

We could understand them.

If I had had to endure their history, if I had been banned for years and years to a nomadic life, going from refugee camp to refugee camp while strangers had moved into my

283

apartment, if my family had been murdered—would I have argued any differently?

But the longer we spoke, the more seriously we explained our convictions, the more openly and more precisely both sides expounded their views and their doubts—the nearer these debates brought us.

This war was not being waged for their sake—they were a useful building block in the American campaign, nothing more.

"The Americans don't want this war because we have such beautiful eyes," says Nasrin Abdulqadar. "We were only an afterthought as a reason for war."

From the beginning, the Americans passed this off as a preventive war, not as a reactive one.

Ius ad bellum, according to the American administration, was the clear and present danger that Saddam Hussein posed for the United States, not retribution or punishment for his crimes against the Kurds or Shiites.

If this had been about the injustice done to the Kurds in northern Iraq by Baghdad, then a humanitarian intervention would have been in order in 1988 or—at the latest—1991. If it had been about the well-being of the Kurds, the international community could have long since freed them from this ambiguous national existence as a hybrid state and have given them an independent status in their region—*within* the territorial borders of their province (and thus without disturbing the borders of Syria, Iran, or Turkey) and combined with a recognition of minority rights of other ethnic and religious groups.

Kurd dosti nia—the Kurds have no friends.

No, they did not have any illusions about it.

284

But we should eat with them, and they patted us amicably on the shoulder.

Often I asked myself, when we were once again invited to dinner by people such as Sadi Pire of the PUK: where do they get this tolerant generosity?

Pire has devoted his entire life to politics.

He could live in Austria with his family, with his children, of whom he is so proud.

Instead he has moved into a bare house in Erbil in order to work in the reunited regional parliament.

He knows that we won't give up our resistance to the war, he laughs about it—his son also belongs "to this pacifist generation"—but we're certainly not averse to good food?

Night after night, Pire invites us over, helps with contacts whenever we ask, introduces us to important contacts. We are always welcome, we may disturb him anytime in his office in Erbil. Not once does Pire reproach us for our political differences.

We disappear for weeks, meet with political opponents, report critically about the war—and Pire is never disappointed or angry.

With enjoyment he receives us in his home, has chicken skewers and salad, hummus and flatbread, cigars and wine served up, and enjoys beating me mercilessly at backgammon while simultaneously discussing politics.

Dr. Mohammed S. Gouma, one of Massud Barzani's advisors, was of a similarly unconditional generosity. Countless evenings we sat at his lavishly set table and argued about the future of the Kurdish province. His house was always open to us, he shared his historical knowledge just as naturally with us as with his educated friends, who arrived at Gouma's every evening and analyzed the course of the war.

The Slow, Creeping War

They do not have much room. In a circle, closely leaning against one another, the Peshmerga squat in the no-man's-land and share their frugal lunch of lentil soup and flat-bread. One false move would be deadly. They have wrested two square yards of grass from the enemy, who has fled. No more. The whole morning long, the squad of mine specialists cleared the gruesome weapons. "A going-away present from the Iraqis," says Rahid, and points with plea-sure to the 340 mines that they dug up from the asphalt in the street between Qosh Tepe and Altun Kupri. "They cannot hinder our homecoming."

However, they'll need patience to get that far.

The Americans are in the land, but without orders, the Kurds may not fight at their side. "We only advance for-ward when the Iraqis evacuate posts and areas," says Nas-raddin Mustafa of the Spi Kirkuk Brigade, and straight-ens the turban on his head. With a colonnade of land cruisers and twenty armed fighters, the commander drives to the Iraqis' most recently vacated position.

He looks out the window: the region of Qosh Tepe, from Altun Kupri to the Kurdish capital Kirkuk, lies be-fore him and his battle-ready soldiers. Nasraddin knows this could be the first victory the Kurds win without a fight. The Iraqi army is exhausted from the bombings; the border has become porous. Every day the Iraqi lines move back several hundred yards—and regroup. "When the Americans want us—we are ready."

Until then, Nasraddin's men from Kirkuk celebrate every yard that they come closer to their lost city as a victory. Right next to the steel border rails, in the middle of barbed wire and damp blankets left behind by the Iraqis in their hurried flight, the Peshmerga dance. The leader sings and waves his red and white scarf above their heads, the whole troop dances in a half-circle behind him and answers the rhythmic song. Only the soldier with the bazooka in his backpack stands in the middle and claps: "The land belongs to us and in freedom we will see it again."

Not even the smallest shadow is cast by the perpendicular sun across the figures on the hill by the river. In the burning heat, Sarhad sits there with the other Peshmerga from Mustafa Nasraddin's Spi Kirkuk Brigade. Crouched, in order not to offer the sun such a large target. Silent, in order to avoid any exertion. Enveloped by dust clouds and the diesel stench of the yellow Kawasaki bulldozer that is clearing the way to the river at the foot of the hill.

There is no bridge across the greenish brown Sab, only a small, fragile wooden boat lies at the claylike bank. Sarhad must wait. For the ferryman. For the trip across in the overfilled boat. For the fight at the front against the retreating Iraqis. For the victory.

"Decades of suffering have taught us patience," explains Sarhad, and looks at the hustle and bustle by the river, above which a spliced steel cable is being pulled taut. Along the cable, the vessel will be pulled across the water against the current. Sarhad, lost in thought, gnaws at the corner of his grayish black Kurdish scarf.

He wants to go across, to the other side, to the open fields and meadows between Altun Kupri and Kirkuk, from which—in the past—Kurdish families had been deported.

He wants to go back to the destroyed Kurdish villages that Saddam had laid waste and buried with bulldozers. His sweat drips onto the stock of the Kalashnikov he is holding in his lap. "The American pilots are leading a technically easy war," says Sarhad, and the Peshmerga, equipped with only a few grenades, waiting in the noonday heat, nod. "And here we are, slowed down by a river."

The ferryman uses a plastic cup to bale out the water that has run into the boat, and then he calls the next load of fighters. Sarhad grabs a rolled-up wool blanket from the dusty ground, climbs into the unsteady boat, and prompts the boatman, who brings the human freight to the other bank—into the war.

Traces of the hectic flight stretch along the ditches around the destroyed Iraqi position. The despairing soldiers have left a blue, half-empty pack of Sumer cigarettes in their lost post. A muddy metal bowl lies right next to the sandbags. The bast roof, reinforced by Turkish plastic tarps, lies to the side of the uncovered ruins. Saddam's soldiers didn't even want to take the colorful wool blankets on their retreat to nowhere. "Allah is our prophet," is written in dark yellow paint on the crumbling inside wall of the empty hut. "The Americans are mercenaries and dogs," on the next wall.

The Peshmerga Mala Bakir wanders through the narrow strip between the wild wheat at the edge of the path and the barbed wire rolled out around the post of the enemy, who has fled.

Even losers can be dangerous, Bakir knows, and the Russian mines between the still green heads of wheat at the edge of the path seem only to wait for careless Kurds.

Every day, the officer of the Spi Kirkuk Brigade comes to the shifting front. He can't be truly glad. Even when the border to Iraq is retreating before him every day. With a motionless face, the Peshmerga looks toward the south in his traditional uniform. "I haven't been home for thirty years," says Bakir. Then he is silent again, as if with that everything were already said about the injustice that Saddam has done to the Kurds.

There are not many days left until the fall of the dictator, this much the experienced fighter knows. He has lived through all the Kurdish revolts against Saddam and this, there is no doubt, will be the last battle. And yet, he does not want merely to be on the winning side in the war. "The Kurds were always merely the victims," he says sadly and shoves a dented metal bowl to the side. Bakir does not want the freedom, which seems so near, for free. He wants to fight for it himself. "But the Americans have another tactic. They don't want our sleeper cells in Kirkuk to begin a revolt." He feels the butt of the pistol in his waistband as if to test whether it's still sitting right. "And we must stick to that."

"Embedded Journalism"—or the Most Intelligent Form of Censorship

Until now, the retreat of the Iraqis had been going peacefully.

Slowly the armies were moving, keeping a steady distance between them, deeper into the Iraqi territory; every day, the Iraqi troops surrendered a few hundred yards more, left meaningless positions behind, and occupied the next strategically important posts in the rear line.

The Peshmerga followed peacefully, took over the abandoned military barracks of the fleeing Iraqis, and sent mine commandos into the buildings.

It's true that several journalist colleagues had already died in the first weeks of the war: through a terrorist attack in the south of northern Iraq and through mine explosions—but our work on the front line had gone relatively peacefully except for a few rare sniper incidents.

And so we were completely unprepared when the war on the northern front suddenly turned brutal.

The Iraqis had given up the old position in Kalak this morning, and the Peshmerga and U.S. Special Forces were moving forward when the Iraqis suddenly fired mortars at the unsuspecting troops.

On both sides of the street, Kurdish and American soldiers crowded behind small mounds of earth.

A grenade lands in the field two hundred yards in front of us. We all throw ourselves on the ground. Nobody knows exactly in which formation the Iraqis have retreated, where the new invisible front line runs, how far their weapons reach.

Commander Babery Sarbast lies among his soldiers from the Kurdish Spi 17 unit on the claylike ground and curses into his radio. Only three small earth walls and two ditches near the street serve as cover against the artillery fire of the Iraqis.

One hundred sixty yards in front of him, the next mortar crashes down and whips the soil into the air. "These damned Iraqis are resisting," roars the radio from the front line, two hundred twenty yards further in the direction of Khaser, the strategically important city on the way to Mosul. "Stay down," whispers the commander, "Don't move."

"This is target practice," says Sebastian.

It is by no means certain that it is safer to move farther back. Since the Iraqis are apparently still adjusting the range of their artillery, it could even possibly be safer a hundred yards ahead than farther back.

All at once it is silent again. Everyone interprets it differently: The Iraqis are pulling back more. They're advancing with their tanks. They're laying mines on the bridge right in front of the city of Khaser. They're preparing themselves for a counterattack.

We wait.

They say that a small commando of U.S. Special Forces is trying to disable the Iraqis.

We decide at least to run up to the next Iraqi post.

A bad decision.

Two hundred twenty yards ahead, to the left of the street, men are lying flat on the ground, wedged against one another; they lie behind the tiny bank. They take us into their midst, between their bodies. Danger threatens here not only through mortar fire, but also through the well-aimed shots of Iraqi snipers. Only a quiet hiss can be heard, invisibly the bullets whistle over our ducked heads.

Salah, a young Peshmerga, pushes himself a few inches forward with his weapon in order to "shoot down" breakaway, attacking Iraqis.

Behind this tiny hill, pressed tightly against the bodies

of the soldiers, between hand grenades and Kalashnikovs, under artillery and sniper fire, I ask myself whether I would be relieved if Salah *hit* his mark as often as possible.

What kind of a thought was that? How could I wish that the person at my side might shoot others to death?

In that moment of existential threat it becomes clear why "embedded journalism" makes critical reporting nearly impossible.

Once underway with a fighting unit, integrated in the band of soldiers, the journalist is at the mercy of these people.

The first victim of war is truth, they say.

Well, truth is the second victim of war, because neutrality is already lost first.

Once under fire, each has an interest in the victory of the troops in whose midst he lies—out of sheer survival instinct.

Once exposed to the same existential threat, an emotional and psychological proximity arises between journalist and soldier, between the author and the one about whom he is supposed to write. It seems to me to have been the most intelligent form of media censorship in this Gulf War to not exclude journalists, but to integrate them into one's own fighting unit, and in this way to co-opt the media.

For hours Salah has been lying among his comrades and has been under fire from the Iraqis. "It is my thousandth deployment in war," he says and straightens the grenade on his waistband, "but now hopefully also my last."

Now the Peshmerga need help from their new American friends, who are crouching with them at the side of the road.

The support comes from the air—and on order. By radio, American soldiers direct their comrades from the Air Force. The Iraqi artillery must be eliminated by bombs. Then Salah and the other Peshmerga can advance further.

The Bush administration had not imagined the war like this. They had believed in a glorious victory from the air—with as little danger as possible—against a weak army. They had assumed that the Iraqi army would quickly be demoralized by continual bombardments and weakened by turncoats and deserters.

But the following day at dawn, the American and Kurdish troops are still trapped in tiny holes in the ground as if in their own graves. Two Kurdish Peshmerga have already died from a mortar on the open field, right next to the post. The whole night long, under artillery fire from the Iraqis, they have been reinforcing their position on both sides of the street. Their white all-terrain vehicles have distributed the fifteen men from the Special Forces onto the field behind small hills. And they themselves have tried to sleep standing and crouching in dug-out holes.

For a few hours all has been quiet, and the American fighters and Kurdish comrades crawl hesitantly out of the protected areas, and rub the sleep from their reddened eyes with their dirty hands. "Heads down," shouts Babery Sarbast, and a quickly approaching grenade lands halfway and sinks into the wheat field to the left of the position.

With the Jeep on the road, we attempt to drive on in the direction of Khaser, but the Iraqis have taken up their positions again and fire on us, but only hit the fields to the right and left.

We turn around. There's no point.

Small Reasons That Could Save Your Life

Whoever writes about wars is once again looking for an explanation for something that can't be explained.

The war leaves us confused, disturbed by the power with which it forces its logic on us, disheartened above all by the pure chance through which destinies are decided.

War teaches a lesson in humility.

Even if heroic epics like to tell how the actions of a few courageous people can determine entire battles, it seems to me above all to be misfortune, error, arbitrariness that have power over life and death.

At least Sebastian and I owe our lives to a mere coincidence.

It was settled over the course of three days.

After the two turbulent days at the front outside of Khaser, where we had come under fire together with the Kurdish Peshmerga, a dramatic excursion into the liberated zones around Altun Kupri followed on the third day, during which our Peshmerga unit became disoriented and got lost right in the middle of the front. We drove right up to an Iraqi post, which luckily wasn't occupied, before we turned around in a panic and after hours of driving around, finally found our way back to Kurdish territory.

A nightmare.

Slightly in shock after these three days, we staggered

into the hotel and discussed our luck at the front. Three times we had escaped; three times we could also have not gotten off so lightly. We forced ourselves to reflect, and decided to get a few hours of rest the next day, Sunday.

We don't want to go to the front, we said to Hemen, our translator.

As an exception, Sebastian and I would stay in the hotel and sift through our material, and settle down a bit. We should meet in the afternoon around two o'clock.

Hemen agreed.

Then we changed and went to the Salahaddin mountain for dinner with Wegih Barzani, son of the Kurds' heroic freedom fighter Mahmud Barzani and brother of the current Kurdish leader Massud Barzani.

For weeks now, Wegih had treated us with favor for incomprehensible reasons.

One evening, one of the generals of the Kurdish army of the KDP had called us in the hotel and announced Wegih's spontaneous visit.

Within ten minutes, the lobby filled with bodyguards, the street was blocked off, and a convoy drove up: Wegih Barzani came and wanted to meet us.

After this first meeting, we encountered Wegih almost daily, at the front, while visiting the troops, on the muddy fields by the American landing strip, in the barracks of the special unit that he commanded, up on the Salahaddin mountain.

Each time the young son of the most famous Kurdish family became warmer and more trusting.

We were able to experience the extent to which the Peshmerga admired him.

Wegih can't stand it for long up on the Salahaddin mountain, where his brother Massud—"the president," as Wegih
calls him—confers with advisors and ministers. He'd rather
visit his overtired soldiers in the foxholes at the front.
Without a bulletproof vest and in an inconspicuous uniform, he stands among the fighters and listens to them.

He's already used five lives, they tell one another about
their beloved leader, who doesn't display any grandiose manners, as would befit the descendant of the Barzani family.

"I have the nine lives of a cat," says Wegih and merely
laughs at the dangers he has escaped. The stories of the
battles that Wegih has survived have become myths, and
this slight, friendly man personifies for the Kurds their
people's will to resistance.

Today we were finally supposed to visit him privately,
without the presence of his bodyguards. Without the entourage of security officials and without protocol. We were
simply supposed to come to dinner.

Accompanied by our translator, Hemen, we drive from
Erbil to the villa high above the city. The heat of the day
has dissipated on the Salahaddin mountain. Wegih is sitting in his beige uniform on the sofa in front of a table set
with Kurdish delicacies.

He has slept for only three hours. For weeks, he has
been living with and for this war. Now, freed from the
corset of military consultations, for once not involved in
political discussions with his brother Massud, without the
train of admirers, protectors, and American partners, ex-
haustion catches up with him in his private surroundings.
"It is not always easy to be a Barzani," says Wegih and
runs his hand over his closely cropped hair with his typi-

cal gesture. "I am infinitely proud of my father, but it is also hard to do justice to the tradition."

Self-pity is foreign to him.

He was not brought up for it. Anonymously, under an assumed name, he was put to the test in basic training. Ruthlessly and without mercy, the wealthy son of the famous clan was mistreated by the officers just like all other recruits.

Like all Kurds, he longed for this war. Despite fame and riches, the Barzani family has experienced suffering like that of the poorest Kurds: they were expelled, driven out, deported, and killed. In this way, they are no different from the others.

We talk late into the night.

He grew up with violence and war, he was trained for war and resistance, and yet he has never been able to get used to it.

"Someday I'd like to have a normal life," he finally says, and then, relaxed and also a bit melancholy, he tells of his love for Spain, and of the pending trip to Berlin that he has promised his daughter. And of the places and bars in Berlin that he likes so much.

Someday.

When he is no longer needed in this land, in this eternal state of war.

We say goodbye well after midnight in the yard in front of the house.

The next morning around ten o'clock, Wegih calls the cell phone of our translator, Hemen.

He wants to invite us to go with him in his car to a liberated area by Dibager. A whole convoy is on the way there.

The Iraqis have pulled back, several Americans would accompany him. Hemen should be so kind as to call me and Sebastian and ask if we want to go with him.

Our translator drops the ball.

Instead—as agreed in such cases—of calling us up and asking if we wanted to accompany Wegih (of course we would have wanted to), he doesn't even bother to tell us. Without obtaining an answer from us, without any authorization, Hemen declines Wegih Barzani's offer.

"No," Hemen answers directly and bluntly, "they aren't working this morning."

While we sit in front of our computers in the hotel with no idea, Wegih Barzani sets off in the direction of Dibager without us.

From countless conversations and interviews the next day, the following events can only be *reconstructed*.

On Sunday morning, Kurdish troops advance farther into Iraqi territory.

In Ser Dibager, the hills outside of Dibager, Americans and Kurds lie together behind an embankment of protective rocks. Tariq Koiy is one of them.

Tariq Koiy has already been waiting with his unit on the hill of Ser Dibager for two days.

The offensive near Dibager is supposed to cut off the strategic connection between Mosul and Kirkuk.

Sixty Iraqis had positioned themselves in front of the hills the night before. Apprehensively lurking, the estranged compatriots lie for hours across from one another—until the Kurd Tariq Koiy calls out in Arabic a promise in the darkness: no harm will be done to deserters.

"Then they came crawling out of their hiding places like hungry animals."

The Kurds take a yellow Toyota pickup truck with four Kalashnikovs as well.

"We gave them cigarettes and two hundred dinars."

Shattered by the losses, the Iraqis finally move on, with seven tanks, along the road between Erbil and Dibager.

Except one of their Soviet model T-54 tanks dies during the retreat due to engine trouble, and so Saddam's soldiers leave the rusted vehicle to the right in the ditch next to the intersection.

Around noon, Wegih Barzani takes off toward Sher Dibager in a convoy with his closest friends and bodyguards and with two American trucks. The British journalist John Simpson and his team from the BBC accompany the line of cars.

Tariq Koiy and his fighters are suddenly surprised by a counterattack by the remaining Iraqis. With tanks, Saddam's faithful followers move against the hill. Two times in a row, the Peshmerga under the commanding officer Mohamad Maghdid, together with the U.S. Special Forces, succeed in repelling the Iraqis.

They fight side by side, but they can't talk to one another.

"We can't communicate," says Tariq.

The soldiers of the superpower don't have a Kurdish translator with them. Finally, the American radio operator calls in distress for help from the Air Force. They are under fire, he announces. Iraqi tanks were moving toward their hill. Three miles outside Dibager, those are the coordinates of our own position.

Wegih Barzani's convoy reaches the intersection just before Sher Dibager.

Tariq's American comrades fire off a smoke bomb for orientation, so that the pilot in the fighter jet can differentiate between the friendly lines and the enemy lines. It lands in the plains between the rocky posts of Sher Dibager, behind which the Kurds and Americans have taken cover, and the attacking Iraqi tanks. However, Tariq has the feeling that "the flare does not ignite correctly." The smoke disperses more quickly than planned.

Wegih Barzani and his companions get out at the intersection next to the broken T-54 tank. Two U.S. bombers approach the intersection. Just as Barzani walks around the cars, the American F-15 pilots drop the bombs on the convoy next to the tank and transform the scene into a flaming inferno. "It's a scene from hell in front of me: burning bodies are lying around me," reports John Simpson for the BBC. "It's a horrible incident of friendly fire— the Americans are shooting their own allies."

Tariq and his fighters hear the powerful explosions behind them.

The frightened American radio operator orders an immediate stop to the bombardment of their own people.

Tariq runs back to the intersection.

The cars are ablaze, giant pieces of metal and shards of glass, ripped-off body parts, blood-soaked cartridge belts lie scattered within a radius of several yards. Due to a flying piece of shrapnel, the bazooka and ammunition brought on the back of one of Wegih's bodyguards are also exploding.

Tariq carries four wounded to the Iraqi pickup truck

that he took just the night before, and races to the Emergencia Hospital.

The bomb rips the legs off Kamran Abdurazaq Mohamaed, the translator from John Simpson's team, and the Kurd bleeds to death before he can be brought to the hospital in Erbil, twenty-two miles away.

The helpers, hurrying over to the scene, finally find Wegih Barzani on the ground in the chaos of screaming and moaning. A piece of metal shrapnel has bored itself through the head of the young Kurd leader. Seriously wounded, he is brought to Erbil. And shortly after is flown to Germany.

Fifteen people die in this so-called friendly-fire attack, forty-five are wounded, some of them seriously.

Only the Iraqi tank is still standing next to the devastated intersection—unharmed and harmless, as before.

The Fall of the Statue in Baghdad

Ali Haider is forty-seven years old. He has dragged all seven kids out of bed. They can always sleep later. They should put on their finest for this late-night party. All dressed up and overtired, they finally sit packed together in his car. Rayan, sitting on Haider's lap in her little silk dress, is only two and a half years old, but she should experience this, this historic day of joy.

Only a few minutes have passed since images of the falling statue of the hated dictator from Baghdad were broadcast on television stations in the north of the divided country, and a flood of rejoicing Kurds is already

301

pouring into the streets of the Northern Province and celebrating the belated triumph.

On the road encircling the citadel of Erbil, the capital city in northern Iraq, Haider stands in a procession of honking cars and weeps silently: "My family should finally for once see me happy," says the Kurd and rubs his eyes. The children push their way onto the backseat of the Toyota and stare with disbelief at the bizarre scenes of ecstasy: uniformed soldiers embrace widows dressed in black, on the sidewalks in front of the bazaar musicians strike up a dance in the middle of the night, and motley semicircles move rhythmically to the song of the lead singer and swing their scarves to the beat, half-naked young men hang out of the open sunroofs of their cars and hold up pictures of George W. Bush and Tony Blair high into the air: "This is the end of Kurdish fear," says Haider. "It has come too late. But I fervently hope that it remains."

We stare at the sea of red-white-and-green and white-red-and-black flags.

It's not the dream of Kurdish independence that is being expressed here. In the moment of greatest euphoria, the people beneath the fortress of Erbil are waving not only Kurdish flags, but also Iraqi ones.

The Imaginary Conflict between Arabs and Kurds

The streets of Baqrata, the tiny Arabic village directly behind Mahmus, are deserted. No stores are open, no children are playing on the street, no veiled women can be seen.

302

The green zone has fallen, American troops have marched into Baghdad, umpteen thousand Kurds have set out for Kirkuk, their secret capital city, and the Arabic residents of the villages have fled, fearing the wrath of the victors.

The Kurdish envoy Sadaq Pshtwan gets out of his car, followed by an entourage of bodyguards and political functionaries in dark suits, and with open arms approaches a very different figure in a black Arabic robe. Abdul Rahman Marky, one hand on the golden edge of his noble cloak, bows before the Kurdish delegation.

It is the end of the war, the rulers in Iraq are changing, and the Arabic tribal leader wants to show the Kurdish victors his respect:

"I welcome you," says Abdul Rahman Marky, "but please come again later. My wife is not here and I am not in a position to honorably receive you."

North of Baqrata, in Mosul, the fighting between troops loyal to Saddam and the coalition army of Americans and Kurds continues, to the south in Kirkuk and Baghdad the incensed masses are already moving through the streets and plundering, but the Arabic leader would like to preserve civilized manners in the midst of chaos.

"Massud Barzani sends me with the following message," replies Sadaq Pshtwan, and under the given circumstances simply transforms the dusty street into a meeting place. "At this time we remember the Arabic-Kurdish brotherhood. The Arabic tribes have been living here for four hundred years and that should not change now. We hold you in high regard and love you, and for you, too, the situation will now improve."

Western media like to present ancient Mesopotamia as

a region in which ethnic wars have always raged, far too often Iraq is represented to us as a territory with apparently irreconcilable conflicts between Sunnis and Shiites, between Kurds and Arabs, as if this were about wild tribes still in their "natural state."

The scene in Baqrata, which we witnessed purely by chance, contradicts all familiar assumptions. The war was scarcely at an end, no international mediators were present, nobody was forcing the Kurds to approach the Arabic patricians in this moment of triumph.

"We have been living together with the Kurds for centuries," the Arabic leader answers. "We are Iraqis. With no distinctions."

The Arabs should have their families return. Nobody will do them harm, the Kurdish delegate assures him. They should feel safe once again. They could even keep their weapons for self-defense.

"And if somebody comes and wants to take the weapons away from you, kill him in my name," says Pshtwan.

Kirkuk

The rooms behind the notorious yellow walls remain off-limits. But the windowpane of the small guardhouse in front of the entrance is already smashed in. Somebody has painted a black heart and a crooked "USA" under it.

The colorful tiles of the mosaic with the portrait of Saddam Hussein splinter with every additional stone thrown by the children in front of the portal. Hundreds line the streets and clap and sing in chorus with the cheering Pesh-merga militia men, who are entering in convoys. The inner rooms of the former headquarters of the Baath Party in Kirkuk have been swept bare. However, Ibrahim Chalil still does not want to enter.

The regime in Baghdad has been toppled—but the Kurd is still afraid. For weeks he has prepared himself for this day as an armed sleeper in the underground resistance. Chalil has smuggled secret dispatches to the Peshmerga on the other side of the green zone. "Again and again, our people were busted and executed by the Iraqis."

The whole night he fought in Kirkuk against the last sol-diers from the regime. Chalil runs his hand over the brand-new rifle from the arsenal they stormed. "This is what Sad-dam's Iraq consisted of: death and weapons. Nothing else."

Right in front of his eyes, two men are already looting the building of Saddam's party: corrugated metal roofs, a refrigerator, and a computer keyboard are added to the three chairs on the bed of the gray pickup truck. Nobody intervenes. The Iraqi police, whom Chalil fears, don't exist any more. Only dancing, veiled women and children who wave the green, white, and red Kurdish flag. The small truck with the stolen goods takes off. "Soon I will celebrate too," says Chalil, "when the fear finally sub-sides. Then we will have triumphed."

One day after the dictator in Baghdad was toppled, Kurds, together with American troops, take over town after town in the north. But soon thereafter, the Pesh-mergas already have to withdraw again from Kirkuk and Mosul. The Americans don't want to upset the Turks.

The gate at the mile-long factory site of the Baba-
gurgur oil field is unguarded. As darkness falls, only the
yard-high flames shine from the burning oil well across
the abandoned parking lot. Palm trees and eucalyptus
groves line the abandoned houses of the Arabic foremen
and engineers. Except for Kassas Abdil, nobody else is
there. "Where should I flee to?" asks Abdil, shrugging his
shoulders. "And above all, with what?"

In the morning, fighters from the KDP came with their
yellow headbands around their foreheads and their Kalashnikovs and had ripped off his SUV. A few hours later,
the Peshmerga from the PUK showed up with their
green flags on their car. They stole the battery out of the
Arabic engineer's second car. "It's strange, first everybody
fights for the oil in Kirkuk, and then nobody comes to
protect it."

In the rapacious chaos of the first hours, the losers in
the war sneak away unpunished. On the street between
Kirkuk and Altun Kupri, those conquered stream home
like a pathetic caravan.

Some come barefoot, the former soldiers of Saddam
Hussein. They have taken off their uniforms, left the tell-
tale laced boots behind next to the tanks and cartons of
ammunition. They've kept only the worn-out green parkas.

"The Kurds are receiving their freedom late," says
Abbas Heidar and wraps a towel, which Kurdish Peshmerga
gave him in the morning cold because he was freezing,
around his shoulders. "We are guilty with regard to the
Kurds, and they still give us food," he says slightly ashamed
and moves on.

Nation Building without Manners

For two days the incensed masses have already been raging through the cities of Baghdad, Kirkuk, and Mosul without the American troops stepping in.

Five hundred fifty yards in front of the city border of Kirkuk, U.S. soldiers sit on their tanks and light military vehicles and look idly on as thousands of cars packed full with stolen goods from the fallen city pass by.

Cars with refrigerators on their roofs pass, trucks with furniture from entire apartments drive by—but nothing happens.

The Kurdish soldiers of the KDP and PUK try desperately to control the anarchic conditions after the fall of Saddam Hussein. But at the behest of the Turkish government, the Americans forbid them to march into Iraq with too many units, and so the Peshmerga are completely overwhelmed.

Even if it is possible to imagine that the troops really were surprised by the plundering in Baghdad on the first day, it nevertheless remains incomprehensible why twenty-four hours later, at the fall of Kirkuk, they had obviously received no directives to stop the criminal activities.

Mosul was defeated by the coalition troops another twenty-four hours later—but here too, the U.S. Army held back as mobs descended on the city and took away everything they could carry.

One day later, the Americans finally moved into the city of Mosul.

At the old, bullet-ridden airport terminal, Colonel

Robert Waltemeyer sets up the new headquarters with his troops.

A delegation of senior city officials and patricians collects in festive dress on the yard in front of the airport and would like to pay their respects to the American colonel. In long black robes and noble garments, the dignitaries stand together in quiet conversation about the events of the past night. Turkmens and Arabs, Shiites, Sunnis, and Christians, everybody has come to give the foreign rulers a good reception, as is proper according to the rules of the millennium-old civilization.

Their city is falling apart, first from the weeks of bombardments by the British-American Air Force, now from the hoards of plunderers.

The Iraqi Baathists in the police and army have fled; there is no other civilian authority.

Only this morning did the Arab leaders succeed in calling together their supporters and setting up civilian posts and checkpoints, and in this way bringing one neighborhood after another to rest.

Without them, Mosul would have fallen into anarchy.

Today they have come to greet these Americans, who have let them down in the past days.

"We are desperate," says Khalid Hashm, an Arab from Mosul. Three of his cousins were killed by marauding bands as they tried to defend their house against the plunderers. "We no longer know who is in charge."

The Catholic priest Dr. Louis Sako watches in disbelief as White, the boyish press officer, diligently draws up borders and zones with tape on the dusty parking lot and pushes the ambassadors from the city of Mosul behind the plastic strips like cattle.

Louis Sako has come to speak about mutual cooperation in Mosul.

Then Colonel Robert Waltemeyer appears.

The slightly dirty gang of international reporters presses closer to the barrier; the noble company of citizens from Mosul are standing next to us.

Waltemeyer positions himself in front of the wooden podium that his aide has made ready for him, as if to hold a speech on the state of the nation, and even before we can get out our notepads, the colonel lets loose.

"First of all, you should understand all the rules here," begins Waltemeyer, as if he were a bad copy of the officers from *Apocalypse Now*, "and I make the rules. I decide here which questions I will answer and which I won't."

Among the press, several exchange amused looks. Can it be that nobody has briefed the colonel on who he has before him?

The representatives of the city of Mosul stand upright in their elegant robes in front of the ridiculous plastic strips and look—as if in shock—at the uniformed man, who neither greets nor receives them, but merely shouts commands and orders.

"Whoever doesn't want to keep to these rules can leave now."

Khalid Hashm becomes restless. He didn't come here for this.

"We're here to offer our cooperation and help," he calls to the foreigner in English.

"When and with whom we cooperate is still decided by us," retorts Waltemeyer brusquely, without even condescending to look at Hashm.

And then he speaks of the American heroic acts, of the patriotism of his soldiers and his pride in their accomplishments—but by then everything is already destroyed and the delegations of Arab, Turkmen, and Assyrian citizens from Mosul go back to their neighborhoods. They have things to do. They have to put things in order and resume their lives after the war. In the new, unstable peace—this much they have just learned—they will have to depend on themselves.

"If the Americans want to be treated with respect by us," says Father Louis, "they must begin their so-called nation building a bit differently."

The Refugee

On each trip there was always *one* special encounter that for me encapsulated the experience with a whole landscape. And there was *one* special conversation as well, *one* special story that stuck with me: Alberto's dog in the favelas of Nicaragua, who bit my hand; Luis, the small son of Fanny, who during the civil war in Colombia sat in my lap while behind him the battle for Comuna 13 raged; Mariam in the Cherat refugee camp in Pakistan, who shook me as if she could in this way straighten the world that had gone awry; Mohammed Shafi, the weeping old man in the hospital at the border between Pakistan and India, who poured out the suffering of a long life; the traumatized girl in the rubble of the old town of Gjakova in Kosovo, who forgot how to speak and didn't even notice; Ahmet, the orphan boy in the junkyards on the periphery of Bucharest, who experienced humanity only through the isolated Gypsy families in the neglected huts.

In northern Iraq and this entire miserable war it was Rashid Yasin whom I will never forget.

All these years he has carried with him the yellowed bundle of paper in a gray cover. Ever since his flight from the attacking helicopters that shot at his village, Biraspan. Through all the years in the camps for homeless deportees. Through the nights in damp tents, as well as in his chilly stone house at the edge of the city of Erbil, in which his wife had died and he had grown old. With trembling hands, Rashid Yasin takes the rolled-up document out of the container that protects the fifty-year-old, thin paper with the entry from the land register. It is the only thing he has left of his farm. Now, since the end of the regime of the dictator from Baghdad is near, Yasin hopes that he will finally see justice before he dies.

The old farmer opens the scroll on his lap and points with his index finger to a stamp that has not been valid for a long time. King Faisal's portrait authenticates the deed to Yasin's property, and it is valid, even though the kingdom of the earlier Iraqi monarch has long fallen apart and been reorganized.

"I can prove it: This land belongs to me," says Yasin and his gold tooth, which sparkles when he speaks, emphasizes his claim to previous riches. "Nobody can dispute my right to it."

Yasin sits in a tiny courtyard on a stool under the only tree.

His shepherd's staff is still hanging on a hook in the trunk within reach, but he has not set foot on the land, across which he could walk with this staff, since 1991.

For a whole year, Yasin had resisted the attempts at intimidation by the Baath Party. One Kurdish neighbor after another fled from Biraspan in the wake of the "Arabization." But Yasin held out on his land. For one whole year he hauled blocks of ice from nearby Kirkuk to his house, because the Iraqis had cut off the electricity in the village and otherwise the food would have gone bad.

"I hold no grudge against the Arabs, only against the government of Saddam and those who plundered and robbed our land."

His house, which Saddam reduced to rubble, had sixteen rooms. He could have put three hundred sheep to pasture on his own land, which has remained untilled since the deportation.

None of his urban sons can really understand the humiliation the old man feels because he has had to work the land of others for years.

A salvaged reaper stands outside on the street in front of the house.

Just in case.

If Biraspan is taken by the Americans or Peshmerga, Yasin wants to return. Even if the entire village consists only of rubble and he can find no roof over his head.

"I would just like to sit on my own land again. Nothing more," says Yasin, "only sit and look at the land. That I would still like to experience."

Two days later, the plateau around Altun Kupri, as well as the old village of Biraspan, is liberated. We drive to Rashid Yasin and ask him if he would like to visit his old farmstead with us. It is, mind you, a strenuous journey, the bridge across the Sab River still not built, and his village perhaps destroyed.

Rashid Yasin does not yet want to set out.

But the news of the liberation of the plateau of Altun Kupri is on his mind.

The eternal refugee continues to wait on his stool in front of his tree in Erbil with the deed in his hand, but his son Bilal should scout out the arduous way home for him.

Bilal was ten years old when Saddam Hussein drove his father from house and home in Biraspan.

The narrow passage to the front at the plateau around Altun Kupri has gotten a bit bigger. The tiny boat on the bank of the Sab, full of holes, has been taken out of service in the meantime. Two tractors, one on each side of the river, now alternately pull a concrete platform back and forth on the river with a steel cable. Reinforcements are desperately needed. Mala Bakir, of the Spi Kirkuk Brigade, steers a jeep across the two rusty iron girders onto the square barge. Then he waves the soldiers to himself, goes back to the bank and shouts the start signal to the tractor driver. From his pickup truck, the officer of the Spi Kirkuk observes how the steel cable jumps up through the water, becomes taut, and then pulls the platform across, grinding. Bilal Yasin reaches the other side along with the Peshmerga.

After an hour through confusing paths, dried-out, stony riverbeds, passing huge rapeseed and wheat fields, Bilal reaches the devastated village of his childhood. A gray-black wall of smoke darkens the horizon in the south. The oil wells around Kirkuk are in flames and the pungent stench also surrounds the ravaged plateau miles away.

Bilal stands there in the middle of sandy ruins. Weeds and wild thistles reach up to his thighs.

Looking for clues in the rubble and in Bilal's memory.

"I'll recognize the stones from our house," he says and he wanders in the shimmering heat, with his Kalashnikov on his back, through the crumbling ruins of a village that exists only in the memory of the survivors.

"That's it." Bilal stands beaming in front of the brownish red claylike mass of a giant ninety-degree angle created by the remains of a wall: "That is our house."

And then he zigzags his way over mounds of earth churned up by wild mice, past overgrown piles of stones, taking his old path to school up to the cemetery of Biraspan. The gravestones have been toppled, the names made unrecognizable.

"This region was supposed to be Arabic, so Saddam wanted to destroy everything that pointed to a Kurdish identity," says Bilal and runs his hand over the crumbling stones, "but us . . . he forgot about us."

When today, one year later, I read in the newspapers about the allegedly endless demands of the Kurds, about the American interim government's resistance to the return of the Kurds to their homeland—then I always think of Rashid Yasin.

When no weapons of mass destruction could be found at the end of the war, new justifications for the operation were hastily made up by the American government. The injustice that had been done to the Kurds was the favorite alibi of the Americans. Only too gladly do they point to the suffering of the Kurds, to their losses under Saddam Hussein—except now that the dictator is deposed, nobody is allowed to remember the losses of the exiles any longer. The victims are suddenly no longer victims, but unpleasant, demanding Kurds.

And I imagine Rashid Yasin, as he continues to sit on his stool under the tree, his shepherd's staff within reach at all times so he can set out to go home, and I picture him, as he looks at his property deed with the likeness of the king and can't understand why the old, certified rights should have no currency in the new, free Iraq.

What did they all die for then? The Kurds, the Arabs, and the American soldiers?

Editorial Note

These letters have had a strange life in the no-man's-land of languages.

Originally, immediately after my return from each overseas assignment, I wrote them in English, so that my friends abroad could share these experiences. For the book version, the letters were translated into German and I then reappropriated the text in my own language and edited the translation. The English book version is an adaptation of the original English letters to the version of the German book, with additional editing by my American publisher. Isabel Cole, Sara Costa, Kristen Hylenski, and Chris Sultan were wonderful translators who helped finalize some chapters for the English manuscript.

One letter was written retroactively. The letter on Iraq was written—for purely contingent reasons—after almost a year's delay, and with the knowledge that the letters would be published.

All letters describe trips I made on assignment for *Der Spiegel* and about which I published various articles during the years 1999 to 2003. The letter on Pakistan and Afghanistan was published in an earlier version as "No Soldiers in the Scenery" in *Radical Society* 29, no. 2 (2002): 67–84. Passages from the letter on Iraq appeared in Stefan Aust and Cordt Schnibben, eds., *Irak: Geschichte eines modernen Krieges* (Munich: Deutsche Verlags-Anstalt, 2003).

Editorial Note

Sources for the epigraphs are as follows: Hannah Arendt, *The Human Condition* (Chicago: University of Chicago Press, 1958); Michael Walzer, *Just and Unjust Wars* (New York: Basic Books, 2000); Simone Weil, *Cahiers I* (1933–1940); Emmanuel Lévinas, *Difficult Freedom* (Baltimore: Johns Hopkins University Press, 1997); Wolfgang Sofsky, *Violence: Terrorism, Genocide, War*, trans. Anthea Bell (London: Granta Books, 2003); Edmond Jabès, *A Foreigner Carrying in the Crook of His Arm a Tiny Book*, trans. Rosemarie Waldrop (Middletown, Conn.: Wesleyan University Press, 1993); Wallace Stevens, "A Clear Day and No Memories," *The Collected Works of Wallace Stevens* (New York: Alfred A. Knopf, 1954); Theodor W. Adorno, *Minima Moralia*, trans. E.F.N. Jephcott (London: New Left Books, 1974); Ingeborg Bachmann, "Every Day," *After Every War*, Eavan Boland, translations from the German (Princeton, N.J.: Princeton University Press, 2004).

Acknowledgments

This book is rooted in an ongoing dialogue with friends: the letters were written in an understanding of my own interwovenness with the thoughts and lives of these friends—so there is more gratitude than I usually owe.

There would not be a single letter if it hadn't been for the trust and encouragement of the heads of the foreign news department of *Der Spiegel*, Hans Hoyng and Dr. Olaf Ihlau, who allowed me to travel and supported my journeys and my work in every respect.

None of my trips would have been possible without the excellent photographers who accompanied me: Sebastian Bolesch, Thomas Grabka, Vincent Kohlbecher, Markus Matzel, and Thomas Müller. Especially those who have been in war zones with me have become friends of a sort previously unknown to me. The trust and attachment formed in these times are incomparable. From each of these photographers I have learned something unique—and I thank them all.

I met Joanne Mariner of Human Rights Watch under the most horrific circumstances during the war in Kosovo. Our friendship has brought us together again and again since. I admire her passion for human rights and her grace under pressure. I cannot thank her enough for

Acknowledgments

her wonderful sense of humor, her closeness during the darkest times, and her generosity during countless New York visits, including one on 9/11. Without her, I don't know how I would have come to terms with what we witnessed.

I have met Elizabeth Rubin in all kinds of possible and impossible situations around the world. Her warmth and wit have been indispensable in often trying times.

The letters talk about strangers who offered help without expecting anything in return. We experienced generosity and hospitality without reason. Strangers entrusted their stories to us, they introduced us and enlightened us, they overlooked our ignorance and invited us gently into their culture and world. The letters are also a belated token of appreciation to all those strangers whose lives and suffering we shared for a brief moment—only to abandon them again in the next.

The letters should also speak of those humans who always live within the radius of violence: Mariam, Mohammed Shafi, Emine, Kujtim Bilali and his nephew Noni Hoxha, Ahmed Tawfiq, Alberto, Fanny Ruiz and her son Luis, and many more.

I am particularly grateful to my mother, who always accepted and supported my desire and need to travel and who managed (despite complete trekking incompetence) to buy me the most wonderful sleeping bag of all time. And I am grateful to my friends in Berlin, Luzia Braun, Uli Broedermann, Rahel Jaeggi, Isabell Lorey, Herbie Rebbert, Martin Saar, Andrea Thilo, Hortensia Völckers, and Beatrice von Bismarck.

320

Acknowledgments

Letters are written for an addressee, the other to whom you talk.

For me this was a collection of friends from all over the world. But some friends were particularly important as listeners, as significant others, and later as encouraging friends who urged me to publish something that was intended as a private dialogue: without Jay Bernstein, Wendy Brown, Kirsten Fischer, Tamara Metz, and David Rieff, these letters would never have been published.

This book was written in various places: in Palermo, in Buenos Aires, and in the apartment of Karoline Duerr in New York, where I was allowed to stay for several months to edit the manuscript. I want to thank Karoline for her incredibly relaxed generosity. I also want to thank Professor Seyla Benhabib for her invitation to teach during the academic year 2003–2004 at her Institute for Ethics, Politics, and Economics at Yale University, where I was able to finish the book. David Apter, Drucilla Cornell, Thomas Dumm, Nancy Fraser, Geoffrey Hartman, Morris B. Kaplan, Nikolas Kompridis, Joanne Mariner, Tamara Metz, Elizabeth Rubin, Susan Sontag, Eli Zaretzky, and particularly Amelie Rorty were important interlocutors and friends during that year in the United States.

I want to thank Silvia Bovenschen for her initiative in showing the letters to a publisher and her commitment throughout. Special thanks to my wonderful editor at Fischer Verlag, Peter Sillem, whose thoughtful and gentle attitude helped overcome all my fears and doubts in the course of preparing rather personal letters for publication. Brigitta van Rheinberg and Eric Weitz I want to thank for their interest in human rights and their amazing support. Madeleine Adams I thank for her wonderfully careful copyediting of the English edition.

Silvia Fehrmann I thank silently.

Rarely in life does one encounter someone who turns out to be amazingly complementary to oneself. Rarely does one encounter a colleague who shares the same professional passion, political convictions, intellectual curiosity, and interest in human rights issues—and whom one continues to find bearable over the course of weeks squeezed together in very limited space.

I have found such an other in the photographer Sebastian Bolesch. His dedication to his profession and his high standards for both photography and journalism are impressive. His understanding of humans beings and their needs, his sophistication, his amazing tranquility, and his incorruptibility allow me to overlook his dreadful passion for Johnny Cash and his morning taciturnity.

I have learned at least as much about the language of images from him as about trust and friendship.

This book is dedicated to him in gratitude.

HUMAN RIGHTS AND CRIMES AGAINST HUMANITY

Edited by Eric D. Weitz

Human rights catastrophes are a recurrent feature of the modern era. They create countless victims, and the societies that have engaged in large-scale atrocities remain haunted by their pasts. To counter such abuses, new standards of human rights protection have arisen and are expressed in an array of proclamations, treaties, and tribunals. Human Rights and Crimes against Humanity provides a forum for publication and debate on the perpetration of large-scale atrocities and the often highly charged political and ethical issues of human rights protection, memory, and redress that develop in their wake. The series uses a broad understanding of crimes against humanity, including genocides, ethnic cleansings, massacres, various forms of slavery, lynchings, mass rapes, and torture. Chronologically, the series runs from around 1500, the onset of the modern era marked by European colonialism abroad and the Atlantic slave trade, to the present. Geographically, it takes in every area of the globe. It publishes significant works of original scholarship and major interpretation by academics, journalists, and other writers. An important goal is to bring these crimes—and the responses to them—to the attention of a wide audience and to stimulate discussion and debate in the public sphere as well as among scholars and in the classroom. The knowledge that develops from the series will also, we hope, help promote human rights standards and prevent future crimes against humanity.